I0815474

DESTINATION MACAO

Born and currently based in London, Paul French lived and worked in Shanghai for many years. After a career as a widely published analyst and commentator on China he is now a full-time author, focusing on China and Asia in the first half of the twentieth century. He has written a number of books, including a history of foreign correspondents in China and a biography of the legendary Shanghai adman, journalist, and adventurer Carl Crow. His latest book is *Her Lotus Year: China, the Roaring Twenties, and the Making of Wallis Simpson* which examines the controversial and revealing period in the early life of the legendary Wallis, Duchess of Windsor – her one year in China.

His true crime book *Midnight in Peking* was a *New York Times* bestseller, a BBC Radio 4 Book of the Week, a Mystery Writers' of America Edgar award winner for Best Fact Crime, and a Crime Writers' Association (UK) Dagger award for non-fiction. His Kirkus-starred book *City of Devils: A Shanghai Noir* focuses on the dancehalls, casinos, and cabarets of wartime Shanghai. Both *Midnight in Peking* and *City of Devils* are being adapted for film and television and have been translated into Chinese.

French is a regular contributor and book reviewer for various publications including the *South China Morning Post, The Mekong Review, China Books Review, Sinica*, and *Crime Reads*. He occasionally works in audio drama-documentaries for the BBC Radio with productions including *Death at the Airport: The Plot Against Kim Jong-nam, Peking Noir,* and *The Defectors*, as well as the twelve-part Audible Original, *Murders of Old China*.

Destination Macao is the third in the *Destination...* series following *Destination Shanghai* and *Destination Peking*.

Praise for *Midnight in Peking*

'A fascinating tale of life and death in a city on the brink of all-out war.'
— *Time*

'He resurrects a period that was filled with glitter as well as evil, but was never, as readers will appreciate, known for being dull.'
— *The Economist*

'The most talked-about read in town this year.'
— *New Yorker*

'A crime story set among sweeping events is reminiscent of Graham Greene, particularly *The Third Man*, while French's terse, tightly-focussed style has rightly been compared to Chandler. *Midnight in Peking* deserves a place alongside both these masters.'
— *The Independent* (UK)

'It is the storytelling flair that marks *Midnight in Peking* so highly above the run-of-the-mill true crime stories: with its false leads and twists, it sucks the reader in like the best fiction.'
— *The Scotsman*

'The shocking true tale, combined with prose you can't drag yourself away from, makes *Midnight in Peking* a work of non-fiction as compulsive as any bestselling crime novel.'
— *Sunday Express* (UK)

'One of the best portraits of between-the-wars China that has yet been written.'
— *Wall Street Journal*

Praise for *City of Devils*

'It's hard to go wrong with dope, decadence, and the demimonde . . . French recounts all this with great energy and brio.'
— Gary Krist, *The New York Times Book Review*

'Wonderfully atmospheric . . . French's two-fisted prose makes this deep noir history unforgettable.'
— *Publishers Weekly* (starred review)

'Nothing lasts forever: In 1930s Shanghai, the no-holds-barred gangster scene was run by an American ex-Navyman and a Jewish man who'd fled Vienna. Their milieu — and its end — comes alive.'
— Carolyn Kellogg, *Los Angeles Times*

'A tale of flash and noir demands a voice to match; fortunately, French combines the skills of a scholar with the soul of Dashiell Hammett.'
— Boris Kachka, *Vulture*

'Move over Weimar: Paul French's *City of Devils*, a history of glam and seedy interwar Shanghai's refugees and criminals, is nostalgic noir at its best.'
— *New York Magazine*

'The story is brought alive by French's Shanghai-noir telling, which echoes Dashiell Hammett and James Ellroy. He grips his reader to the end.'
— *The Economist*

'French's louche and moodily lit recreation of Shanghai is thrillingly done.This atmospheric survey hangs on the zoot-suited shoulders of the two leads. French's story chops and changes between Jack and Joe as they make their wayward ways east until fates and hardscrabble fortunes collide in the dive bars and dancehalls of Shanghai's Blood Alley.'
— Laura Freeman, *The Times* (UK)

'A story with the dark resonance of James Ellroy's novel *L.A. Confidential* and the seedy glamour of Alan Furst's between-the-wars mysteries . . . Reader advisory: By the time you are done with this extraordinary book, you will believe in devils, too.'
— Mary Ann Gwinn, *Newsday*

Praise for *Her Lotus Year*

'French is a fine and compelling writer, acclaimed author of a dozen books about old China. His painstaking, forensic research proves beyond reasonable doubt that although there was some truth in these sly and scandalous tales, none of them could have involved Wallis: the dates simply do not add up. She was certainly no angel, but nor was she the monster created by an establishment whispering campaign.'
— *Financial Times*

'French's book — beautifully told through meticulous historical research and examination of contemporary literature and film — gives the reader a vivid picture of what China must have been like for an American expat in the 1920s, and in fact tells a more interesting story.'
— *The New York Times*

'In this briskly debunking book Paul French, an old 'China hand' himself, makes it clear that the woman who had been born plain old Bessie Warfield in Pennsylvania in 1896 did not sign a pact with the Devil during what she later called her 'lotus year'.'
— *The Sunday Times*

'A new account of the months Simpson spent in China debunks the well-worn gossip about sexual adventures and opium addiction and even invites admiration for a 'buccaneering' woman.'
— *The Observer*

'Those who already appreciate French's talents as a historical storyteller will find a story to savour. For those who haven't yet had the pleasure, *Her Lotus Year* is an excellent place to start.'
— *Asian Review of Books*

'Paul French depicts a glitzy period the future Duchess of Windsor spent in China … The story of Wallis's Chinese awakening is worth telling.'
— *The Daily Telegraph*

'*Her Lotus Year* stays in the mind as a bright, shining, lively snapshot, delightful to read.'
— *The Spectator*

'The rumours about Wallis — collected in a so-called "China Dossier" - were unfounded, but the truth about her year in China s well documented by French — and is, perhaps, more interesting. For those who wish to follow in Wallis's footsteps, a surprising amount of what she saw still remains...'
— *The Times Luxx Magazine*

'In the newly-published *Her Lotus Year*, biographer Paul French forensically takes apart the most damning evidence — the China dossier — and proves that the stories made up around Wallis were never anything more than desperate and shabby inventions.'
— *Daily Mail*

Also by Paul French

Her Lotus Year: China, the Roaring Twenties and the Making of Wallis Simpson
Destination Peking
Strangers on the Praia: A story of Refugees and Resistance in Wartime Macao
Murders of Old China (an Audible Original)
Destination Shanghai
City of Devils: A Shanghai Noir
Midnight in Peking: How the Murder of a Young Englishwoman Haunted the Last Days of Old Peking
The Badlands: Decadent Playground of Old Peking
Bloody Saturday: Shanghai's Darkest Day
Supreme Leader: The Making of Kim Jong-un
Betrayal in Paris: How the Treaty of Versailles Led to China's Long Revolution
The Old Shanghai A-Z
Through the Looking Glass: China's Foreign Journalists from Opium Wars to Mao
Carl Crow – A Tough Old China Hand: The Life, Times, and Adventures of an American in Shanghai
North Korea Paranoid Peninsula – A Modern History

DESTINATION MACAO

by

Paul French

BLACKSMITH BOOKS

DESTINATION MACAO

ISBN 978-988-76748-2-5

Published by Blacksmith Books
Unit 26, 19/F, Block B, Wah Lok Industrial Centre,
37-41 Shan Mei Street, Fo Tan, Hong Kong
Tel: (+852) 2877 7899
www.blacksmithbooks.com

First printing 2025

Edited by Paul Christensen

For Anne. Sorry it rained.

Contents

HEONG-SAN
Nove-Ilhas
(Kau chau)
Cat-tai
Cattoi (Alfandega)
Passa Leão
Chin-San
Casa Branca
Alfandega
Pta Passa Leão
Apo-Siac
Pac-Siac
Canal de Tam-chau
Sanei
Pac-San
Tan-chiu
MACAU
Portas do Cerco
I. Verde
AREIA PRETA
de Mong-ha
Macau Siac
Ft D. Maria
PATANE
Guia
Farol
PORTO ARTIFICIAL PROJECTADO
Porto interior
S. Francisco
Bom Porto
Ft S. Tiago da Barra
CANAL PROJECTADO
Pedra Areca
BANCO DE MALAU-CHAU
Alfandega
I. Malau-chau
(Bugio)
ILHAS DA TAIPA
Pta Maria
Pta Cabrita
Pta D. João
ILHA PATERA
OU
ILHA DA LAPA
Mte de Lapa
Van Chai
Cuan San
R. Grande
Anan
Guanhang
Tai-liu
Sai-lio
I. CHA UAN SAN
Kuen Siec
Mahon San
Kua Teng
Enseada dos Piratas
Kien-Siac
Hang-mi
RIO
N
S
28'
30'
32'
34'
36'
38'
16'
14'
12'
10'

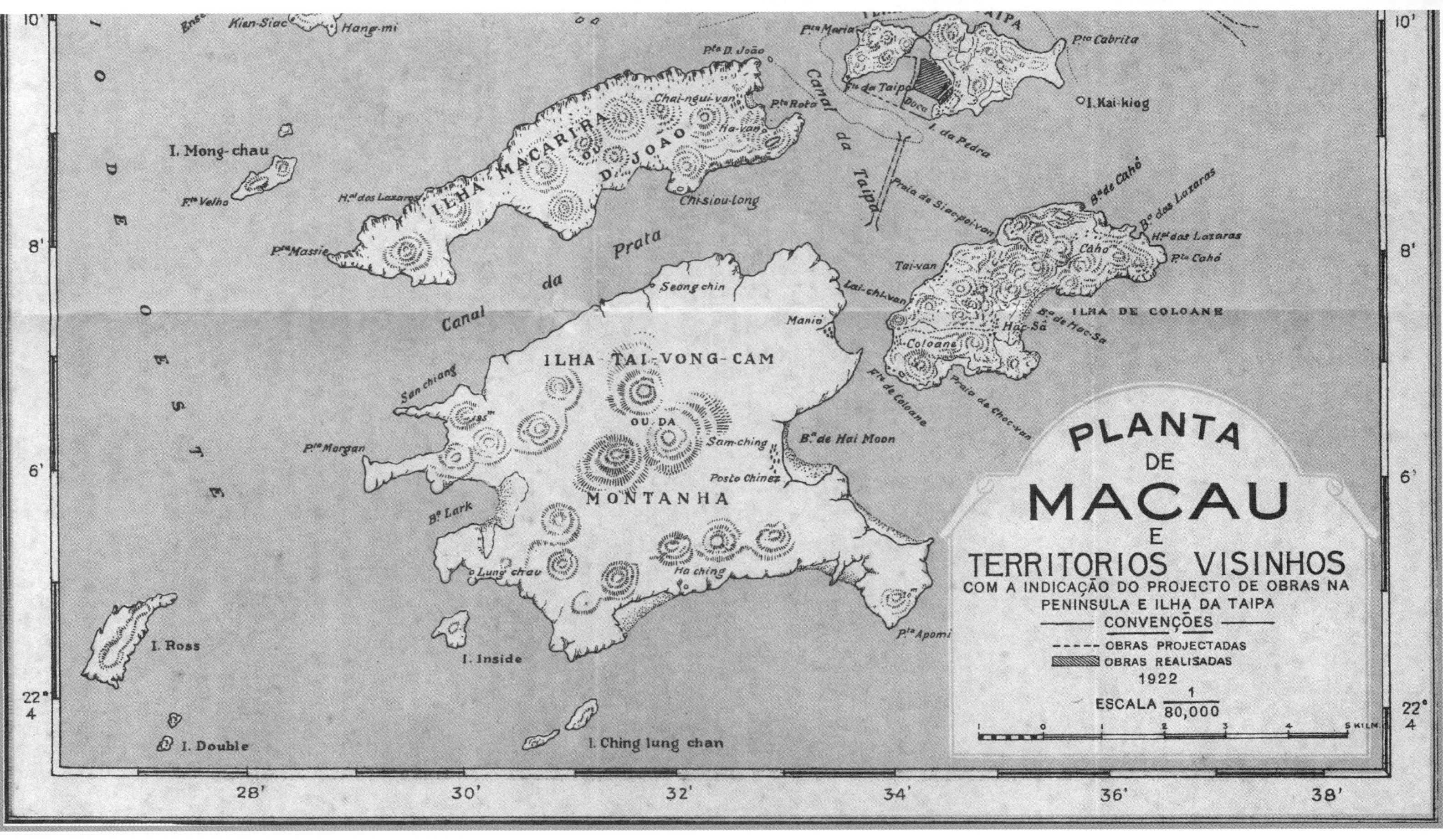
PLANTA
DE
MACAU
E
TERRITORIOS VISINHOS
COM A INDICAÇÃO DO PROJECTO DE OBRAS NA
PENINSULA E ILHA DA TAIPA
CONVENÇÕES
OBRAS PROJECTADAS
OBRAS REALISADAS
1922
ESCALA 1/80,000
ILHA MACARIRA OU D. JOÃO
ILHA TAI-VONG-CAM OU DA MONTANHA
ILHA DE COLOANE
Canal da Prata
Canal da Taipa
I. Mong-chau
I. Ross
I. Inside
I. Double
I. Ching lung chan
I. Kai-kiog
I. da Pedra
Kian-Siac
Hang-mi
Pta D. João
Pta Rota
Pta Maria
Pta Cabrita
Pta Massie
Pta Morgan
Pta Apomi
Pta Cahó
Chai-ngui-van
Ha-van
Chi-siou-long
H.al dos Lazaros
Fte Velho
Seong chin
Manio
San chiang
Sam-ching
Posto Chinez
Ba de Hai Moon
Ba Lark
Lung chau
Ha ching
Tai-van
Lai-chi-van
Coloane
Hac-Sa
Ba de Hac-Sa
Cahó
Ba de Cahó
Ba dos Lazaros
H.al das Lazaras
Praia de Si-ac-poi-van
Praia de Choc-van
Fte de Coloane
Fte da Taipa
Doca
O D E O E S T E
28'
30'
32'
34'
36'
38'
10'
8'
6'
22° 4

Introduction: The Gem of the Orient

A weed from Catholic Europe, it took root
Between the yellow mountains and the sea,
And bore these gay stone houses like a fruit,
And grew on China imperceptibly.

Rococo images of Saint and Saviour
Promise her gamblers fortunes when they die;
Churches beside the brothels testify
That faith can pardon natural behaviour.

This city of indulgence need not fear
The major sins by which the heart is killed,
And governments and men are torn to pieces:

Religious clocks will strike; the childish vices
Will safeguard the low virtues of the child;
And nothing serious can happen here.
– WH Auden, *Macao: A Sonnet* (1939)[1]

Gem of the Orient earth and open sea, Macao!
– Sir John Bowring, Governor of Hong Kong (1854-1859)[2]

1 'Macao: A Sonnet', *Journey to a War* (London: Faber & Faber, 1939). According to Edward Mendelson this sonnet wasn't part of the original manuscript sent to Faber. Auden and Isherwood had planned to write another book, *Hongkong-Macao: A Dialogue*, but then dropped the idea and incorporated their brief thoughts on Hong Kong (but not Macao) into *Journey to a War* with Auden adding a sonnet on each location. See Ed. Edward Mendelson, *The English Auden*, (London: Faber & Faber, 1986), p.425.

2 The phrase comes from a sonnet written by Sir John Bowring while visiting Macao in July 1849 – 'Gem of the orient earth and open sea/Macao! That in thy lap and on thy breast/Hast gathered beauties all the loveliest/Which the sun smiles on in his majesty.'

The Macao of the Mind

Macao, on the western shore of the Pearl Estuary, is where the search for the earliest traces of an organised foreign presence in Asia might begin. The phrase 'Gem of the Orient Earth' comes from a sonnet written by Sir John Bowring while visiting Macao in July 1849 – 'Gem of the orient earth and open sea/Macao! That in thy lap and on thy breast/ Hast gathered beauties all the loveliest/Which the sun smiles on in his majesty.' Five years later Bowring became the fourth Governor of Hong Kong and fortunately seems to have not had time to write any more sonnets. The few early wanderers, such as Marco Polo, aside it was the establishment of Portuguese trading posts at Canton and Macao around 1514 that initiated the collective involvement of Europeans, Americans, and others in what would become known as the "China Trade". That commerce comprised the importation of opium (the Portuguese traded *ópio* into China from Macao from 1729) and the exportation of Chinese silk, cotton, wool, artworks, tea, rhubarb, and porcelain. The story of Macao is essentially the origin story of the foreign presence in Chinese history.

Portugal acquired a permanent lease of Macao from the Ming dynasty in 1557 (the Portuguese being the only Europeans to have serious contact with the Ming). Lest we forget, this was a year before Elizabeth I succeeded to the throne of England and 63 years before the *Mayflower* sailed to what became Massachusetts. Macao was a success. In 1587 King Philip II of Spain (and also King of Portugal from 1580) declared Macao *Cidade do Nome de Deus* (City of the Name of God). Regaining independence from Spain in the 1640s, King João, *o Restaurador* (King John IV, the Restorer), added the motto *Não há Outra Mais Leal* (None is More Loyal). The Reverend Father António Francisco Cardim of the Jesuit Seminary at Macao wrote in 1640: 'Macao is put together of very fine buildings and is rich by reason of the commerce and traffic that go there by night and day.'[3] Fine buildings indeed: 1640 was the year construction was completed on the impressive Igreja de São Paulo (the

3 Quoted in Richard Hughes, *Hong Kong: Borrowed Place – Borrowed Time*, (London: Andre Deutsch, 1968), p.129. Cardim (1596-1659) spent several periods of time in Macao in the 1620s and 1630s.

Church of St. Paul), the ruins of which still dominate the central parish of Santo António today. Destroyed by fire in 1835, the frontage remains, impressive to all visitors, as the writer Han Suyin described it, '…divested of any inside or any walls behind it, an abandoned stage prop, high on a hill, framing the evening sky in its doors and windows.'[4]

The city grew. Macao's waterborne trade into China came to supplant the old Silk Road in the far north, devalued by disruption from constant skirmishing in Central Asia and improvements in European shipbuilding and maritime navigation. Macao was now the major landmark of arrival in the Chinese world for vessels sailing from Europe and points east of Europe. At the same time Macao saw a dual influx of missionaries and merchants, a hub for the trade in souls as well as goods.

Despite always having a majority Chinese population Macao was also something akin to a mini-Portugal in the South China Sea. Apart from small details and the occasional Gothic church or mansard roof Hong Kong does not look like Georgian London nor Saigon really resemble Haussmann Paris, yet the historic centre of Macao has always felt distinctly Portuguese and constantly been described as such. Old Lisbon was destroyed by an earthquake in 1755 and so had to be almost entirely rebuilt. Arguably the north Portuguese city of Porto (or Oporto) with, as the English writer William Kingston noted, its apparent abhorrence of right angles in its street layout, feels more like Macao.[5] Macao's plethora of small *praças* (squares or plazas), churches, convents, theatres, vibrant shops and markets (though admittedly lacking a major river to rival the Douro) mirrors Porto more than the Portuguese capital.

The bay (the *Porto Exterior* or Outer Harbour) is Macao: its raison d'être, main entry point, and the locus of trade and migration for centuries. It is where missionaries, Canton traders, navies, and Hong Kong ferries have all arrived, and where they, along with galleons destined for Japan, Manila, Malacca, as well as the indentured labourers bound for Cuba, Brazil, Peru, all departed from. The settlement extends from the bay, up past the Praia Grande (Great Bay) into the peninsula parishes of Santo António, Nossa Senhora de Fátima, and Sé. Macao has since spread far and wide: once quite distinct villages of Taipa and Coloane

---

4 Han Suyin, *A Many-Splendoured Thing*, (London: Jonathan Cape, 1952), p.99.

5 William HG Kingston, *Lusitanian Sketches of the Pen and Pencil*, (London: JW Parker, 1845), p.30.

are effectively now suburbs; the islands once named Lapa, Dom João and Montanha (collectively the Hengqin Islands) have been absorbed by reclamation, landfill, and levelling. So too as Canton boomed off the back of the China trade, the colony of Hong Kong consolidated and provided a constant flow of ferries. Later when the county town of Shum Chun became the kernel of the mega-city of Shenzhen, and even once humble Chuhai expanded to become the Pearl River entrepôt of Zhuhai, Macao came to adjoin southern China and Guangdong province in a way that feels far more intimate today than a century ago. And certainly more so than over 465 years ago when Macao was first leased from the Ming.

*

The story of colonial Macao would culminate on December 20, 1999, with the return of Macao to China. Yet despite its 500-year history the Macao bookshelf remains limited. Macao's first serious historian, Carlos Augusto Montalto de Jesus, in his book *Historic Macau* in 1902, observed that Macao, 'uncommonly rich and significant as it is, has been allowed to remain buried in obscurity, belittled by superficial writers whose prejudices and inaccuracies are always perpetuated.'[6] It is to be hoped that this collection does not fall into that category.

Previous books in this series have added (unapologetically) to the already groaning shelves of Shanghai- and Beijing-related books. Works of travel writing, novels, histories, and memoirs of both cities by foreign writers number in the hundreds if not thousands. Macao, on the other hand, suffers from a paucity of texts, both in English and other languages European and Asian. If you go back to the eighteenth and nineteenth centuries, the odd book in French or Spanish appears, a couple of travel memoirs in German and Dutch, a few studies in Chinese, a couple in Japanese.[7] On trips to Lisbon and Porto I have spent several days scouring

6 Carlos Augusto "CA" Montalto de Jesus, *Historic Macao*, (Hong Kong: Kelly & Walsh, 1902), p.i. Montalto de Jesus is also a potential warning from history for anyone writing about Macao. Though the first edition of *Historic Macau* was well received and reviewed, a second revised edition (1926) was burned by the Portuguese colonial authorities for alleging they were unfit to run Macao and that its administration should be handed over to the League of Nations.

7 There are local writers working in both Chinese and Portuguese in Macao today of course. I would note the poets Agnes Lam and Un Sio San, the historical novelist Joe Tang, author of *The Lost Spirit, Assassin,* and *The Curse of the Lost City*, that are all

bookshops, a patient local friend from my Portuguese publishers dragged along to help, looking for anything on Macao. My search yielded only a couple of historical romance novels with Macao settings and a sun-faded cookbook.[8]

I should stress that, as with the previous volumes in this series, *Destination Macao* does not in any way seek to provide a comprehensive history of the Portuguese colony, nor serve as a complete catalogue to the most famous residents and sojourners. It is rather a gallimaufry of people, events and themes that have caught my attention over the years. And this particular *Destination…* collection is as much about the Macao of the mind as it is about the reality of Macao's history and former denizens. The historian César Guillén Nuñez, in an introduction to a reprint of the English colonial official Austin Coates's *A Macao Narrative* (1978) noted, 'Western historians of his generation had to contend with a literature not yet fully developed, in which parts of the city's history had been fictionalised.'[9] This collection too deals with the fictional as well as the real Macao – it is incomplete, partial, and fragmentary by design.

City of Sin

While its presence may be lacking in serious works, Macao has certainly been a staple of effervescent hack journalism. This began in the mid- to late-nineteenth century, following the First Opium War (1839-1842) and continuing into the early twentieth century. A chief concern was the eclipsing of Macao as an entrepôt port, military garrison, and financial centre, by the new and dynamic British colony of Hong Kong. By the time of World War One this eclipse was total and so discussion throughout the inter-war years resorted to tropes of Macao as a city of sin, sex, opium, and piracy. This exotic impression remained on constant repeat after World War Two through to the 1970s by which time Macao, to all

set among key historical moments in Macao's past. Also, those late writers including the poet and defender of Macanese Patuá, José Inocêncio dos Santos Ferreira, aka Adé (1919-1993); Henrique de Senna Fernandes (1923-2010); Leonel de Barros, aka Neco (1924–2011) and others.

8 There is a partial, but not complete, list of other texts on Macao not otherwise noted in the footnotes throughout in the acknowledgments at the end of this book.

9 César Guillén Nuñez, Foreword to Austin Coates, *A Macao Narrative*, (Hong Kong: Hong Kong University Press, 2009).

intents and purposes, largely dropped off the map, lost in the shadow of a booming Hong Kong and then of a reviving post-Maoist southern China. If mentioned at all Macao was noted as nothing more than a haven for smugglers, gamblers, and gold dealers, seemingly beyond any law – perhaps a place for adventurers but containing little of modern relevance.

Nevertheless, this hack journalism has much to reveal, whether from the likes of adventurer-journalists such as Aleko Lilius, or seekers of sin cities such as Hendrik de Leeuw and Maurice Dekobra in the 1920s and '30s, through to the numerous pulp fiction writers and then film makers who found a ready-made exotic locale in Macao. This was a vogue that continued with post-war visitors including the American journalist Harrison Forman, James Bond creator Ian Fleming, and the French writer Joseph "Jef" Kessel.[10]

Macao was represented as an island of debauchery, shadiness, and assorted villainy, whilst simultaneously being an idle, slow-paced, island of tropical lassitude and sleepy backwater boredom. A sultry Mediterranean town where little happened but that by chance was anchored to mainland China. It was also the vibrant, exciting 'Monte Carlo of the East'. Could Macao really be both simultaneously? This apparent duality was in stark contrast to Shanghai's unquestionable sin city reputation of rampant debauchery coupled with bare-knuckled capitalism, arch modernism, and the free-for-all appropriation of the city's east-west fusion. Nobody ever doubted Shanghai's credentials. Could Macao ever really be both sin and lassitude, sex and siestas? The frustratingly slim Macao bookshelf provides no conclusive answers.

City of Poets

I make no apologies for the fact that several stories in this collection – notably the chapters on the cinema of Josef von Sternberg and the fictional writings of Maurice Dekobra, concern movies and books by directors and authors who spent little or no time in Macao. Others who left us images of Macao, the artists George Chinnery and George

10 The American newspaper correspondent Harrison Forman's Macao diaries are held as part of the Harrison Forman Collection, University of Wisconsin Library (Milwaukee). Joseph Kessel, *Hong-Kong et Macao*, (Paris: Gallimard, 1957).

Smirnoff, as well as the writer Deolinda da Conceição, spent more time in Macao but were influenced by outside locations (England, Ireland, British India, Harbin, Tsingtao, Hong Kong and Shanghai among them) and artistic movements (Chinnery was a classic portraitist in oil or crayon, though considered 'new' at the time he developed his style in the 1790s; Smirnoff excelled at 'wash' painting).[11] Including them is intentional, and it is because Macao has been so much an imaginary place over its entire history that separating the "idea", or "dream", of Macao from the reality is difficult if not impossible. They are hopelessly intertwined.

Even those who lived in Macao often preferred to dream of it, creating their personal visions of it. The one-eyed *Lisboeta*, street brawler, jailbird, and moody denizen of Portugal's mid-sixteenth-century *demimonde* Luís de Camões (c.1524-1580) was expelled from Portugal to North Africa for his politics (where he probably lost his eye in Ceuta). Further trouble ensued – female related – which led to duels and a more distant banishment to Goa. There he was offered prison or exile to the furthest reaches of the Portuguese Empire. He chose Macao.

Luís de Camões, 1577

Camões's entire biography is splendidly wreathed in myth and rumour. The epic poem *Os Lusíadas* (*The Lusiads*, or *Song of the Portuguese*) which would make him the great bard of Portugal is essentially a voyage of the mind imagining Vasco da Gama's sea route to India.[12] Legend has it *Os Lusíadas* was (or at least the last three cantos were) written in Macao during his sojourn around 1557 (no one is entirely sure of his dates in

11 'Wash' is a technique in which the brush is made very wet with solvent and paint that is then applied to a wet or dry support such as paper or canvas.

12 Macao acquired an Avenida Vasco da Gama in 1898 to commemorate the fourth centenary of da Gama's discovery of the sea route to India, though the boulevard no longer exists. The Jardim de Vasco da Gama (Vasco da Gama Gardens) – between Rua de Ferreira do Amaral, Calçada do Gaio, and Estrada da Vitória – was also originally laid out in 1898 with fountains and a bust of da Gama added in 1911.

the colony), sheltering from the sun in a cave, right where the Jardim Camões now stands.[13] Whether or not he wrote all, or just some, of *Os Lusíadas* (published in 1572 after surviving heat, shipwreck, and the censors) in Macao or not, he did have one of the most extraordinary jobs while resident there. He was Trustee for the Dead and Absent, taking care of the deceased's belongings and arranging for transport to their next of kin. He made no money from *Os Lusíadas*, despite its being recognised as a paean to the nation. He died in Lisbon impoverished in 1580, his grave unrecorded. Though he wrote next to nothing directly about Macao he has been consistently lauded there – the first record of a monument to Camões in Macao is as early as 1631. He left to return to Goa, as ever under a cloud and in some disgrace (alleged theft, misappropriation of goods/funds it seems), and so perhaps he preferred to gloss over his time as Trustee for Macao's Dead and Absent.

Wenceslau José de Souza de Moraes in Macao, 1893

Writers abounded in Macao. The Orientalist writer Wenceslau José de Souza de Moraes (1854-1929) is most closely identified with Japan – a symbolist poet and translator of *haiku* poetry often compared to Lafcadio Hearn. Serving in the Portuguese Navy in 1889 he was assigned to assist the Captain of the Port of Macao (essentially the highest ranked naval officer in the colony). Macao was very much a base for Moraes who spent time in the Kingdom of Siam, Portuguese Timor and Japan. However, he did form attachments to Macao during his decade there. He married a Macanese woman named "Atchan" with whom he had two sons José (born 1893) and João (born 1894).[14] He also began work on his first book *Traços do*

13 Macao has certainly long claimed Camões's *Os Lusíadas* but at best it was only partly written in Macao and also partially, in Ormuz in the Persian Gulf as well as in Goa too. Camões is often spelt "Camoens" in English texts. The Jardim Camões includes a bust of the poet, large boulders, and originally small palm trees designed to be reminiscent of Portugal's colony in Brazil. Indeed, several busts had to be cast in Lisbon as the first two or three were defaced, indicating perhaps not everyone was a fan.

14 Atchan, aka Mo Wong-shi and Wong Ioc-chan, is variously described as Chinese, Anglo-Chinese and Macanese. She left Moraes in 1894 while pregnant and moved to

Extremo Oriente (*Traces of the Far East*, published in 1895).[15] He left to establish Portugal's first consulate for Kobe and Osaka in 1898.

Moraes overlapped with the slightly later Portuguese poet Camilo Pessanha (1867-1926), who arrived in Macao in 1894, five years after Moraes and over three centuries after Camões. It was an inauspicious arrival being a year of terrible and deadly plague outbreak across southern China. He came ostensibly to teach philosophy, but also wrote poetry. Pessanha remained for 32 years living an unconventional life, ignoring the disdain of the colony's rather more strait-laced Portuguese administrative class for his somewhat Bohemian lifestyle.

Camilo Pessanha

Still, Pessanha was useful to the colonial elite. He advised the Lisbon-appointed governors (*governadors*) and acted as a lawyer, whilst also collecting Chinese art. He was decidedly more curious than most colonists about the local culture. His poetry was a hobby, largely intended to be read by his friends, and next to none was published during his lifetime. But he was clearly simultaneously dreaming of Macao while actually living his life there.

Pessanha's work (and dreams) were influenced by the nineteenth century French poets Rimbaud, Mallarmé, Verlaine and Baudelaire. Pessanha's best-known poem *Clepsydra* (or *Clepsidra*) was written around 1920.[16] It appeared just six years before his death and catapulted him into the position of the leading figure of Portuguese symbolist poetry, for which there was a sizeable vogue in the country. But *Clepsydra* was not officially published until 1945. *Clepsydra*, and other of his works written

Hong Kong with the children.

15 Wenceslau José de Souza de Moraes, *Traços do Extremo Oriente — Sião, China e Japão* (Lisbon: AM Pereira, 1895).

16 The most recent English translation being by Adam Mahler, *Clepsydra and Other Poems,* (Amherst, MA: University of Massachusetts Press, 2022).

in Macao, reject naturalism and realism favouring dreams, visions, and derangement to interpret the world (all admittedly perhaps helped along by his opium addiction).[17] He has been described as the 'most pure of the Portuguese Symbolist poets', and 'perhaps the purest of Macao poets – balancing the actual and the imaginary; melancholia and wistfulness; the Macao of reality and the Macao of the mind'.[18]

Such remembrance is an integral part of writing and thinking about, as well as visiting and living in, Macao. Apart from the dense cluster of streets and squares around the central *Leal Senado* (Loyal Senate House, built around 1784 with a number of later refurbishments in 1904 and 1936), Macao's cityscape has altered beyond all recognition since the period this book covers (the nineteenth and the first half of the twentieth century). Of course, it is also true that Peking and Shanghai have seen wholesale heritage destruction, precious little serious preservation, and massive population expansions too, but Macao's changes are arguably more fundamental. A small preserved historical area sits alongside the garish new casino buildings of recent years. But this process in Macao is accentuated in dreamlike fashion by the preponderance of illusory fanciful recreations littering modern Macao's gaming house-strewn landscape – Fisherman's Wharf, The Venetian, The Londoner, The Parisian, and Treasure Island, and among them faux relics of old Portuguese Macao.[19]

17 Christopher Chu & Maggie Hoi, *Camilo Pessanha's Macau Stories,* (Macao: Os Macanese Publicações, 2023).

18 Pessanha as described by the Portuguese journalist, playwright, and film director Reinaldo Ferreira (aka Repórter X). A *clepsidra* (or clepsydra) is an ancient form of water clock. Pessanha's work combined sonnets, scattered, and fragmentary verses, poetry, and translated Chinese poems. In 1914, Pessanha published translations of eight Chinese eulogies in the Macao newspaper *O Progresso.* A statue of Pessanha stands in the Jardim das Artes (Arts Garden) on the once banyan-tree lined Avenida de Amizade in Sé, while he is buried in St Miguel Arcanjo Cemetery (St Michael the Archangel) on Beco do Alm. Costa Cabral.

19 Incongruously the Fisherman's Wharf development includes a replica of Rome's Colosseum. The Venetian is a sister property to the one of the same name in Las Vegas and includes a section of the San Luca Canal with gondoliers etc and a replica Rialto Bridge. The Londoner Macao includes a model Houses of Parliament, Big Ben, and a Changing of the Guard show. Should you wish, you can stay in "Suites by David Beckham". The Parisian of course includes a 525-foot replica of the Eiffel Tower and a 'Parisian style' fountain.

All old maps are redundant, reduced to antique curiosities. Substantial landfill created Cotai, the strip that now links the once distinct Coloane and Taipa into one island, and the 34-mile-long Hong Kong-Zhuhai-Macau Bridge (HZMB). To traverse the HZMB at night, atop a double-decker bus, is to leave Macao and plunge into near-total darkness for 45 minutes with perhaps only the faint lights of a Kowloon- or Pearl River-bound cargo ship, only to then reappear into a brightly lit Hong Kong, and a very different historical trajectory.

Visiting Macao in the twenty-first century it is almost impossible to separate illusion and reality. The imaginative visitor to Macao's UNESCO World Heritage-listed official "historic centre" (*Centro Historico de Macao*), with its remaining traditional shophouses, churches, art-deco, and *Português Suave* deco architecture, can sense a time past. Elsewhere are buildings inspired by the Bauhaus as well as Le Corbusier-influenced Brutalist architecture, and a few examples of the stripped-back and traditionalist architecture favoured during the authoritarian *Estado Novo* period (in opposition to "decadent modernism").[20] You can feel you might encounter Robert Mitchum in *Macao* (1952) disembarking on the Porto Exterior destined to intertwine his fate with Jane Russell, or perhaps Jennifer Jones and William Holden strolling along the Praia Grande (before it was hemmed in by land reclamation) hand-in-hand in *Love is a Many Splendored Thing* (1955).[21] Or maybe join Erich von Stroheim in the French film *Macao, l'enfer du jeu* (1939) in a fan-tan house, or the adventuring journalist Aleko Lilius among the *cho* seagoing junks as he encounters (or imagines) Lai Choi San, the Pirate Queen of

20 There are any number of art-deco structures in Macao, both in the historic area and elsewhere, for instance in Coloane. Examples include the combined cinema-retail-residential development, Teatro Apollo, on Avenida de Almeida Ribeiro. *Português Suave* was a style advocated by the authoritarian Salazar *Estado Novo* regime. Originally termed *Estilo Português* (*Portuguese Style*) it became more commonly known as *Português Suave* after a popular cigarette brand. It incorporates elements of modernism with what some see as a provincial traditionalism. Le Corbusier's influence can be seen in the late 1950s Rainha D Leonor residential building (on Avenida do Infante Dom Henrique). The *Estado Novo* style was built principally in the 1940s and 1950s and can be found in several buildings including the Carmo Post Office in Taipa (1954).

21 The writer and former Hong Kong colonial district officer Austin Coates recalled, perhaps somewhat apocryphally, that 'you could picnic in the middle of the Avenida de Praia Grande without getting in the way of the traffic' in the 1950s. Ramon Rodamilans and Austin Coates, *Souvenirs and Letters*, (London: Athena Press, 2007), p.93

the 1920s South China Seas.[22] And alongside these fictions are the self-invented, yet true, characters of Macao – Stanley "King of Macao" Ho, or Dr Pedro "Golden Grandfather" Lobo.

Fernando Pessoa, 1914

One more poet. The dreamscape Macao wrought by Camões and Pessanha is compounded by another Portuguese poet, Fernando Pessoa (1888-1935). Writing under one of his many heteronyms, Álvaro de Campos, he imagined himself to be in Macao at one in the morning… awaking with a start…hearing a cry in Cantonese 'Yhat-loh-oh-oh-oh-oh-oh-oh-oh-oh-oh-oh…Gea-…' Yet Pessoa never visited Macao. He only dreamt of it, perhaps discussed it with his friend Pessanha in Lisbon or Porto. His early morning Cantonese cry is an invention, an imagining.[23] For Pessoa Portuguese history, its empire, the national identity, and by extension its colonies, including Macao, were all at their root myths, inventions, creations.[24]

22 *Cho* – A Macanese word for a seagoing junk derived from Cantonese "t'so". Also, as fan-tan will come up repeatedly throughout this book it is perhaps worth noting that it is a game, long popular in Macao (both in old Macao casinos and in just about every literary evocation of the colony) and one of pure chance. Fan-tan is played by placing two handfuls of small objects on a board and guessing the remaining count when divided by four. After players have cast bets on values of one through four, the dealer or croupier repeatedly removes four objects from the board until only one, two, three or four beans remain, determining the winner.

23 *Álvaro de Campos (aka* Fernando Pessoa), *Passagem das Horas* (*Time's Passage*), translated by Richard Zenith, included in *Fernando Pessoa & Co.: Selected Poems*, (New York: Grove Press, 1998), pp.146-168. Pessoa preferred the term heteronym to pseudonym as he felt his alter-egos had their own independent intellectual lives, physiques, and biographies. Pessoa saw de Campos as a well-travelled naval engineer turned Sensationist poet from the Algarve who drank absinthe and smoked opium.

24 For Pessoa on Macao and myth see Arnaldo MA Gonçalves, 'Macau in the Myth of the "Quinto Império" by Fernando Pessoa', *Pessoa Plural* (A Journal of Fernando Pessoa Studies), No. 21, Spring 2022.

When I first visited Macao in the early 1990s it was most often talked about in terms of languor, ossification, a symbol for a sort of slow tropical decay. It was dismissed as frivolous when discussed alongside wealthy Hong Kong, the booming mega-cities of southern China, and the re-emergent Shanghai. It briefly perked up and attracted attention in 1999 – sensational triad street wars and machine gun battles faded into the handover and a sterner hand on the tiller. And then a 180-degree shift to vast casinos, money, glitz, and mainland gambling-driven tourism. The new Macao was born, but there were also continuities.

City of Indulgence

American author Sherwood King's bestselling novel *If I Die Before I Wake* (1938) formed the basis for the Orson Welles and Rita Hayworth film noir *The Lady from Shanghai* (1947). Welles had a major hand in the script as well as directing.[25] He moved the action from King's New York State's country estates and courtrooms onto a yacht to heighten the movie's claustrophobic tension. Quite where the "Shanghai" bit came in is unclear, though of course in 1947 the city's name was a byword for vice and corruption, appealing to Welles. In the film Hayworth explains the back story of her character (Elsa "Rosalie" Bannister, speaking in the third person):

> 'Her parents were Russian, White Russian. You never heard of the place where she comes from…'

Elsa comes from Chefoo in northern China's Shantung province. The Welles character (Michael O'Hara, a sailor-vagabond type) claims to know Chefoo:

> 'It's the second wickedest city in the world.'
> 'And the first?' Elsa asks,
> 'Macao. Wouldn't you say so?', answers Welles/O'Hara, to which Hayworth/Elsa replies:
> 'I would. I worked there…How do you rate Shanghai? I worked there too…You need more than luck in Shanghai.'

25 Sherwood King, *If I Die Before I Wake*, (New York: Simon & Schuster, 1938).

And finally, one of the potentially great accounts of Macao that we never got was that from WH Auden and Christopher Isherwood. The pair were commissioned in 1939 by the publishers Faber & Faber to highlight the war in China and research and write *Journey to a War*, which was published later that same year. They initially visited Hong Kong, which didn't impress them much. They then took the ferry to Macao. However, their experiences never made the book, except for Auden's sonnet where he dubs Macao, 'This city of indulgence…' The sonnet's opening lines in 1939 were:

WH Auden, 1939

A weed from Catholic Europe, it took root
Between the yellow mountains and the sea,
And bore these gay stone houses like a fruit,
And grew on China imperceptibly.

But Auden later updated the sonnet, perhaps feeling he had been a little too flippant in believing that nothing serious could ever happen in Macao. The new opening lines read:

A weed from Catholic Europe, it took root
Between some yellow mountains and a sea,
Its gay stone houses an exotic fruit,
A Portugal-cum-China oddity.[26]

This volume – like the previous *Destination Shanghai* and *Destination Peking* – does not aim to tell those stories of Macao that have, in my

26 In *The Collected Shorter Poems* published in the 1960s, and *Auden's Collected Poems* published in the 1970s, the original opening lines were replaced by those, slightly amended, quoted here.

opinion, been told before in greater depth. It is by design some aspects of Macao's history and representation that have caught my attention and intrigued me enough to delve a little further. I should perhaps note that I am, like Auden, English, and so what jumps out to my non-Chinese, non-Macanese, non-Portuguese eye is, I think, sometimes different than what has often previously attracted Chinese and Portuguese writers on Macao. Though ultimately it is that *Portugal-cum-China oddity* that these contributions seek to tease out.

Paul French – December 2024

A note on names and spellings

Names in this book reflect the spellings commonly used in the first half of the twentieth century. Hence Peking and not Beijing; Canton and not Guangzhou. Where Chinese people were commonly known by Western names to foreign audiences, these are used, rather than the pinyin romanisations. Additionally, I have used the best-known variations of some Chinese names rather than their more modern variants, such as Sun Yat-sen rather than Sun Zhongshan. And where people are better known to an English-speaking readership by their anglicised, adopted or, in the case of many, additional English names I have used these, for instance Ho Hung-sun, who is more commonly known in English as Stanley Ho.

"Praia" in Portuguese, as in Praia Grande, simply means a beach, a place beside the sea (a promenade), and was often spelt "Praya" by English-language newspapers and sources. "Porto", as in Porto Interior and Porto Exterior, is simply a harbour.

Macao or Macau?

The etymology of Macao is disputed, with various theories, though it most likely derived originally from the (still surviving) Temple of A-Ma, or Ma Kok Temple, in the Barra district, dating back to 1448. Portuguese sailors understood Ma Kok (or some variant thereof) as Macao. The earliest Portuguese spelling for this was *Amaquão* (or *Amacão*) until Macao became common during the seventeenth century.

The 1911 reform of Portuguese orthography standardised the spelling as Macau, though Macao remained in common usage in English and other European languages. The standard Mandarin Chinese for Macao is *Aomen*, or *Oumun* in Cantonese.

Macao is invariably now rendered as "Macau" in Portuguese. Before 1955 (i.e. the period of all but a couple of the essays in this collection), the spelling Macao was used in most official documents. However, spellings have varied depending on the user's preference and the shifting spelling reforms in Portugal beginning in 1911, as well as various orthographic agreements between Lisbon and its colonies (notably Brazil). Generally now there are too many exceptions for there to be a hard and fast rule.

The official spelling of the Portuguese language in Macao is currently fixed by legal decree (Law #103/99/M) agreed in December 1999 and recognised by the *Governo da Região Administrativa Especial de Macau (*Government of the Macau Special Administrative Region of the People's Republic of China).

Additionally, the term "Macanese" is often used to describe people of predominantly mixed Cantonese and Portuguese (as well as Malay, Japanese, English, Dutch, Sinhalese, Indian and other) ancestry. The major Macanese diaspora communities live in Hong Kong, North America, Brazil, Australia, and Portugal. Macanese can also be applied to cultural phenomena – cuisine, art, literature, patois, that have all emerged in Macao. To differentiate between Macanese as an ethnicity and as a descriptor, the sociologist Zhidong Hao uses the term "Macauan". But I find this a little clumsy, though perhaps more accurate, and so have stuck to Macanese and hope that the context in which I am writing is obvious within the text.

Throughout this book therefore I use Macao, unless in an original quotation where the author used Macau. I hope it is not overly confusing or dogmatic.

The Myths and Realities of Macao (1513-Present Day)

Macao as a stereotype, 1902

'To me Macao appeared as a beautiful little Portuguese city. There is population but of ruins, of avenidas, of lovely gardens tended by hands long forgotten (...). The pale pink and pale green houses, with balustrades and verandahs, take one for a few seconds back to the Tagus.'

– Alfred Harmsworth (Lord Northcliffe), *The Times* (1928)

'There is no question that Macao harbours in its hidden places the riffraff of the world, the drunken ship masters, the flotsam of the sea, the derelicts, and more shameless, beautiful, savage women than any port in the world. It is a hell. But to those who whirl in its unending play, it is one haven where there is never a hand raised or a word said against the play of the beastliest emotions that ever blackened the human heart.'

– Hendrik de Leeuw, *Cities of Sin* (1933)

Finding Incident and Adventure

In June 1903 Shanghai's *North-China Daily News* urged any Shanghailanders heading south not to forget Macao. 'Visitors who go over from Hongkong for a day little realise how full of incident and adventure the story of Macao is.'[27] Many did go, wandered the *avenidas*, alleyways, compact *largo*-squares, and *travessa*-junctions. They found shelter from the sun under spreading gnarled banyans on the Praia Grande and in shady corners of public parks. They ate in Portuguese-style restaurants that could have been on a Lisbon or Porto street, took cocktails on the verandas of comfortable *pousadas* (inns), and drank strong coffee in cafés and the foyers of charming *pensão* small hotels, escaping the intermittent tropical downpours. And along the way they all found their own personal versions of Macao.

The British newspaper magnate Alfred Harmsworth, Lord Northcliffe (immortalised as "Lord Copper" in Evelyn Waugh's 1938 satire of sensationalist journalism, *Scoop*), certainly found a more wistful Macao than the once popular Dutch travel writer of rather licentious tastes and a consistently flowery pen, Hendrick de Leeuw. Was Macao a place of gambling and debauchery, or solitude and lassitude. Of swashbuckling Chinese pirates raiding its shores and foreign adventurers seeking their fortunes, or Chinese fisherman hauling heavy nets while Portuguese colonists sat fanning themselves on the docks of the Porto Interior?

Harmsworth was on a world tour with a punishing schedule. He decided Macao would be a relaxing place for a weekend – and so it was for him. De Leeuw travelled the world seeking out the buzzwords of the day – "fleshpots", "white slavery" "red light districts" – and he too found in Macao what he sought. The Finnish-American journalist Aleko Lilius chose, in the 1920s, to see a place frozen in time, defined by tradition. This too suited Lilius's narrative, which he repeated *ad nauseam* in newspapers, and books, describing pirate haunts seemingly unchanged for centuries. What visitors seemed to find easily was the particular Macao they desired. And Macao always seemingly obliged their whims.

But to many others, less lofty than Lord Northcliffe, less obsessive than de Leeuw, less desperately in search of readers than Lilius, Macao

27 *North-China Daily News*, June 23, 1903.

was something else. The Russian émigrés, Canton gangsters on-the-lam, debt-laden London painters, persecuted Japanese Christians, ambitious Timorese clerks, "lost" New York debutantes, Cantonese resistance fighters, Jewish wartime refugees, Armenian moneylenders, wandering Azorean poets, *Lisboeta* political rebels, disgraced Shanghai cops, Parsee traders, Portuguese army deserters, opium dealers of a dozen countries, numerous Jesuits, Lazarists and a few Protestants – to all of these Macao was to be a place of refuge and potential opportunity.[28]

For centuries each inhabitant, colonist, sojourner, exile, refugee, or simply casual day-tripper has taken what they wanted from Macao; selecting what they needed at that moment in time; picking and choosing from its offerings as, by turns, sanctuary (political, religious, economic), opportunity, strategic career move, haven, staging post, or hide-out. Others had less choice. Chinese "coolies" tricked into indentured service in Macao, or black African slaves from Portugal's colonies brought to *Provincia de Macao* and sold.[29]

The Water-Lily Peninsula

Despite the power of the Macao of the imagination, of course there is a real history. One of the attributes that makes Macao unique and especially fascinating is its longevity as the oldest European settlement on the China Coast. Galleons sailed east from Lisbon, out past the Torre de Belém into the unknown throughout the early 1500s. They edged ever more eastwards to the Maghreb, down the African coast, across to India and the Straits of Hormuz on the eastern side of the Persian Gulf. From Bengal, Coromandel, Gujarat, *Goa Dourada* (Golden Goa and

28 Macao was of course especially important to the Jesuits (The Society of Jesus – formed c.1540s) for their missionary-trading activities in both China and Japan. Following their expulsion from Portugal in 1759 their property was confiscated; many were imprisoned, and the missionaries expelled from all Portuguese colonies as well as officially from Macao in 1762.

29 The presence of black slaves, brought directly from Africa, sometimes Brazil and occasionally via Portugal, has a long history in Macao, certainly back to at least the 1630s. Zhidong Hao refers to the Portuguese Captain-Major (*Capitão-mor* or sometimes the Captain-General – effectively the Governor at the time) Diogo de Pinho Teixeira punishing a soldier who raped a black slave woman in 1710. Zhidong Hao, *Macau: History and Society*, (Hong Kong: Hong Kong University Press, 2011), p.33.

sometimes referred to as the "Second City of Portugal" it returned such wealth[30]) and onwards to Malacca, Siam, and always creating new trading centres and sometimes colonies along the way. Macao was, via the Cape of Good Hope, approximately 15,000 miles in total sea voyage terms.

The Portuguese explorer Jorge Álvares is usually credited with having first arrived in Chinese waters in 1513. After some objections Portugal eventually formally leased Macao as a trading post from the Ming Dynasty in 1557, the year the first fleet from Lisbon appeared in Chinese waters. It was not until over three centuries later that the Qing, hoping to forge an alliance to fight south China's scourge of piracy, granted Lisbon perpetual occupation rights in 1887.[31] The Portos Interior and Exterior became crowded with galleons and *nao* carracks as well as traditional *choa* junks, sampans, sloops, and the distinctive "egg-boats" of the Tanka people that housed whole families.[32]

The British historian of Portugal's maritime history (as well as a Hong Kong spy chief, and partner of *New Yorker* correspondent Emily Hahn) Charles Boxer dated the oldest original documents in the archives of the *Senado da Camara* (Town Council) from 1712.[33] However, there are incomplete records that appear to date back further to the 1630s. The *Leal Senado* (Loyal Senate) was established in 1583, by which time already 900 Portuguese ("Portingalls" as the English often called them then) were officially registered in Macao. The earliest reference by a founder of the colony is, again according to Boxer, from Father Gregório Gonçalves, who first went to Macao around 1554. He was describing Macao at a time

30 Though not much thought of today the link between Macao's early sustenance and prosperity and Goa is crucial. As David Howarth, author of *Adventures: The Improbable Rise of the East India Company, 1550-1650,* (New Haven & London, Yale University Press, 2023) succinctly puts it: 'Although 3,835 nautical miles lie between Goa and Macao, as the albatross flies, Macao could not have been sustained without Goa as a stop-off for carracks that had already travelled the 9,710 miles from Lisbon.' p.200.

31 These "rights" were subsequently renewed several times, including by the Nationalist (or Nanking) government of Chiang Kai-shek in 1928.

32 RM Ballantyne's *Man on the Ocean*, (London: Nelson, 1862) notes 'At sundown the boat-people anchor their craft in rows to stakes, cut lengthwise, they are called in the Chinese language "egg-boats". A large family will sometimes pack itself into an egg-boat not much more than twelve feet long and six broad.'

33 Charles R Boxer, *O Senado da Cãmara de Macau*, (Lisbon: Livraria Castro e Silva, 1997).

when the colony already had approximately 500 houses, a "priestery", three churches (all Catholic, one Jesuit), and a hospital. Macao was as much a religious outpost as a commercial colony, trading with China, the Philippines and Japan (eventually, with the Portuguese opening a trading post at Nagasaki in 1571), and at the same time proselytising where it could. Gonçalves refers to Macao in 1555 as the 'Water-Lily Peninsula', a nomenclature that predates the better-known and more dramatic *Cidade do nome de Deus* (City of the Name of God).[34]

*

In the early nineteenth century Macao was home to a majority Chinese population living alongside the Portuguese colonists, various Jesuits and Lazarist missionaries, and those in the fledgling Canton Trade. The traders moved back and forth between Canton and Macao as cargoes arrived and departed and Chinese official whim allowed. The Portuguese port offered at least some protection from the twin ravages of the South China Seas – piracy and typhoons. Qing dynasty officials allowed the traders to stay in Canton at their "factories" – basically warehouses with offices and living accommodation attached – in a small, concentrated area of the city to which they were largely confined (and all foreign women forbidden). But, out of the trading season – the spring and summer months – or if the local authorities were displeased, the foreigners retreated to Macao.

It was a small but vibrant colony – as a trading settlement soon eclipsing Malacca in importance for the Portuguese. An entrepôt with cargoes of silk, nutmeg, saffron, cinnamon, rhubarb, pearls, *guayacan* bark, tamarind, Japanese silver, and Chinese porcelain all passing through. The Macao *pataca* was yet to be introduced and so merchants, traders, and ships' captains did business in Portuguese *ducados*, *bazarucos*, *pardaus*, *réis*, and *tanga*, Brazilian *cruzados*, Goan *rupias* and *xerafins*, Chinese paper dollars (and later Hong Kong dollars), Mexican and Spanish-American *doubloons* and silver dollars, Japanese bronze and silver *mon*, gold *oban* coins or paper *yen*, Philippines *pesos*, French Indochina *piastres*, Dutch *guilders*, British pounds, shillings and pence, Chinese silver *taels,* and gold

34 Charles R Boxer, *Portuguese Society in the Tropics: The Municipal Councils of Goa, Macao, Bahia, and Luanda 1510-1800,* (Madison, Milwaukee: The University of Wisconsin Press, 1965), p.42. I believe the archives he refers to are the *Arquivo Histórico Ultramarino* (Overseas Historical Archive) in Lisbon.

bullion from around the world.[35] All these currencies circulated, as well as Chinese promissory notes or deposit certificates, known as *pangtans.*[36]

However, after the First Opium War (1839-1842) and the establishment of Hong Kong as a British Crown Colony, Macao gradually receded into something of a backwater. Hong Kong offered a deep-water harbour, better typhoon shelters and an end to reliance on Portuguese largesse. After an economic boom – British builders in Hong Kong initially ordered 10,000 bricks a day shipped from Macao to the new colony[37] – Macao's key role in the early China trade was usurped by a thrusting and aggressive mercantile Britain and its new fortified base on Hong Kong Island. The Macao-favouring English artist George Chinnery, who visited Hong Kong Island once for a few months in 1846 lamented that the new colony would be the death of Macao. Hong Kong was the embodiment of greater British imperial power throughout the East as well as the rising dominance of the British China traders and their allies and "frenemies" the Parsees, Danes, and Americans.

When the British departed Macao to colonise Hong Kong they took a lot of the entrepreneurial investment and trade from Macao with them. Simultaneously the French were consolidating their Indochinese empire.[38] The historian CA Montalto de Jesus commented that 'history repeated itself: as Bombay had doomed Goa, so Hong Kong now doomed

35 Incidentally, the *pataca* was introduced in Macao (and Portuguese Timor) in 1894 to replace the previously widely used Portuguese real at a rate of 450 to 1. *Pataca* is a Portuguese word that roughly translates as "metallic coin". The *pataca* finally became indexed to the Portuguese *escudo* in 1935 (following the British government's decision to link the Hong Kong dollar to the pound sterling).

36 *Pangtans* continued to be a feature of Macoa commerce, especially in times of instability and restricted money supply, such as during World War Two.

37 There was a rash of construction of brick works including a major centre of production, The Macao Cement and Brick Works, on Lapa Island, shipping the bulk of output straight to Hong Kong.

38 We should also note alongside the colonial populating of Hong Kong the exodus of Europeans and Americans to various Chinese coastal trading posts too as the first treaty ports opened in the early 1840s. The British and Americans were quick to seize particularly on Shanghai's opportunities. The French were slightly later with the first French ship, *La Bayonnaise*, sailing to Shanghai from Macao in 1849. Mathilde Kang in her book *Francophonie and the Orient* (Amsterdam: University of Amsterdam Press, 2018) talks of 'the French Macao-Pondicherry-Canton-Shanghai-Indochina-Kwangchowan (Guangzhouwan) itinerary.' (p.181).

Macao.'[39] Portugal's position *vis-à-vis* China was considerably diminished by the fluctuation and structural changes of that trade and the growth of neighbouring Hong Kong.[40]

In the later nineteenth and early-twentieth centuries Macao was not in great economic shape. By the 1920s the local economy still consisted largely of dried fish, matches, teak handicrafts, groundnut cooking oil, some stone cutting, and a little canned fruit production.[41] There was also some Chinese liquor distilling, a traditional fireworks and firecrackers industry (employing thousands of people at its height, mostly based on Taipa, and which fairly regularly saw spectacular explosions and deaths of workers), mixed in with a little licensed opium selling, and gambling (at the *jai-alai*, greyhound and horse racing, as well as in casinos which had been licensed since the 1850s) all combining to provide the bulk of the colony's economy. There were, of course, also the traditional illicit businesses of prostitution and smuggling – salt to heavily salt-taxed Lantau Island; high priced kerosene into Macao from Indochina or the

39 Montalto de Jesus, *Historic Macao*, p.309.

40 Not that Portugal didn't gain some advantage out of Britain's victory and became more emboldened towards China. Jingzhen Xie argues that 'After the First Opium War, the Chinese authorities were no longer respected and obeyed by the Portuguese residing in Macao. In 1849 the then Portuguese governor João Maria Ferreira do Amaral expelled all the Chinese officials from Macao', Jingzhen Xie, *The French in Macao in the Nineteenth and Early Twentieth Centuries: Literary, Cultural and Historical Perspectives*, (London: Palgrave Macmillan, 2022), p.15. However, Amaral (1803–1849), known as the 'one-armed governor' having lost his right arm in the Battle of Itaparica in Brazil in 1823, was soon after assassinated in Coloane by several Chinese men over a dispute involving the construction of a road that required the relocation of Chinese graves. His stabbing and beheading caused the Battle of Passaleão (or Baishaling) between Portugal and China. Incidentally due to the power vacuum in Macao's government after Amaral's murder two Royal Navy and two American warships entered Macao's Praia Grande while some British Royal Marines were landed to defend Portuguese civilians and British nationals if necessary (the first British troops to land in Macao since 1808 – see Chapter 2 *A Scurvy Business*). A statue of Amaral, by the Portuguese sculptor Alves Maximiano, astride his horse and wielding a stick as a weapon, was erected in Macao in 1940. However, it was removed in 1991 at the insistence of the director of Beijing's Office of Hong Kong and Macao Affairs and sent to Lisbon where it now stands in a suburb near Lisbon Airport.

41 Fruits included lichees, longan, loquat, pomelo, bananas, plums, pears, and tangerines. The Portuguese introduced papaya, guava, custard apples and pineapples (as well as peanuts).

Dutch East Indies; cigarettes and wines from China and Indochina; silver from Manila; and gold (which Portugal began to source from Brazil as early as 1699).

Many local industries established in the mid-nineteenth century had slumped into decline by the start of the twentieth century. Some were by now long gone, such as the sixteenth- and seventeenth-century once-booming Macao specialisations of cannon and church bell forging, as well as the grey amber (or ambergris) trade to China.[42] Matchmaking had also been significant, exporting to Hong Kong, Southeast Asia, Malacca, Mozambique, and South America. However, matches, joss-sticks, and incense made in neighbouring Kwangtung province were cheaper by 1900 and the home-based "sweated" trades of making match boxes and incense sticks unpopular with all but the most financially desperate.[43] The groundnut pressing factories that produced cooking oil closed due to constant pirate raids and extortion.

Parsimonious subsidies from Lisbon had scarcely added to Macao's economy. Inward investment was minimal. The second decade of the twentieth century saw little more than the Lisbon-funded slight expansion of an 1880s-built cement factory (which was used locally and also exported to Manila, Hong Kong, and Japan) on the Ilha Verde, the establishment of a small Chinese-funded tobacco factory, and a new spinning mill employing 800 female workers. These were just about the only industrial enterprises in the colony by the time of World War One.[44]

At the same time it seemed Macao had to import just about everything from charcoal, kerosene, firewood, coal, and cork, to paper fans, tea (manufactured rather than grown), sugar, Kwangsi cassia-leaf oil, and

42 Ambergris (the solid substance produced in the digestive systems of sperm whales) was a much sought after item in China supplied largely by the Portuguese from their East African and Indian Ocean colonies.

43 The joss stick and incense industry also depended on imports of spices, incense powder, binder, coloured powder, wrapping paper and sandalwood as well as sweated labour.

44 According to Jingzhen Xie, commenting on the writings of the French traveller and photographer Alfred Raquez (1862-1907) who visited in 1898 'many of these workers were considered pretty and of mixed races of Chinese and Macanese. Several had bound feet. Some carried a baby in a bag on their back, so these children passed ten hours in the spinning mill with their mothers, who made 0.3 French francs each day.' *The French in Macao*, p.110.

silk, all of which naturally had to be paid for in cash. When typhoons swept Macao causing damage to buildings, bamboo scaffolding poles (first noted by foreigners in 1699 as being used by builders[45]) and roof tiles all had to be imported along with daily supplies of pigs, poultry, eggs, and most foodstuffs to supplement the colony's meagre market gardens. Anything engineered – machinery, electrical components, bicycles, rickshaws (and before them sedan chairs), cars, modern ships, and planes – had to be imported, as did even very basic manufactured products, such as lightbulbs.

By the start of the twentieth century the British in Hong Kong had secured Kowloon and their 99-year lease of the New Territories to support life on Hong Kong Island with food, water, and power, as well as expanding the colony's port facilities and dry docks. They were encouraging additional farming of pigs (for local consumption as well as salted and sold to ships' captains), poultry, eggs, vegetables (including of potatoes) and dairy cows, which were almost solely for the consumption of Europeans, herb farms specializing in cultivating for the Chinese medicinal trade, light engineering, and manufacturing. Macao had no such equivalent natural resources and developed little modern industry. Consequently, the colony's balance of payments was increasingly distinctly unfavourable.

'A Beautiful Little Portuguese City…'

Yet, unlike Hong Kong, Macao had charm. The signature long curve of the Praia Grande faced the Porto Exterior. It was protected with granite boulders to prevent flooding. About half a mile in length, it ran between the grey stone São Francisco Fort and the Bom Parto Fort.[46] The Praia Grande was lined with camphor, pine, Chinese banyan, and pagoda

45 Noted by the Italian traveller Giovanni Francesco Gemelli Careri in the late 1690s. Gemelli Careri, *Giro Del Mondo: Part IV*, (1699).

46 The São Francisco Fort was built around 1692. The Bom Parto Fort, being fully the Forte de Nossa Senhora de Bom Parto, was built around 1608, rebuilt in 1775, and abandoned in 1892. It was subsequently incorporated into the grounds of the Hotel Bela Vista (Boa Vista). The Bom Parto Fort was especially important as it guarded the peninsula end of Macao's telegraph cable.

Macao's Praia Grande, 1930s

trees.[47] Large private residences (many later to become consulates) had covered verandas in the Corinthian-style, columns and colonnades, and were all painted in bright colours and washed with lime (by order of the Portuguese authorities, who also stipulated there could be no commercial signs on the Praia Grande). The bay below was constantly packed with junks, schooners, cutters, *lorchas*, and Tanka sampans and egg-boats.

Especially grand residences included the East India Company's (EIC) residence, which was actually three or four houses joined into one. There was also the house of the Portuguese Governor with its guard of African soldiers.[48] The Praia Grande was constantly referred to as resembling the grand, but old and rather ossified, *la Junqueira* waterfront of Lisbon, or Naples's old waterfront, the *Chiaia* – both un-redeveloped strips of

47 In the late 1890s the visiting American journalist and occasional poet Margherita Arlina Hamm (1867-1907) noted the addition of banana, fig, olive, lemon, guava, and orange trees to the pagoda trees (*styphnolobium japonicum*) along the Praia Grande and in its adjacent gardens. Margherita Arlina Hamm, *Manila and the Philippines*, (London/New York: F Tennyson Neely, 1898).

48 Austin Coates maintained that inside the EIC's Praia Grande conjoined houses resembled 'nothing so much as what it was, a superlatively luxurious men's club in typical London style.' (Coates, *City of Broken Promises*, p.31.) The King/Queen (George III, George IV, William IV, and Victoria over the residency's existence) and "the directors" of the EIC were toasted nightly at supper.

former glory left to slowly stagnate and rot in the heat.[49] Visiting in 1836 the British surgeon Charles Toogood Downing described the bay as resembling an amphitheatre, while the Hong Kong civil servant Austin Coates wrote that, 'I always associate Macao with Venice. Whichever one I am in, I always wake wondering which one it is.'[50]

An egg boat, from The Fan-Qui in China by Charles Toogood Downing, 1836

Macao was initially a typical Portuguese colonial port merged into a southern Chinese village (complete with temples to Kwan Yin).[51] In the early days the harbours were crammed with galleons, galleasses, the early trading caravels, then the later and larger *nao* (or carrack in English and

49 The comparison of Macao's Praia Grande to the Bay of Naples – the bay, the Mediterranean feel of the town, the hills (Mount Vesuvius can at a glance resemble the non-volcanic Hengqin Islands) in the distance is made often and throughout the nineteenth and twentieth century. It's impossible to know who first made this comparison but it is certainly asserted in Osmond Tiffany, Jr., *The Canton Chinese, or the American's sojourn in the Celestial Empire,* (Boston: James Munroe & Co., 1849), p.261 – 'There is nothing Chinese in its [Macao's] appearance; it bears a striking resemblance to Naples in its curving beach and hills, and in its buildings.'

50 Charles Toogood Downing, *The Fan-Qui in China in 1836-7,* (London: Henry Colburn Publishers, 1838), p.25; Coates, *A Macao Narrative,* Preface. (Searching for books in Lisbon I did spy a Portuguese translation of Austin Coates's *A Macao Narrative* with the title *Macau – Calçades da Histōria* published in the 1980s.

51 Quan Yin – Goddess of Mercy, protector of women, children, sailors, fishermen, anyone in trouble, and the sick, disabled, and poor, most commonly venerated throughout southern China's coastal communities.

up to 900 tons), both great floating crescents symbolic of Portuguese shipbuilding, mixed in with the local *proa*, junks and sampans.

The Bay of Naples, so often compared to Macao

The China-Japan-Macao trade (technically illegal in the sixteenth and seventeenth centuries, the Chinese emperor having banned direct trade with Japan) saw entire shipyards constructed at Goa, Cochin (Kochi) and Bassein (Vasai) where the teak was suitable and plentiful for Portugal's carracks. The Portuguese very profitably became middle-men for the Sino-Japanese market. Portuguese "Japan ships", (the Japanese called them the "Black Ships") carried mixed cargoes of cotton cloth from India, glassware, ivory, Spanish velvet, olives and olive oil, and wines.[52] The circuit of Macao-Canton-Malacca-Nagasaki became standard in the 1600s – Chinese silk one-way, Japanese silver the other, pepper, cloves, and aromatic woods from the Malay Peninsula for China. And always a percentage for the Portuguese in between. Missionaries sailed to Japan with traders and sought souls, at least until their expulsion in 1620 by the Tokugawa Shogunate.

Into the twentieth century Macao remained what seamen called 'a coasting port' rarely, if ever, visited by deep-water ships. Neither the Porto Interior (lying between the peninsula and Lapa Island), or the more suitable Porto Exterior, were ever meaningfully developed to become

52 The Japanese dubbed the initial foreign ships arriving the "Black Ships", *kurofune*, as the Portuguese carracks had hulls painted black with pitch.

anything more than shallow anchorages. Perhaps this didn't matter in the early days when Portugal's revolutionary caravel ships that could handle shallow coastal waters (Macao's anchorages, Goa's ports, as well as the majority of the Spice Islands and Malacca) arrived, but it would become a long term drag on Macao's development in the following centuries. Additionally, the outflows of mud from the Pearl River Delta caused Macao's waters to become silted and remain shallow. They were never meaningfully dredged, and so the problem persisted. Even in the 1830s vessels that drew over three feet of water could not moor up quayside.

The second half of the nineteenth century saw an age of advancement in Portugal (combined with improved political stability) and a significant growth in transport infrastructure and engineering projects – often dubbed *Fontismo*.[53] Despite continued cyclical economic ups and downs, as well as large budget deficits in Lisbon, roads, railways, bridges, tunnels, harbour entrances, lighthouses, and the country's key deep-water port at Leixões all appeared. But not much effort was directed towards the colonies and when it was, in the late nineteenth century, it was focussed on keeping Lisbon in the European "Scramble for Africa" rather than upgrading little Macao.

Visiting in 1923 the American travel journalist Harry A Franck wrote of the 'wharfless Praya Grande' noting the lack of waterfront commerce.[54] Larger ships had to head to the Macao "Roads", just off Taipa.[55] It was as Austin Coates noted '…a minute segment of land surrounded by water, yet not quite an island.'[56] By the 1950s the Porto Interior would be little more than a collection of cheap eateries, noodle shops, barefoot-dentists, cobblers, pedicab driver rest-stops, and a Caltex petrol station with a solitary pump.

53 *Fontismo* is the name given to the period between 1868 and 1889, perhaps extending into the early twentieth century, of centralised initiatives to promote public works and modernize Portugal's infrastructure. *Fontismo* derives from the name of Fontes Pereira de Melo (1891-1887), a leading political figure of the period who championed the policy.

54 Harry A Franck, *Roving Through Southern China*, (London: T Fisher Unwin, 1926), p.215 and also included in the excerpted version of this text in the China Revisited series from Blacksmith Books (Hong Kong: Blacksmith Books, 2023).

55 "Roads" being a body of water sheltered from rip currents, tides, or swells where ships can lie reasonably safely at anchor without dragging or snatching.

56 Coates, *A Macao Narrative,* Preface.

The Tung Hing Match Factory

As the Porto Interior and Exterior were never seriously upgraded to become a viable modern port Macao remained unable to welcome modern commercial shipping or the new larger naval gunboats. Subsequently Macao was never to become – unlike Canton, Hong Kong, Shanghai, or even the smaller treaty ports of Amoy, Foochow, or Ningpo on the China coast – a major transit point and entrepôt.

Post the Great War a small naval air station at Taipa was constructed in the 1920s so Portuguese naval planes could support British Royal Navy piracy suppression initiatives, but little else in the way of new infrastructure development occurred.[57] Portugal was in a dire economic state after World War One and the economy close to collapse. The Frenchman Charles Ricou, a pioneer of electricity connection in the region and also owner of the Macao Ice and Cold Storage Company, formed The Macao Aerial Transport Company. He built a temporary hangar for his five Curtiss Model F flying boats situated in the Porto Interior. They flew goods, mail, and a few passengers back and forth to southern China. Unfortunately, and despite aviation becoming a rapidly

57 This was small at first but expanded in the 1930s to accommodate trainee pilots, mechanics, technicians, and radiotelegraphy operatives. It was then renamed the Centro de Aviação Naval (Macao Naval Aviation Centre).

growing business in Hong Kong and China, his Macao aviation business only lasted a couple of years.[58]

Macao had indeed fallen far economically since António Bocarro, Portugal's most important official in India in the first half of the seventeenth century, had described the colony as the most profitable Portuguese settlement in the Indies.[59]

Exodus

With little opportunity and dwindling living standards, people left the colony in large numbers. Portuguese and Eurasian-Macanese (often the offspring of soldiers, *soldados,* who never returned to Portugal, and local Chinese women) departed to economically more vibrant Hong Kong. Additionally, there was a growth of smaller 'Oriental Portuguese' diasporas appearing in Foochow, Canton, and Shanghai.[60] They worked as clerks, translator-compradors (local agents for European firms), teachers, administrators, and colonial government bureaucrats. Many had begun working for British and American traders in the Canton Factories and followed them to Hong Kong. A list of names of early Hong Kong officials from the 1840s, as well as those of traders and bank clerks, printers, sail makers, typesetters, and newspapermen among other occupations, betrays their origins – D'Almada, Remédios, Grand-Pré, Carvalho, Barretto, Braga, Almeida, Noronha, Basto, Vargas.

Already by the early 1850s a total of 322 Portuguese men and 137 women had relocated to Hong Kong. Despite discrimination from the British they mostly stayed. By 1897 more than half of Hong Kong's

58 Ricou became a permanent resident of Macao and was also involved with the Far East Electric Company. His aviation service should have worked – twenty minutes to Hong Kong rather than the then standard four hours or so the ferry took. Quite why it failed is unclear.

59 CR Boxer, ed., *Seventeenth Century Macau in Contemporary Documents and Illustrations*, (Hong Kong: Heinemann Asia, 1984), p.14. António Bocarro (1594-1693), Portuguese historian and geographer whose career was focussed on Portugal's eastern colonies. He was employed first as a soldier in Goa and Cochin, later as controller of customs in South India and Goa's official historiographer.

60 The term 'Oriental Portuguese' is used by David Brookshaw in his Introduction to Henrique de Senna Fernandes's 1970s novel *A Trança Feiticeira*, translated by Brookshaw and published as *The Bewitching Braid*, (Hong Kong: Hong Kong University Press & Instituto Cultural do Governo da RAE de Macau, 2004).

Portuguese population had been born in the British colony. Macao's loss was Hong Kong's gain. Hard working taxpayers, these Macanese settlers were also instrumental in building out the Kowloon suburbs where many had settled.[61] By 1911 over 2,500 Portuguese lived in Hong Kong (the vast majority of them having come from Macao after differing lengths of stay, or the offspring of relocated Portuguese), though prejudice remained. The Hong Kong-based *China Mail* newspaper wrote in 1921 that these 'Portuguese' …

> '…were settled in the tropics, thoroughly acclimatised, and apparently not recruited to any extent from Europe. In one sense therefore they are indigenous; but in another alien, as they retain their allegiance to their own country, and their connection with the Portuguese Colony of Macao…'[62]

Historian Vaudine England has described the Portuguese of Hong Kong as 'a good example of both a cosmopolitan sensibility and coexisting communalism' with families, business ties, and friendship networks in both colonies and making regular trips between the two.[63]

Many Chinese took the same route across to Hong Kong as the Portuguese, often from southern China via Macao. They went into shopkeeping, stevedoring, or construction as well as a host of entrepreneurial enterprises. Other Chinese embarked as indentured labourers from Macao for Cuba and the Antilles' sugar industry, Peru's guano trade, Trinidad, or Demerara (now Guyana) – the so-called "Coolie Trade".[64] In 1866, according to Victor Tissot, a Swiss traveller,

61 As well as Club Lusitano in Central (opened 1866) and Club de Recreio (1906) in Kowloon, the Portuguese-influenced Catholic Church of the Holy Rosary on Kowloon's Chatham Road, the Escola Camões (now Po Leung Kuk Camões Tan Siu Lin Primary School) in Yau Ma Tei, there is also Soares Avenue and Julia Avenue in largely Portuguese-developed Ho Man Tin; the Braga Circuit on Kadoorie Hill, Rozario Street in Sheung Wan, and Boa Vista ("Good View") at Tai Tam while, until land reclamation pushed the boundaries ever outwards across Victoria harbour, the Hong Kong waterfront was generally known by the Portuguese term as the Praia.

62 *The China Mail* (Hong Kong), 76th Anniversary Edition, March 1921.

63 Vaudine England, *Fortune's Bazaar: The Making of Hong Kong*, (London: Corsair, 2023), p.136.

64 Both these "coolie labour" destinations proved profitable for the Portuguese authorities in Macao. The British banned their nationals from involvement in the

Macao's gross domestic product was 1,188,000 Swiss francs. Among this number, 500,000 francs came from gambling while over 300,000 francs was derived from the opium and "coolie" trade.[65]

Ship wrecked in a typhoon, 1920s

The Atlantic slave trade, from which Lisbon had profited greatly, was outlawed by Portugal in 1836. However, the Coolie Trade was begun in 1851 and Macao was a centre of this pernicious business. Run largely by unscrupulous Europeans and ship captains who tricked country peasants across southern China, and as far as the Annamese Mountains

---

passage to Cuba and Peru in the early 1850s. However, the Portuguese continued to work with the "coolie traders" – receiving commissions, overseeing the loading process, and checking documents – until the mid-1870s. An estimated 200,000 Chinese embarked from Macao to Havana, the *Chincha Islands,* and Callao (though many were Cantonese or Fujianese transiting through Macao to the Caribbean and South America). See Evelyn Hu-Dehart, *Chinese Coolie Labor in Cuba in the Nineteenth Century*, Contributions in Black Studies, Volume 12, Article 5, 1994. According to the French traveller Ludovic de Beauvoir who visited Macao in 1867, approximately 5,000 Chinese "coolies" left for Havana and 8,000 for El Callao every year. *Java, Siam, Canton. Voyage Autour Du Monde*, (Paris: Henri Plon, Imprimeur-Éditeur, 1870). Additionally, Jingzhen Xie notes some French involvement in the coolie trade via Macao. Jingzhen Xie, *The French in Macao,* p.164.

65 Jingzhen Xie, *The French in Macao*, p.94.

in Indochina, with offers of wealth it was an often vicious and violent trade. Enticed to Macao the labouring men ("coolies") were kept in large, invariably unsanitary, buildings known as "barracoons".[66] Attempts to escape and desperate mutinies were common and brutally put down until the trade itself was suppressed in 1874. Though many decried the business – in their reports back to London British consuls in the region referred to those involved as "manstealers"[67] – many were implicated in some way: Spanish and Portuguese "merchants", the local Chinese "agents" (or "crimps" in vernacular criminal slang), British, French, and American ship captains, and the Hong Kong dry dock firms who fitted out vessels as coolie transports.

Diverse Macao

Importantly we should not fall into the trap of seeing Macao as a binary between Portuguese colonists and the Chinese population. That latter population ebbed and flowed with people from Kwangtung, Fukien, Kwangsi, and other provinces, as well as Hoklo (Hokkien) people from various points and the Tanka boat people (so often painted by the Macao-based artist George Chinnery) – what has been termed Macao's "internal diaspora".[68]

The early days of the Canton Trade saw British, Americans (at least from 1784 and the arrival of the *Empress of China* in Chinese waters), Dutch, French, Prussians, Austro-Hungarians, Italians, Spanish, and various Scandinavians moving seasonally between the Canton Factories and Macao.[69] Armenian traders were also present, borrowing money

66 The term, a corruption of the Portuguese barracão/barracãoes (and Spanish and Catalan terms, all for "hut"), was already being used for such holding facilities on the Atlantic slave trade.

67 Wm Fred. Myers, NB Denys, and Chas. King, *The Treaty Ports of China and Japan: A Complete Guide to the Open Ports of Those Countries, Together with Peking, Yedo, Hongkong and Macao*, (London and Hongkong: Trűbner and Co./Shortrede and Co., 1867), p.22.

68 Again from David Brookshaw's introduction to *Visions of China, Stories from Macau,* (jointly published by Gávea-Brown Publication of Providence, Rhode Island, and Hong Kong University Press, 2002), p.11.

69 Though from an early stage (even when the crowns were united) Spanish-controlled Manila was considered a rival to Macao in the Chinese and Japanese trade. While a handful of Spanish resided in Macao and a few Portuguese in Manila there

cheaply in Macao to lend at high rates of interest in Canton to smaller merchants in the Canton Trade who were invariably in debt between arriving consignments (and those debts worsening if the cargoes were lost to typhoons, pirates, shipwrecks, or Chinese injunctions that excluded the merchants from Canton periodically). Portuguese financiers also did good business lending to supercargoes whose finances were a bit stretched between trading seasons.

Macao's foreign population was a mixed bag of overlapping interests – business, personal and diplomatic. Take the case of Anders Ljungstedt, a Swede who had worked in Russia. He was later hired by the Swedish East India Company. But the Company folded in 1813 and Ljungstedt, already in Canton, opted to settle in Macao as a merchant, from which business he became seriously wealthy and threw the most lavish soirées.[70] In 1820 he was appointed Sweden's first Consul General to China and also took on the role of Russia's Honorary Consul in Macao.[71] Ljungstedt claimed the Macao climate suited him. He was painted by Chinnery, wrote a history of the Portuguese in China, was instrumental in establishing the Protestant Cemetery, and eventually, in 1835, was buried in it.[72]

Europeans and Americans aside, a number of Malay labour agents, *ghaut serangs*, based themselves in Macao to supply the merchant fleets with Lascars, as well as Malay *duennas* (governesses), and domestic servants who worked in Portuguese households.[73] Many were Muslim

---

was a constant antagonism between the two rival entrepôts and often between the two countries.

70 Ljungstedt competed closely with Magdalenus Jacobus Senn van Basel, the representative of Dutch diplomatic interests in Macao until 1848, to throw the biggest parties in the colony.

71 Incidentally, in 1820, there was a liberal revolution in Portugal though Macao reportedly had to wait two years to find that out. My thanks to Macao-based journalist Hugo Pinto for that tit-bit.

72 Ljungstedt wrote *An Historical Sketch of the Portuguese Settlements in China, and of the Roman Catholic Church and Mission in China; with a Supplementary Chapter, Description of the City of Canton*, (Boston: James Munroe & Co., 1836). A street in Macao is named after him, Avenida Anders Ljungstedt.

73 "Lascar" is a notoriously tricky category to classify, though was frequently used between the seventeenth and early twentieth century. A perhaps useful explanation is provided by the former merchant seamen Jan de Hartog in his autobiography *A Sailor's Life*, (London: Hamish Hamilton, 1955), p.81. 'To help the young sailor out: there is no such race as "Lascars." It is the name for all Oriental and especially Indian sailors

A Goan policeman on patrol, 1920s

and attended the Macao Mosque (and associated cemetery) on Ramal Dos Moros in Nossa Senhora de Fátima district which was built originally by South Asian Muslims who served with the Portuguese colonial army. The centrality of the Armenians and Malays to the Macao-Canton trade, in terms of financing and managing seamen respectively, has been long overlooked.[74] Additionally numbers of South Asians, including Sikhs, Malabars, and Goans (Canarins) were recruited to the police force and as watchmen, while many Timorese made their way to Macao in search of better opportunities within the Lusophone Portuguese colonial world.[75]

which has been adopted into the Merchant Shipping Acts, without any definition. "Lashkar" was first applied by the Portuguese to an inferior class of sailors in the seventeenth century.' Many included in the category were also Malays.

74 England, *Fortune's Bazaar*, p.33.

75 Malabars are people from Kerala. The Canarins are the Konkani people from Goa. In the late nineteenth century Macao effectively acted as a cutout between Lisbon and Timor with the Portuguese Timorese budget being set and approved by the Governor of Macao.

Regiments of black soldiers from Portuguese East Africa in khaki summer uniforms with red fez hats were stationed almost continually in Macao.

Many of the dynamic Parsees in the Canton Trade also made the same Canton-Macao commute.[76] However, most of them, such as the Macao-based oil, gems, and silks dealer FM Talati, moved to Hong Kong when it became a British colony along with the majority of Europeans and Americans. The Parsee merchant Heejebhoy Rustomjee had traded in the Portuguese colony since the 1830s, but still decided to make the move from Macao to Hong Kong. The family acquired land in the British colony and subsequently moved their businesses. Dhunjibhai Rustomjee (no relation to Heejebhoy above) moved from Macao and Canton early and became a founding director of the Hong Kong, Canton, and Macao Steamboat Company. The Parsee Anjuman (traditional community centre) moved from Canton to a new more permanent home in Hong Kong via a short period in Macao.[77]

And, inevitably, there were intermarriages and mixed relationships that created a sizeable and vibrant self-identifying Eurasian community. This community was to be found at all levels and ranks of Macao society. To many at this time of economic decline in Macao, the Portuguese community, along with the so-called *mestizos* (or *mestiça* in Portuguese) and Eurasians, were no longer seen as part of the colonial class, or even the privileged European elite, but something "other" and in between.

Concerning particularly French views of Macao at the time the academic Jingzhen Xie writes that, 'The Portuguese residing in Macao were seen as those who had been transformed from great explorers to small clerks working for big American and British firms. As a result, they became unfamiliar and even somehow "other" to the French.'[78] It became commonplace in European and American reporting of the time to note inter-racial mixing with some distaste in every article or travelogue

76 The Parsees (or sometimes "Parsis") had long been a presence in Macao constructing their own Zoroastrian cemetery (at the foot of the Guia Fortress) as early as 1829. It is located on Estrada Dos Parses and contains fourteen graves. They are occasionally noted as "Persians", particularly in French language sources – Parsi means "Persian," and the community did originally descend from Persian Zoroastrians who emigrated to India to avoid religious persecution.

77 For more on the Parsees-Macao connections, and their relocations to Hong Kong see England, *Fortune's Bazaar,* pp.30-31.

78 Jingzhen Xie, *The French in Macao*, p.viii.

concerning Macao. According to the globe-trotting Austrian diplomat Joseph Alexander von Hübner who visited in the late 1870s, only twelve families in Macao were a hundred per cent Portuguese by race.[79]

All of this – the ending of the old Factories-based Canton Trade system and the exodus to Hong Kong after 1842 – meant population fluctuations. In the nineteenth century Macao's population had grown slowly. In 1874 the population was approximately 68,086 and in 1897, reached 78,706.[80] By 1915 the population was only 80,000, a negligible growth in nearly two decades, and nine-tenths Chinese. However, after World War One the population doubled to 160,000 by the late 1930s as war clouds gathered, refugee numbers grew, and Portuguese in Hong Kong and mainland China opted for a safer locale. Additionally, this was also the period of Macao as a 'pleasure resort for South China' stimulating the hotel, casino, and related 'sin' businesses.[81]

Most of the population spoke Cantonese (or in some cases another Chinese dialect), though Portuguese was the language of the colonial power and many middle-class residents. The Macanese (mostly Eurasian) often spoke a nineteenth-century creole known as Patuá (which has certain affiliations with the "Papia Kristang" of Malacca mixing medieval Portuguese, Cantonese, various languages of the Indian sub-continent and even some Japanese) part of Macao's unique Luso-Chinese heritage.[82]

But along the way Macao had become a trope...

79 A very unscientific survey and more a random observation from Joseph Alexander von Hübner, *Promenade autour du monde*, (Paris: Hachette, 1877), pp.418–19. Noted in Jingzhen Xie above.

80 James Dyer Ball, *Macao: The Holy City, The Gem of the Orient Earth*, (Canton: China Baptist Publishing Society), p.4.

81 As discussed in various chapters later Portugal was neutral throughout World War Two. But World War One had been more complicated with Lisbon initially declaring neutrality but, after repeated clashes with German troops in Africa and naval clashes around Germany's U-Boat activity, joined the allies in 1916. Robert Bickers in his book *Out of China: How the Chinese Ended the Era of Western Domination*, (Cambridge: Massachusetts, Harvard University Press, 2017), p.19, reports that during the 1918 victory celebrations the Boy Scouts Association of Macao (Associação de Escoteiros de Macao) 'trampled on Germany's flag and then burned it'.

82 Patuá – a Portuguese-Asian Creole considered a "critically endangered" language by UNESCO and now with perhaps a few dozen speakers in Macao and possibly a couple of hundred in Hong Kong, Portugal and the Macanese diaspora.

Opium at Your Bedside

Looking through European and American newspapers between the world wars for stories featuring Macao yields little more than exotic travel pieces and feuilletons written in clichéd prose and almost all noting the hack writers' familiar quartet of pirates, opium, prostitution, and fan-tan houses. Macao had become an international cliché for Asian tropical torpor and loose morals, a day trip from Hong Kong, an Asian sin city. This was to be a theme that continued through to the 1950s and '60s.

My personal favourite piece, and one that illustrates just about every pre- and surviving post-war trope about Macao, is from *Variety* in 1954 and headlined:

> *Adventure Still Rules Macao; Gals Serve Your Opium at Hotel Bedside*
> 'Gambling is the chief relaxation with fan-tan operated by smiling Chinese girls…dancehall hostesses wear slit skirts and high-necked blouses…for 32¢ the tourist can smoke a single pipe of opium in any number of dingy dens; for a little more the pipe of forgetfulness can be delivered to your hotel room – by a comely serving girl to heat the joy gum by your bedside…Prosties work only in the *maisons de joie* and there are no *femmes du pave*. Neither a recent government ban nor the efforts of the churches have been able to close down the brothels which provide a variety of Eurasians, White Russians, Chinese and Japanese attendants.'[83]

Variety's view of Macao was not, of course, totally unwarranted. The Portuguese authorities had encouraged casinos. They had licensed (and taxed) them since the mid-nineteenth century and they did register all prostitutes and insist they work in licensed houses. Efforts to restrain their number and limit the associated worlds of prostitution and taxi-dancing (which could tip over into prostitution at times) had all been half-hearted

83 Dick Larsh, 'Adventure Still Rules Macao; Gals Serve Your Opium at Hotel Bedside', *Variety*, August 11, 1954. Larsh spent a lot of time in Asia – drafted into the US Army in the Pacific in 1942 and subsequently working for the US Occupation authority in Japan as an intelligence officer. He freelanced for a while (including here for *Variety*) until joining the army newspaper *Stars and Stripes* in Tokyo before finishing out his career as an editor with the *Honolulu Advertiser*.

at best. If *Variety* was right that *femmes du pave* (streetwalkers) were not taking to the cobblestone alleyways around their traditional haunts by the famous Rua da Felicidade red light area, then this was a recent occurrence and only temporary.

The inter-war years saw new and old forms of entertainment (and government revenue generation) appearing. Lotteries such as the *Pacapio* had always been popular – the trick was to legalise (and tax) them.[84] The authorities restarted horse racing and the construction of a hippodrome after a break of eighty years in 1927.[85] They permitted the building of canidromes for greyhound racing from 1931.[86] Lotteries, horses, and dogs were all activities that appealed to all social classes, both the Chinese population and Portuguese colonists, and the curious tourists disembarking the steamers from Hong Kong which were timed to arrive in time for the racing and depart when it finished.[87] Jai-alai could be added to that list too, as could cricket fighting which nobody ever thought, or bothered, to regulate, tax or ban (though the betting was reputedly heavy).[88]

84 *Pacapio* is a traditional game introduced to Macao in the early twentieth century and involves making wagers on pigeon racing. The birds are identified with names and bets placed on the competing pigeons. This racing eventually changed to a game similar to a lucky draw, in which players bet on ten of 80 characters written on a piece of paper, with 20 characters drawn to match. Players win if five or more chosen characters match the drawn characters.

85 And then, rather suddenly, horse racing ended again in Macao on April 1, 2024 and the Macao Jockey Club was ordered to cease all racing activities by the government.

86 The Macao Yat Yuen Canidrome, otherwise known as the Macao Canine Club or Macao Greyhound Racing Club, was founded by a group of Americans and Chinese investors led by Fan Che Pang, the owner of Hou Heng Company, who ran casinos. It closed just before World War Two and didn't open again till 1962. It finally closed in 2018 though the deco-inspired structures remained as of 2023.

87 For more on the history of horse and dog racing in Macao see Catherine S Chan, *Greyhounds in a Sin City: Animal Welfare under Macao's Gambling Culture*, Cultural History, Vol 12 Issue 1, April 2023, pp 98-119. As a side note there were several conversations in Macao over the decades about introducing Portuguese-style bullfighting with *cavaleiros* and *forcados*. However, despite some events in a temporary arena in the mid-1960s it never became a permanent fixture in Macao.

88 The definitive history of competitive cricket fighting in Macao is yet to be written! However, competitions were held in the Central Hotel on the Avenida de Almeida Ribeiro and champion crickets were brought from Hong Kong to challenge local

In the 1930s Macao presented itself to the outside world largely in terms of leisure with only limited manufacturing (the old stalwarts of fireworks, firecrackers, matches, etc limped on) with a promotional exhibition at the 1934 Portuguese Colonial Exposition, a world's fair, in Porto's Palácio de Cristal.[89] The centrepiece of Macao's exhibit was a reproduction of the Guia Lighthouse (built 1865) along with a traditional teahouse, and Chinese musicians. Macao would also be featured prominently at the *Exposição do Mundo Português* (Portuguese World Exhibition) held on Lisbon's vast Praça do Império (Empire Square) some years later in 1940.[90] This time an entire, and highly detailed, typical Macao street was constructed. Three million people visited.

The plan worked…to a point. Visiting English aesthete Harold Acton, living in Peking at the time, reported that in 1936 he struggled to get a room at the Riviera Hotel – all booked out for the races.[91] However, as everywhere with such activities, much of the income slipped through the tax net and never saw a government coffer. The balance of payments remained negative and the *Ministério das Colónias* in Lisbon was consistently disappointed.

In Portugal the *Estado Novo* authoritarian dictatorship of António de Oliveira Salazar (1933-1974) did attempt somewhat to resist these tropes through the regime's colonialist justification theory of *Lusotropicalismo*. "Luso-tropicalism" assigned to the Portuguese empire a high degree of originality and racial harmony when compared to other European colonial projects. The *Lusotropicalismo* concept was paid little attention outside of Portugal though, as the previous 1921 *China Mail* quote about the Portuguese in Hong Kong shows that similar thinking, for different reasons perhaps, was going on in British minds.[92]

---

insects. Tournaments often went on for days with medals awarded and large sums bet on the outcomes.

89 The Exposition was inspired by France's *Exposition Coloniale Internationale* event in 1931. The Exposition also featured so-called "human zoos" in which men, women, and children, from the various colonies, were exposed in their "habitats".

90 Organised to mark 800 years since the foundation of the country and 300 years since the restoration of independence from Spain.

91 Harold Acton, *Memoirs of an Aesthete,* (London: Methuen, 1948), p.297.

92 *Lusotropicalismo* was developed by the Brazilian anthropologist and cultural historian Gilberto Freyre (1900-1987). In his earlier works on colonial Brazil. Freyre argued that the Portuguese were better colonisers than other European nations due

The Balancing Act

Macao's position in World War Two echoed that of Portugal's and strove for neutrality. At most 1,500 Portuguese (and mostly Portuguese colonial) troops were stationed in Macao with at least 60,000 Japanese troops across the border in southern China. It was a tricky balancing act as the later chapter covering Stanley Ho's wartime exploits shows. In a sense this was once again the colony following the colonial master's lead. At many points in Macao's history domestic politics in Portugal were to dictate events, be that the Napoleonic Wars, the shifts from absolute to constitutional monarchy, from there to a republic, and then the establishment of the authoritarian and semi-fascist *Estado Novo* under Salazar that instituted the neutrality policy.

During the war Macao was entirely surrounded by Japanese-held territory. When Hong Kong fell on Christmas Day 1941, 9,000 British subjects became refugees, along with Macanese and any Portuguese who had been living there. With an additional influx of Chinese refugees from Kwangtung Macao's population swelled to half a million. With both the Allied and Axis powers maintaining consulates, a plethora of spies on all sides, and the fear of Japanese takeover at any time, Macao was dubbed a "Far East Casablanca". The fears were real. Japanese troops did invade both Portuguese and Dutch Timor to oust the small and under-equipped combined British, Australian and Dutch force occupying the territories.

By late 1942 conditions were tough. Combined wartime privations, food shortages, multiple disease outbreaks in the hastily established refugee camps, and a particularly cold winter, resulting in a record 16,000 deaths (the average had been 3,000-4,000 per annum throughout the 1930s). Refugee numbers continued to swell – newspapers reported wandering armies of child street beggars, many orphans, driven to Macao from Japanese-occupied southern China. Tensions with the Japanese

---

to Portugal's warmer climate and that this gave them a better ability to adapt to intermingle, intermarry, and indulge in cultural interchange. In the 1930s and 1940s Salazar initially rejected Freyre's ideas as promoting miscegenation, though he gradually, and perhaps grudgingly, came to support the concept in the 1950s. Of course, Lusotropicalism is essentially a justification of Portuguese colonialism, an attempt to spin a unitary narrative out of a series of unequal encounters and forced migrations.

did boil over several times leading Tokyo to demand the installation of Japanese "advisers" to oversee Macao. Lisbon resisted. However, the colony was faced with rampant inflation, a massive black market, and continued shortages of crucial items such as rice and kerosene.

Macao Street at the Exhibition of the Portuguese World, Lisbon, 1940

Violent war came to Macao in January 1945 when the United States claimed that the colony's balancing act was tilting too far one way. They claimed that Macao was planning to sell aviation fuel to Japan. Aircraft from the carrier *USS Enterprise* bombed and strafed the hangar of the Macao Naval Aviation Centre, targeting the colony's fuel dump. Throughout the spring the US Air Force raided strategic targets including the Porto Exterior and the Fortaleza de Dona Maria II (Dona Maria II Fort). Following the Japanese surrender in August 1945, the Portuguese government protested to Washington DC and, in 1950, the United States paid damages in compensation to Lisbon.

The brief respite between the end of World War Two and the 1949 Communist Revolution in China saw Macao somewhat adrift. Hong Kong, despite having been occupied, seemed to bounce back to economic life faster. Refugees from the Chinese Civil War still dribbled into the territory. Macao did have a flourishing gold bullion business, encouraged by the colony's economic tsar and long-term head of its Economic Services Bureau Dr Pedro José Lobo, but the main business was fishing and a resurgent tourism. Day trippers from Hong Kong booked out the hotels, went to the races, crowded the fan-tan tables, and picked up goodies not then available in Hong Kong like Aqua Vita spirit and Bols liqueurs.

The Chinese revolution was to test Macao's balancing act yet again, this time in the Cold War. The Salazar dictatorship in Lisbon was virulently anti-communist and blockades by the western powers of China, as well as some blockading of Macao as a transit point also occurred. Border clashes between Portuguese and People's Liberation Army soldiers, refugees arriving from Shanghai and other parts of mainland China, and the fear that the People's Republic might invade, all combined with another economic dip. Macao's answer was, over the next few decades, to become a centre of gold bullion dealing and to reinvent and expand its gambling and entertainment sector. In this strategy were the seeds of the Macao Chinese Special Administrative Region that we see today.

Though the Portuguese are gone, Macao and its population are still carefully managing the balancing act it has negotiated between itself and China since the 1500s.

A Scurvy Business

The British Are Coming: From Hesitant Encounters to Invasion (1635-1808)

Commodore George Anson

'...the barbarians had arrived. The Chinese Emperor in Peking gave them a tiny permanent base at Macao in southern China and agreed to trade silks for silver...Soon trade was flourishing. Both countries prospered. The middlemen, the Portuguese, grew rich, and their priests – Jesuits mostly – soon became vital to the trade.'
– James Clavell, *Shōgun* (1975)

'...a little point of rock of no importance.'
– Richard Cocks, head of the East India Company trading post at Hirado Island, Nagasaki, describing Macao (1617)

Pursuing the Portingalls

Elizabethan England had heard tell of Portugal's far off enclave of Macao from Richard Hakluyt's *Principal Navigations* as early as the late 1500s.[93] But outside this source London had scant reliable intelligence. Until the acquisition of Hong Kong and before the First Opium War (1839-1842) Britain had had to rely on Macao as its springboard to China. The East India Company's (EIC) supercargo at Hirado in Japan could dismiss Macao as '…a little point of rock of no importance' in the early seventeenth century.[94] However, a century later Hirado was long forgotten and the British uneasily reliant on Portuguese Macao for their Far East trade.

It is hard when considering the British in Macao, and any decisions taken towards the colony, to gauge the level of sectarianism between the British Protestants and the Portuguese Catholics. Yet it was a fundamental and often vitriolic difference. Protestants met to worship in a room at the offices of the EIC on the Praia Grande until, in 1821, the Portuguese authorities allowed for the purchase of land for a chapel and burial ground (now the Old Protestant Cemetery and the attached Morrison Chapel). The first recorded ceremony at the chapel was a marriage in 1833. Similarly, the first Catholic Church in Hong Kong, the Cathedral of the Immaculate Conception, began construction at the junction of Pottinger Street and Wellington Street in 1842, shortly after the colony was founded. It's hard to know the personal enmities between the different Christian schisms in Macao but officially, by the nineteenth century at

93 Richard Hakluyt, *The Principal Navigations, Voyages, Traffiques and Discoveries of the English Nation*, (1589–1600).

94 A supercargo being the name given to the representative of the EIC merchant ships responsible for overseeing the cargo and its sale in Macao and Canton. Cocks (1565–1624) ran the EIC outpost at Hirado between its establishment in 1613 and 1623, when it closed due to bankruptcy. He died a year later sailing home to England. His comments on Macao may be tainted by the fact that, earlier, when employed as a spy monitoring English Catholic exiles in Spain he was cheated out of a large amount of money by a Portuguese conman resulting in him being broke and having to accept the commission to go to Japan to try and re-establish himself. See *Diary of Richard Cocks: Cape-Merchant in the English Factory in Japan, 1615-1622* (edited by Edward Maunde Thompson), (New York: Burt Franklin for The Hakluyt Society, 1883).

least, everyone was getting along fairly well. Religious difference clearly overlapped with competition for imperial gain and trade advantage, often with religion coming third. Britain had to deal with Macao, and by extension Portugal, one way or another – peacefully in co-existence or by threatening invasion and occupation. London's policy veered between the two poles over the centuries…

After several aborted missions eastwards Britain had severely lagged behind both the Portuguese and the Dutch in penetrating far into East and Southeast Asia. Queen Elizabeth I was just granting the EIC its founding charter in London in 1600 as Dutch vessels were already entering Portuguese-controlled waters around Macao. The EIC's creation was in part due to the urgent need to compete with the "Portingalls" and for Britain to look more decidedly eastwards.

The British presence in Macao prior to the mid-nineteenth century was due to imperial rivalry, occasional concordats with Portugal (against Spain or Napoleonic France), linked to the emergent trade with Japan, or latterly, related almost entirely to the state of the China Trade at Canton. The relationship waxed and waned depending on treaties and alliances, wars in Europe, and colonial scramblings on the one hand, and mutual suspicion and religious sectarianism on the other.

The initial wealth of Macao – as all its earlier historians attest including Montalto de Jesus, Charles Boxer, José Maria Braga, Austin Coates through to Rogério Miguel Puga – was initially from the trade with Japan, not China. Portuguese sailors first visited Japan in 1543, becoming the first Europeans to reach the islands and trade – the so-called "Black Ships". The trade was lucrative, 1,600-ton Portuguese treasure ships riding the annual monsoon winds the thousand miles between Nagasaki and Macao, then primarily a Portuguese base for the China trade (and home to a sizeable group of Portuguese-armed dissident Japanese Christians turned *ronin* mercenaries that the Jesuit missionary-traders neglected to tell the Japanese about). The Black Ships sailed from Macao to Nagasaki full of silks bought at Canton and usually more than a hundred thousand ounces of Chinese gold. This hefty investment in the China-Japan trade was the accumulation of the Portuguese traders not just at Macao but also those stationed in Goa and Malacca (and perhaps, depending on the state of Madrid-Lisbon relations, also Spanish traders at Manila too). Silks sold, Japanese manufactures purchased, the Black Ships returned to

Macao (and often from there to Goa and then Lisbon) on the November monsoon winds.

The British finally reached Japan 70 years later in 1613 establishing a "factory" on Hirado Island in Nagasaki prefecture. Not having a permanent base in East Asia the British hoped that Hirado might potentially act as a launchpad to China, allowing them to bypass reliance on Portuguese (and Catholic) Macao. That plan didn't work out, but the arrival of the British (and the Dutch before them) in Japan meant Portugal lost its monopoly on the market to the EIC and the Verenigde Oostindische Compagnie (the Dutch East Indian Company or VOC).[95] The stakes for Portugal in Asia were high. James Clavell's novel of this period – *Shōgun* – has his fictional English pilot-adventurer John Blackthorne declare, 'Without silk Macao dies, without Macao, Malacca dies, then Goa! We can roll up the Portuguese Empire like a carpet.'[96] To add to their woes, Japan became untenable for Portugal after their Jesuit missionaries were expelled and Japanese Christian converts persecuted further, eroding the earlier promising Portuguese-Japanese relationship.

But by 1620 the *Inglês* and the Portuguese had a common interest in keeping the Spanish away from Macao, cobbling together the so-called Fleet of Defence to curb Madrid's expansionist tendencies. Further into the 1600s, thanks in part to the treaty between King João IV and King Charles I, the situation was a dichotomy of a strong Anglo-Portuguese alliance back in Europe, but intense and growing competition between British and Portuguese traders across Asia. Crucially, although the Spanish had a base in the Philippines, the Dutch at Batavia (Jakarta) on Java, and the Portuguese at Macao, the British were still left roving and homeless in the region.

Springboard to Canton

In 1635 the *London* arrived – a British ship under a secretive charter to the Portuguese. Heavily armed, the *London* was designed to show opposition

95 The EIC deemed Hirado unprofitable as they were not permitted to buy Japanese raw silk to import to China. Faced with bankruptcy they closed the factory in 1623.

96 James Clavell, *Shōgun*, (London: Hodder & Stoughton, 1975), p.325. Clavell's John Blackthorne is loosely based on the life and times of William Adams, the first Englishman to reach Japan, sailing under a Dutch flag, and challenge Lisbon's dominance of "the Japans".

to any thoughts the Dutch might have had about expansion in the region between Singapore and Macao. The deal was the protection the *London* afforded Portuguese traders in return for letting British supercargoes trade at Macao. The British had arrived…and the Portuguese had chartered the vessel they arrived on. There was of course plenty of disgruntlement among the Portuguese traders who liked the protection but didn't like the competition, fearing the British would subvert Portugal's favoured position *vis-à-vis* the Chinese. There was also some religious sectarianism from the bishops resistant to any of the Protestant faith even setting foot in Macao.

Then in 1637, a fleet of four British ships under the command of Captain John Weddell, the first to overtly fly the Union Jack, anchored off Taipa and Coloane, then still undeveloped islands of small fishing villages.[97] Aboard was the extraordinary Cornish memoirist Peter Mundy, whose diaries would prove so useful to early geographers of the region (and later to historians of the period). The Portuguese were hesitant about the Protestant British coming ashore but, having brought Jesuit missionaries from Malacca, they were eventually indulged. The British were impressed by São Paulo (St Paul's) Cathedral – which must then have been a staggering European-style edifice to encounter so far east. 'The rooffe is of the fairest arche that yet I ever saw to my remembrance' said Mundy, who recalled a colourful city of painted and tiled residencies, women in Malay *batik* sarongs, cork-soled shoes, and Japanese *kimono*.[98]

The British desperately wanted trading rights in Canton, which the Chinese were far from keen to grant. The Portuguese, in the form of Governor Domingos da Câmara de Noronha, were unwilling to help them obtain the sought after rights. It was clear to Weddell (after a fairly daring pilot-less voyage up the Pearl River) that, unlike Goa or Malacca, Portuguese writ did not run untrammelled in the region. Ultimately it was the Chinese who held sway. The four ship British

97 As a charter the *London* had flown the flag of the chartering nation, Portugal.

98 Ed. Sir Richard Carnac Temple, *The Travels of Peter Mundy, in Europe and Asia, 1608-1667: Volume III, Part 1: Travels in England, Western India, Achin, Macao, and the Canton River, 1634-1637*, (London: Hakluyt Society, 2010). It has been suggested that what Mundy identified as a *kimono* may have been either a Chinese *quimao* (a form of shirt without collar or buttons), a *baju* (a form of short, loose jacket worn on Malay peninsula) or a traditional *sherazzee*, a popular type of shawl in Macao at the time. Either way it indicates Macao's contacts with the China coast, Japan, and/or Malacca.

fleet, after some aggressive cannon firing upriver towards Canton, slunk out of Macao's waters that same year having achieved precisely nothing except having antagonised both the Chinese and the Portuguese. Still, from the Admiralty's position, the British had shown the flag in Macao and now more ships would come – not just from England, but from British possessions in Bombay and Calcutta. The EIC declared trade with China 'desirable' and 'profitable'. They wanted to buy silks, porcelain, and pearls, and sell the Chinese English manufactures.

The British sailed for Macao again in 1689, though that mission also ended in rancour. A decade later the *Macclesfield* arrived with an EIC supercargo aboard and the *Hoppo* (the Emperor's representative at Canton) agreed that the ship could proceed upriver to Canton. In 1704 the *Streatham* brought one of the first shipments of Indian opium destined for Canton and made anchor initially at the Taipa Roads, which afforded excellent shelter with few direct threats ashore. At that time Taipa had a population consisting of little more than a solitary Chinese customs house that measured ships to determine the dues payable before allowing them to proceed to Canton. With the arrival of the *Streatham* a new trade, one that would shape Anglo-Chinese relations, and by extension Macao-China relations, for a century and a half had commenced.

The EIC was finally beginning to prize open China to British trade, although all commerce had to be conducted via Macao, by order of the *Hoppo*. And then only in season which meant that all foreigners were expelled from Canton back to Macao between March and September annually. The British though were also looking to trade along the mainland coast – Amoy, Foochow and across to the island of Formosa (Taiwan).[99] Macao was still seen as indispensable as a summer sojourn, reprovisioning stop, and possible sanctuary in typhoon season.

Blood and Treasure

In November 1742 *HMS Centurion*, under the command of Commodore George Anson, became the first Royal Navy ship to arrive in Macao's waters. Anson had been on an around the world voyage to disrupt and

99 Incidentally the name Formosa derives from Ilha (Island) Formosa ("Beautiful Island"), noted in a Portuguese ship's log in 1542 when passing what they assumed was an uninhabited isle.

harass Spain, and particularly to capture any treasure laden galleons associated with Madrid. However, it had been a much-troubled endeavour, with ships in the squadron lost, sunk, captured, shipwrecked, mutinied. Anson himself had sailed from Tinian in the North Mariana Islands via Formosa to Macao (getting lost a couple of times along the way) with extremely low provisions and a significantly depleted crew due to waves of scurvy either killing or disabling his men. *Centurion* had to be helpfully guided into the Taipa Roads by a Portuguese-speaking Chinese pilot for $30. Anson eagerly paid. The logbook of the *Centurion* recorded an almost continuous fleet of Chinese fishing vessels stretching from Formosa across the South China Sea to Macao. Anson saluted the Governor with an eleven-gun salute, which was returned by an equal number of blasts.[100] The crew of 227 set up a tent village on Taipa while the *Centurion* had a refit.

Despite persistent overtures the Chinese refused Anson permission to visit Canton. Britain was at war with Spain (the so-called War of Jenkins' Ear), then effectively an ally, at least in terms of trade, to China.[101] Rumours came to Anson that the Spanish at Manila were surreptitiously planning to set fire to his ship. So the *Centurion* set sail again despite being desperately short of men. Anson's crew was somewhat bolstered thanks to Macao's role as a centre for the Malay labour agents. Anson had been able to hire on a couple of unemployed Dutch seamen and, through the *ghaut serangs*, about 20 Lascars.[102] Originating from a family of long-time Portuguese Macao-Japan-China traders the Governor, Diogo Pereira, despite being no fan of the English (he was very close to the Jesuits), still politely accorded Anson a departing 15-gun salute.

After a major sea battle in June 1743 Anson spectacularly captured the Manila treasure galleon *Nuestra Señora de Covadonga* (*Our Lady of Covadonga*), as well as the 1,313,843 pieces of eight and 35,682 ounces

100 Richard Walter and Benjamin Robins, *A Voyage Around the World in the Years MDCCXL, I, II, III, IV by George Anson*, (London: Oxford University Press, 1974), p.318. Originally published in London in 1748.

101 The War of Jenkins' Ear between Great Britain and Spain had begun in October 1739 and eventually merged into the War of the Austrian Succession (1740–48). It had started when Robert Jenkins, captain of the British brig *Rebecca*, had his ear allegedly severed by Spanish coast guards searching his ship for contraband.

102 Walter and Robins, *A Voyage Around the World*, p.332.

HMS Centurion capturing the Nuestra Señora de Covadonga, 12 November 1742, by John Steven Dews

of silver aboard.[103] Anson took the galleon back to Macao, sold the ship to the Portuguese, her cargo to the Chinese, deposited most of the Spanish prisoners at Canton (except a portion who wished to hire-on with the *Centurion*), and then departed home to England. The *Centurion* arrived at Spithead, off Portsmouth, in June 1744 as the nation's latest great naval success. The taking of the *Nuestra Señora de Covadonga* meant great personal wealth for Anson and the equivalent of 20 years wages for most of his surviving (British) crew.[104] It should also be noted that Anson's

103 Manila Galleons were the ships that conducted trade between Spain's scattered empire from Mexico to the Philippines. 'Pieces of Eight' is one of many names for the large silver coins issued by the King of Spain, much prized by pirates and English raiders alike. The prize of the *Nuestra Señora de Covadonga* (sometimes *Cabodonga* in English accounts) included the captain General Don Jeronimo de Mentero (a Portuguese working for the Spanish), 492 crew as prisoners (67, mostly officers killed by marksmen on the *Centurion*, were killed in the battle and 84 wounded. Anson lost just two men with 17 wounded), 36 mounted guns, 28 four pounders (*pedresoes*) and a cache of small arms.

104 There are any number of accounts of Anson's round-the-world squadron, his brief time at Macao and his spectacular capture of the *Nuestra Señora de Covadonga* including in Captain SWC Pack (RN), *Admiral Lord Anson: The Story of Anson's Voyage and Naval Events of His Day*, (London: Cassell, 1960); *Walter Vernon Anson, The Life of*

capture of the *Nuestra Señora de Covadonga*, despite his being outmanned and outgunned, was an awesome lesson to the Portuguese of the Royal Navy's potential fighting power in southern Chinese waters.

The Dominance of the Canton Trade

As the Canton Factories grew and expanded so did the need for support services in Macao – reprovisioning, chandlery, crew services, dry docking, the exchange of intelligence on China, translation and legal services, warehousing, and the gathering of flora and fauna and items of interest for transport back to Europe (ceramics, paintings, curios, fans, embroideries, etc). There was also the mini-industry of secret Chinese teachers in Macao, as the emperor still banned foreigners from learning Chinese and the Chinese from teaching it, though instructors could be found in the colony. And, darkly, the buying of slaves from the Portuguese.[105] In general the British became lucrative customers for the Portuguese in Macao, a crucial part of the local economy, rather than (or also as) simply mercantile adversaries.

Whatever rancour existed the British presence was now continual and consistently profitable to Portuguese service businesses and property landlords (only Portuguese could own property in most parts of the colony) and this would remain so until the founding of Hong Kong in the 1840s. By 1776 eight British supercargoes and two private British traders were renting residences in Macao from Portuguese landlords while the EIC was leasing any number of warehouses. The number of British in residence had doubled a decade later to 14 and the British community would keep growing through to the mid-nineteenth century.[106]

Admiral Lord Anson: The Father of the British Navy 1697-1762, (London: John Murray, 1912); and Anthony Bruce, *Anson: Royal Navy Commander and Statesman, 1697-1762*, (Warwick (UK): Helion & Co., 2023). Anson also appears, albeit briefly, in David Grann's *The Wager: A Tale of Shipwreck, Mutiny and Murder*, (London: Simon & Schuster, 2023), *HMS Wager* having originally been part of Anson's fleet sent to disrupt and hassle the Spanish.

105 The import of slaves was banned in European Portugal in 1761. However, slavery within the African Portuguese colonies was only abolished in 1869.

106 The *Leal Senado* (Senate) would occasionally issue prohibitions against Portuguese renting properties to British and other foreigners, hoping to force them to live on their ships. But these injunctions never lasted long and were rarely, if ever, effective.

Macao became a stop for the increasing British sea traffic in the region.[107] The British Empire was booming, from India to Australia and elsewhere. Simultaneously it seemed Portugal was stagnating as an imperial power and proving weak as a naval force.

According to the historian of early Macao, Rogério Miguel Puga, as early as 1717 the British trade in tea alone had overtaken Portuguese commerce in the region. The British supercargoes of the EIC became pivotal to Macao's economic fortunes.[108] Indeed the increase in the volumes of tea shipped by the British were truly spectacular – 22 million pounds in 1803 rising to 30 million by 1813 (despite additional taxes being imposed by the London Treasury). According to one historian of the trade 'Goods from Canton accounted for 67 per cent of all EIC sales income earned in London between 1803 and 1808. From there also came delicate high-value goods such as raw silk, nankeens, pepper, and spices.'[109] Certainly by 1760 the British were the largest traders on the China coast, the EIC dominant, and the emergence of private, so-called "country traders" (meaning private traders, or, to the EIC whose control they avoided, "interlopers") burgeoning as they brought cotton, pepper, and opium from Bombay and Calcutta.

The Chinese had issued an imperial edict as early as 1729 outlawing opium but the British paid it no heed and just smuggled. Lacking a base, British smugglers and supercargoes simply used Portuguese frontmen – a problem for the Portuguese authorities but profitable for all those

107 Most notably perhaps in December 1779 *HMS Resolution* and *HMS Discovery* called at Macao on the way home as part of Captain James Cook's third, and final, voyage. Cook, of course, was killed in Hawaii in February 1779. Now under the command of Captain Charles Clerke *Resolution* and *Discovery* headed to the Kamchatka Peninsula in another attempt to find the Northwest Passage, but Clerke too died that August. Under Captain Gore the two ships turned for home, down the coast of Japan and then to Macao, before departing in January 1780 via the Sunda Strait and Cape Town to Britain.

108 Rogério Miguel Puga, *The British Presence in Macau, 1635-1793*, (Hong Kong & Macao: Hong Kong University Press, Royal Asiatic Society Books and Universidade de Macau, 2013), p.5.

109 Roger Knight, *Convoys: The British Struggle Against Napoleonic Europe and America*, (New Haven & London: Yale University Press, 2022), p.193. In monetary terms Knight records this as £5.9 million, of which £3.4 million (57 per cent) was tea in 1809, quoting Parliamentary Papers, *Fourth Report of the Select Committee on the Affairs of the East India Company* (1812), p.493.

concerned. Of course the situation was building towards the First Opium War in 1839 which would itself lead to the establishment of Hong Kong and the wholesale relocation of the British from Macao.

Macao's Goa-born Governor from 1790 to 1793 Vasco Luís Carneiro de Sousa e Faro wrote to Lisbon to tell them that by the end of 1792 British capital represented approximately 90 per cent of the trade which moved business in the city. It was also the case that the Americans were becoming far more significant, and of course there were Danes, Parsees, Swedes, Dutch, and the French involved as well. Far from wanting, as many of his predecessors had, to rid himself of the British, Carneiro de Sousa e Faro actually feared that they would up sticks, leave, and establish their own colony on Lantau Island and from there ferry both opium and sundry other goods into Canton bypassing Macao. That didn't ultimately happen (although of course Lantau Island would eventually become part of British Hong Kong and effectively the boundary of Hong Kong's waters), but the Governor's fears showed how dominant British influence had become in the colony and how dependent on British cash and trade Macao now was.[110]

But back in Europe, Napoleon Bonaparte was causing problems.... problems that would affect far off Macao...

Just Take It?

Before considering why the Royal Navy felt the need to come ashore at Macao in 1808 we should perhaps just ask whether or not the British could just have taken Macao by force at pretty much any point in the eighteenth century? Britain was in its imperial ascendancy. Why build anew on Lantau when you could just take Macao as Britain's latest imperial possession? What was Lisbon going to do if London decided it wanted Macao for itself?

It was a question seriously posed at the highest levels. In the 1780s the British had considered a permanent settlement – perhaps Dane's Island (Changzhou Island) at Whampoa (Huangpu), 14 miles from Canton, or Macao itself. David Scott, a Scottish director of the EIC and

110 Trade statistic quoted in Puga, *The British Presence in Macau*, p.120. The Lantau theory is posited in Jorge Santos Alves, *Governadores de Macau*, (Lisbon: Labirinto de Paixons Editorial, 2013).

a merchant who had tried (unsuccessfully) to sell sea otter furs from the Pacific Northwest at Canton, sent a letter to the directors of the EIC (later published as a pamphlet to try and take his cause public) arguing that 'the Portuguese gain nothing by Macao; if it could be purchased by our company, it would be a most consequential acquisition.' The EIC rejected the idea.[111] But it lingered on in some minds.

The Barrier Gate by John Thomson, c.1870s

Lord Macartney (and his Mission to Peking) stayed at the luxurious Casa Garden in June 1793 en route to the Chinese capital (ultimately to fail…) to negotiate trading rights for Britain directly with the Qing Emperor.[112] Macartney echoed Governor Carneiro de Sousa e Faro, noting how British money appeared to be almost completely supporting Macao. So why not take Macao by force, or perhaps at least, why not just buy it from Lisbon? Macartney noted in his diary: 'If the Portuguese

111 'Remarks and ideas upon the export trade from Great Britain to India. With a plan and proposals for the increase thereof.' Submitted to the consideration of the directors of the East India Company, by letter from David Scott, dated April 3, 1787.

112 Casa Garden was built in 1770, the park and residence was originally the home of a Portuguese merchant, Manuel Pereira. It was later rented out to William Fitzhugh of the EIC who used the property to house the Company's senior officials and visiting supercargoes. Today it is the home of the Fundação Oriente in Macao in the Praça Luís de Camões.

make a difficulty of parting with it to us on fair terms, it might easily be taken from them by a small force from Madras [Chennai] or with as little trouble and with more advantage we might make a settlement in Lantao [Lantau Island] or Cow-hee [the eastern end of Lantau Island], and then Macau would of itself crumble to nothing in a short time.'[113]

The answer was that they could have, certainly militarily, and probably only needing the Navy and India-stationed sepoy troops. The Portuguese Navy was in decline, the Royal Navy in the ascendancy. The EIC had its own battleships. The British consolidation in India made mass troop mobilisation more convenient and the Portuguese were, at the time, depending on less reliable and inadequately trained colonial troops to garrison Macao. But London knew full well that the Chinese would oppose any takeover of Macao. They would slam shut the Portas do Cerco (Barrier Gate) at the northern meeting point of Macao and mainland China, starve the English out, and probably also loose pirates on British shipping (who would not be unbeatable, but would certainly be a nuisance). The plan was scrapped.

And so, back to Bonaparte, the British, and Macao….

Invading Macao

The social historian Zhidong Hao has written that, 'At one point in 1801, the British were thinking about asking the Portuguese to surrender Macao to them. When that idea was dropped, the British troops forced their way into Macao in 1808, led by Rear Admiral William Drury, in the name of protecting their interests in China, and "defending" Macao from possible French and Spanish attacks.'[114]

It's forgotten now. It's not commemorated anywhere in Macao, Portugal, or England. It doesn't even rank as a footnote in the vast history of the British Empire. It's a minor detail rarely, if ever, noted in the histories of the Peninsular War (1807-1814) where Britain and Portugal

113 Lord Macartney, *An Embassy to China: Lord Macartney's Journal, 1793-1794,* (London: Routledge, 2000), p.211. Macartney specifically mentions Lantau and presumably heard this notion while mixing with British company in Macao.

114 Zhidong Hao, *Macau: History and Society (Second Edition)*, Hong Kong/Macao: Hong Kong University Press & Universidade de Macau, 2020), p.21.

combined to fight the First French Empire of Napoleon Bonaparte on the Iberian Peninsula.

But the fact remains that the British temporarily threatened Macao with invasion and occupation twice – once in 1802 and again in 1808. In 1801, the Portuguese army suffered a setback in the battle against French and Spanish united forces, losing the Alentejo region in southern Portugal to the enemy. The British had sent an army to Lisbon to successfully repel the French, but there were concerns in the EIC that France would move to seize Portugal's overseas possessions. The British sent troops to Goa and other places in Asia in the name of helping Portugal to defend its Asian colonies, safeguarding their own trade lanes, but also attempting to occupy Macao by taking advantage of that favourable situation.

The rather aptly named *HMS Arrogant* was sent to China convoying three EIC ships to Lintin Island near Macao.[115] Each ship contained a detachment of British troops intent on landing on Macao. The Governor at Macao, José Manuel Pinto, was strenuously opposed to any landing. However mixed messages were flying about, including that France and Portugal had concluded a truce and were now both united against Britain. Richard Wellesley, the first Marquess Wellesley and at the time Governor General of India (and the older brother of Arthur, who would become famous as the Duke of Wellington) demanded that Macao be put under British control. The Portuguese resisted, the Select Committee that governed the EIC wavered, everyone knew once Macao came under British control it would never revert to Lisbon again and Anglo-Portuguese relations would be ruined, perhaps beyond repair at a time of necessary unity against France.[116] Ultimately, the suggested landing mission was aborted and British soldiers were not landed on Macao.

*

Still, throughout the Napoleonic Wars the Royal Navy maintained a presence in the waters between Canton and Macao to protect Britain's China Trade and discourage any French ships from thinking of occupying Macao themselves. The British historian of Portugal Neill Lochery has written that 'although it [by now the Peninsula War] was a European war,

115 Now Inner (or Nei) Lingding Island close to Chuhai (Zhuhai).

116 Austin Coates, *Macao and the British, 1637-1842: Prelude to Hong Kong,* (Hong Kong: Hong Kong University Press, 2009), pp.92-94. Originally published 1966.

its effects reached well beyond the shores of the continent. In this respect, it was one of the first truly global conflicts.'[117]

William O'Bryen Drury

This global nature of the war in Europe affected Macao directly in 1808. In September of that year six British warships carrying 300 musket wielding soldiers under the Commander of the Royal Navy's East Indies Station's Rear-Admiral William Drury anchored in the Taipa Roads. The Select Committee of the EIC told Drury that without the prior consent of the Portuguese authorities in Macao, it would be out of the question to ask the Qing government to permit the British troops to land in Macao (worried that the whole slamming shut of the Portas do Cerco leading to starvation scenario would ensue).

British officers immediately visited the Governor of Macao, Bernardo Aleixo de Lemos Faria, and proposed that the British troops defend Macao together with the Portuguese troops under the Governor's command. The proposal was, unsurprisingly, flatly refused by the Governor though he must have realised that this was most serious challenge to Portuguese rule since the Dutch attack in 1622.[118] The governor, aware that the few Portuguese troops stationed in Macao were no match for the British, had no choice but to talk tough as the *Leal Senado* rather vaingloriously publicly swore to fight to the death to defend Macao. The governor claimed Macao was under Chinese domain and any landing would cause war between Britain and China.

Despite this the British landed unopposed and remained in Macao for three months. However, they never removed the Portuguese flags that flew over the two military forts of Bom Parto and Guia that they occupied. Drury maintained he was only in Macao to assist in resisting any French

117 Neill Lochery, *Porto: Gateway to the World*, (London: Bloomsbury, 2020), p.32.

118 The Battle of Macao in 1622 took place during the long running Dutch-Portuguese War of 1598-1663. The Portuguese, though outnumbered, repelled the Dutch in a much-celebrated victory on June 24 after a three-day battle.

incursion and so left the Portuguese flags flying. The resistance the *Leal Senado* had promised did not materialise – it was all too clear any resistors would be swiftly wiped out and the only result was that Macao would become a part of the British Empire.

Step forward the Azorean aristocrat Miguel José de Arriaga Brum da Silveira, the *Ouvidor* (or Chief Justice) since 1802. He (usually referred to simply as Arriaga), along with Governor Lemos e Faria, counselled caution and to pass the British problem along to the Chinese. They hurriedly contacted the *Hoppo* in Kwangtung requesting him to forbid the British troops to land. The Portuguese authorities also wrote to a Portuguese missionary in Peking, Padre Jose Bernardo de Almeida, asking him to try to report to the Jiaqing Emperor (Yongyan) about how the British coveted Macao. Everyone then awaited the Chinese response.

*

Thomas Manning

Even at this rather fraught time some saw Macao as a peaceful and balmy enclave. The early Sinologist Thomas Manning (who had previously been an English prisoner of war of the French in Paris) first visited Macao not long after having arrived in Canton in the early 1800s courtesy of the EIC. After an intense period of living in the Factories, witnessing mass brawls between British sailors and local Chinese, as well as the hubbub of Canton life he wrote home to England of Macao's more relaxing and liberated atmosphere. Within the Factories the foreigners were confined to a small area whereas in Macao they could roam pretty much wherever they wanted. Manning, who craved direct contact with the Chinese, immediately liked Macao, a feeling he suggests was not shared by most of his fellow English in the Portuguese colony:

> 'We spend the summer at Macao, a romantic, tho' barren, spot of ground near a hundred miles south of Canton. I can find nobody that takes any delight in it but myself – I hear it vilified twenty times a day

– it is a dull place, I grant that – but the sea breeze – the reposing bay by lofty hills and mountain tops, the ocean opening at a distance; the contrast between real repose, & ideal tumult & traffic upon the sight of passing ships, the luxurious heat (…) the religious buildings, solidly handsome, tho' plain; the Portuguese superstitions; the memory & marks of their former activity of mind & body; the memory of the Jesuits excited by the organs, the bells &c, with which those active, learned & extraordinary men have endowed this place. Those and other little bundles of delight are sufficient for *me*.'[119]

*

A Chinese response inevitably eventually came. The *Hoppo* suspended all trade in Canton and cut off food supplies to the Factories. The British supercargoes there were forced to flee to Macao. Drury lost the initiative with the Chinese and also started to lose control of his men who, bored, began to plunder, drink heavily. They lost Drury any potential Chinese support in Macao by desecrating a Chinese graveyard. London feared a diplomatic crisis with China it neither wanted nor desired… just yet.

Three months after he had landed, Drury weighed anchor and sailed away from Macao on December 20, 1808. Angry at their humiliation London demanded the firing of Arriaga and Lemos Faria. A weak Lisbon, who referred to Drury's actions as "piracy", agreed and Lemos Faria left the Governorship on December 26, 1808, to be replaced by Lucas José de Alvarenga, who had been a lawyer. Arriaga managed to stay in post. The Chinese, now highly suspicious of British intentions towards Macao, searched Macao's forts suspecting a secret British force had been left behind. Only once they ascertained that Drury had really left with all his men did they allow trade to resume in Canton on January 1, 1809.

Britain remained committed to developing and opening up the Canton trade. In 1809 a total of five convoys (59 ships in total) departed British ports (invariably either Spithead or Cork) for the Far East; in 1813 slightly more were still sailing east annually. Admittedly the China and East Indies trade was not growing as fast as the West Indies trade (28

119 Edward Weech, *Chinese Dreams in Romantic England: The Life and Times of Thomas Manning*, (Manchester: Manchester University Press, 2022), pp.108-109. Manning was not Catholic but did admire the Jesuits' curiosity and learning about China. He is perhaps the only person to praise the heat and it's a mystery quite what he means by 'little bundles of delight.' The italic is Manning's.

convoys in 1809; 37 in 1813, or around 1,702 merchant ships), but it was still growing in importance.[120]

The Napoleonic Wars rumbled on for another seven years until Bonaparte's defeat at Waterloo. The British stayed active in the waters between Macao and Canton but did not threaten to land troops again. HB Morse, a historian of the EIC, summed up the British humiliation:

> 'Admiral Drury in his encounter with passive resistance was defeated without the loss of a man on either side, and in the eyes of the Chinese he must have appeared to have saved all except honour. He had come to Macau to aid the Portuguese in defending it against the French – this aid was rejected by the Portuguese, by the Chinese, and the very British merchants whose business interest he had come to enhance.'[121]

A Scurvy Business

Potential strategic land grabs during the Napoleonic Wars aside, did the French ever really want Macao any more than the British? Of course, a French controlled territory that could interfere with or even curtail Britain's Canton trade would annoy London, the EIC, and the growing number of private traders immensely. Just as the French would soon come to detest British incursions on the borders of Indochina in Yunnan. The French saw Indochina and the western borderlands as their zone of influence, just as the British, even roughly 40 years before the acquisition of Hong Kong, had begun to see southern China as their zone of influence and any incursion into it something to be resisted.

In reality there was little chance of a threat from Portugal. The country was officially a British protectorate between 1808 and 1821, even after the Peninsular War had ended and the French withdrawn back across the Pyrenees. There was a serious power vacuum in Lisbon. The reasons for this are beyond the purview of this book, though Liberalism (Constitutionalism, and a dose of Freemasonry) which had been fueled by the revolutions in France and America finally gained enough traction

120 Convoy data from Knight, *Convoys*, p.184.

121 Hosea Ballou (HB) Morse, *The Chronicles of the East India Company, Trading to China, 1635-1834. Vol I,* (Oxford: Clarendon Press, 1926).

to challenge the monarchists (or Absolutists) back at home.[122] These arguments would be fought out in Macao too. Either way Portugal, and by extension Macao, remained in the doldrums post-war compared to an assertive and victorious Britain. The establishment of the British colony at Hong Kong was still some way off, but after 1815 British dominance in southern China, both militarily and in the China Trade, was total. Portugal was eclipsed. Indeed, some historians have gone further and suggested that Portugal's glorious "era of empire" comes to a juddering halt in 1807 and 1808, having begun in 1415 with the conquest of Ceuta in North Africa.[123]

Of course later, after the First Opium War, the British would no longer need any reliance on the Portuguese as they developed their own colony on Hong Kong Island that soon overshadowed Macao in terms of trade, wealth, and military power. Not that the occasional Anglo-Portuguese tension didn't linger. In 1849 the *Hongkong Register* newspaper reported that on June 7 that year a Mr. J Summers, attached to the Protestant mission at Hong Kong, was imprisoned at Macao for refusing to take off his hat on passing the host at a religious (one assumes Catholic) festival.[124] He had to be rescued by Captain (later Admiral) Henry Keppel and the men of *HMS Maeander* then stationed at Hong Kong. This involved the Captain and his crew storming the gaol to release Summers. Unfortunately, a Portuguese soldier (identified in the *Register* as "Roque Barrache") was killed during the scuffles, three others were injured, and

122 Freemasonry is estimated to have been present in Macao from 1759. Portuguese lodges preceded the creation of British Lodges slightly later in Hong Kong. 'Lodges and Masonic groups emerged incorporating Portuguese, expatriates, and relevant members of the Macanese community, along the administrative bureaucracy, the local companies, the liberal professions, and the circle of intellectuals…' See Arnaldo Gonçalves, *Freemasons in China: The Portuguese Link*, (Social Science Research Network, January 2014).

123 Among the historians arguing for 1808 are AR Disney, *A History of Portugal and the Portuguese Empire*, (Cambridge: Cambridge University Press, 2009) and AJR Russell-Wood, *The Portuguese Empire, 1415-1808: A World on the Move*, (Baltimore and London: The Johns Hopkins University Press, 1998). Among the dissenters from this opinion is Charles Boxer in *The Portuguese Seaborne Empire*, 1415-1825, (London: Hutchison, 1969), as Boxer wishes to include the 1825 Treaty of Rio de Janeiro between Portugal and the Empire of Brazil, which recognised Brazil as an independent nation.

124 Whether Summers's action was accidental, an oversight, or intended as an insult to the Catholic faith is unclear.

the daughter of a gaoler fell 20 feet to the ground, suffering severe injuries. The Queen of Portugal was reportedly furious, while it wasn't quite clear who sanctioned Keppel's rescue effort. The British apologized and paid reparations to Portugal.[125]

Still, the 1808 "invasion" of Macao can be seen as rather a fool's errand. It did little but stir up rancour between London and Canton, as well as with Peking, and obviously Lisbon. And, despite the ongoing Napoleonic Wars it does not seem to have caused any great alarm in Paris, which did not appear to have had any grand strategy as regards extending the Europe-wide conflict into the South China Seas.

Thomas Manning, long wary of British aggrandizement in the Far East, was in no doubt that the 1808 "invasion" of Macao was an error – a 'scurvy business' and 'not much to our [Britain's] honour I'm afraid.'[126] Sojourning in Macao at the time, Manning wrote in his notebook, 'If I was to qualify that senseless expedition with the epithets I think it deserves, I might seem harsh.'[127]

HMS Meander by Oswald Walters Brierly

125 *The Treaty Ports of China and Japan: A Complete Guide to the Open Ports of Those Countries, Together with Peking, Yedo, Hongkong and Macao* by Wm Fred. Myers, NB Denys and Chas. King, (London and Hongkong: Trűbner and Co./Shortrede and Co., 1867), p.63.

126 Weech, *Chinese Dreams in Romantic England*, p.119.

127 Ibid, p.194.

Once There Were Islands – Remembering the Hengqins

Isla Dom João, Isla Montanha, and Lapa (1644-2024)

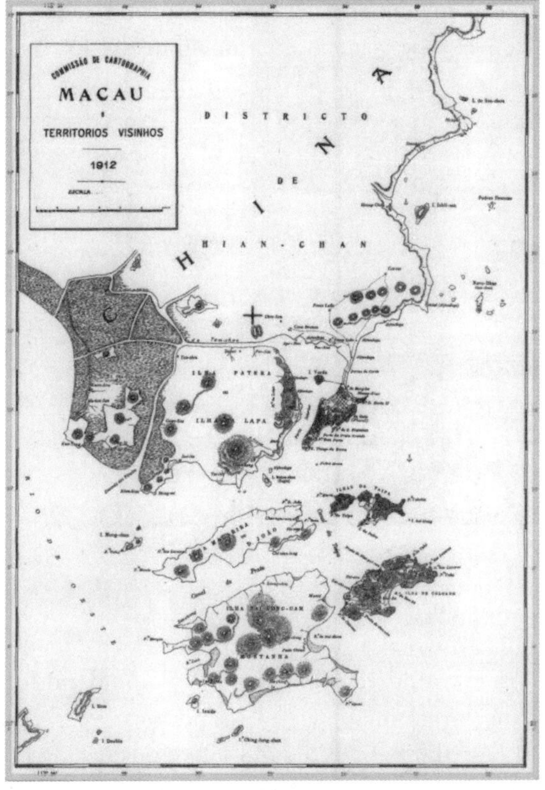

The Hengqins, 1912

'...on the opposite shore rose the majestic Lapa, towering seemingly to the skies.'

– Caroline H Butler, *Recollections of China*, 1844

Once Were Mountains....

It's hard to believe it now when one passes through the soulless, desolate, semi-industrial strip between mainland China and the Macao Special Administrative Region, but there were once three mountainous and verdant islands that lay between the Portuguese colony and the mainland of China. The Portuguese named the islands Dom João (sometimes known as San João and in English records occasionally as St John), Montanha (also known as Tai Vong Cam), and Lapa (or sometimes Lappa). Collectively the island were known as the Hengqins. Lapa was by far the largest of the Hengqins, occupying roughly 30 square miles. Later the islands became known in Chinese respectively as Xiao (Little) Hengqin, Da (Big) Hengqin, and Wanzai.

The Porto Interior, looking across to Lapa Island, 1864

The two Hengqins, which directly faced Coloane and Taipa, were eventually joined by land reclamation to form a single island, while Lapa/Wanzai, a mere few hundred metres from Macao's Porto Interior with its muddy shoreline, saw its inclines levelled and became a peninsula. Visitors to Macao will pass through all the old Hengqins if they use the Wanzai border crossing or have driven over the *Ponte Flor de Lótus* (the Lotus Bridge) from the more recent landfill of Cotai across to Zhuhai.[128]

128 The *Ponte Flor de Lótus* remains especially interesting as it has approach roads on the mainland Chinese side with an almost unique arrangement to facilitate switching traffic from the left-hand side (Macao still drives on the left-hand side as in Hong Kong) to the right-hand side for the PRC. Macao kept driving on the left even though Portugal and all its other colonies switched to driving on the right in 1928.

Hengqin was for a long time a bleak Special Economic Zone of truck parks and industrial units. The Wanzai industrial suburbs are no longer anything close to the once verdant mountains that rose 200 to 300 feet and appear in every old painting of Macao (and often lead to confusion with people misidentifying the location due to these now departed mountains) – the Bay of Naples and Mount Vesuvius being the most common mis-labelling.

Reports have been circulating that China's central government in Beijing may hand over Hengqin to the Macao SAR. The idea is that perhaps the Macau Urban Renewal Ltd (MUR) and the Guangdong Macau In-depth Cooperation Zone quangos can diversify away from the reliance on gaming and tourism with a little more light industry.[129] There's also the development of a massive housing project to accommodate Macao citizens into the Greater Bay Area (GBA) – the 4,000 household Macau New Neighbourhood includes 5,000 sq m of commercial space. There is room – Hengqin covers 106.46 sq km, approximately three times the size of Macao SAR at present and, *The Macao News* reported in 2024, 11,000 people from Macao now live and work in the Hengqin area.[130] This, and the regulatory infrastructure it requires, is all gradually happening – Hengqin became an autonomous customs territory in March 2024. Hengqin has been, as of September 2022, offering cash incentives to listed companies in mainland China and Hong Kong to relocate or expand there.[131]

Perhaps this new spotlight on Hengqin then is a good time to consider that before the warehouses and factories, the highways and housing units, the subsidies and the marketing campaigns, there was a lot of history on the old islands of Dom João, Montanha, and Lapa – storms, gunfights, pirates, and global conflicts played out among the now long-gone hills and mountains.

129 The MUR, with offices on the Avenida da Praia Grande, is a company formed by the Macao SAR Government, the Macau Industrial and Commercial Development Fund, and the Science and Technology Development Fund. QUANGOs are quasi autonomous non-governmental organisations (though this definition is hazy given central government controls in the PRC and Hong Kong/Macao SARs).

130 *The Macao News,* January 4, 2024.

131 Martin Choi, 'Hengqin, an island near Macau, offers cash incentives to listed companies in mainland China and Hong Kong to move there', *South China Morning Post,* September 16, 2022.

The Mountains of Lapa

It was the closest and more easily accessible island of Lapa that most often found itself mentioned in newspapers and memoirs of nineteenth century Macao. In 1844 Caroline Hyde Butler, the intrepid wife of an American tea and silks merchant, noted in her diary that she had climbed to Macao's A-Ma Temple dedicated to the sea-goddess Mazu in São Lourenço and that, '…on the opposite shore rose the majestic Lapa, towering seemingly to the skies.'[132] Passing through almost a century later than Hyde Butler, around 1930, the Dutch travel writer Hendrik de Leeuw noted, 'behind the beautiful bay, the Praia Grande…the ancient forts and modern public buildings, rise the summits of the mountains of Lapa.'[133] Lapa was home to some moderately successful market gardeners cultivating rice, cabbages, turnips, gourds, pumpkins, peas, and beans. Amid them were small communities of impoverished day labourers who often experienced long periods of unemployment. A few farmers experimented with sugar cane, but it never really took; others ground abrasive paddy-husks to make Chinese tooth cleaning powder.

1644 – For a time Lapa had been known as the Ilha, or island, of Padres. Alternatively it was often simply referred to as Patera, a Japanese corruption of padre – Priests Island. This indicated that the island's early Christian Jesuit associations were strong. Dutch mariners in the seventeenth century noted a fortified battery and a dock at Lapa that had been built by Christian missionaries. Writing in 1902, Montalto de Jesus noted that in 1644 the Chinese government at Canton had granted a tract on Lapa as a burial ground for a Jesuit, João Rodrigues (known in China as Lu Ruohan) who had been influential at the court in Peking.[134] In 1645 the Jesuit's tract of land was enlarged by a further imperial grant. Writing in 1869 an Englishman who had lived in Japan and was also for many years a medical practitioner in Canton, Walter George Dickson, maintained that a group of Japanese Christian convert/refugees also once

132 Caroline H Butler, 'Recollections of China', *The Columbian Lady's and Gentleman's Magazine*, Vol 1 (1844), p.131.

133 Hendrik de Leeuw, *Cities of Sin,* (London: Noel Douglas, 1934), p.147.

134 Montalto de Jesus, *Historic Macao*, p.202.

lived on Lapa along with the Portuguese Jesuits, and that they built a large structure known as the *yat-pon-lao*, or Japanese Hall.[135]

1764 – The official Portuguese representatives in Macao reported to the Viceroy of Portuguese India, the grandly named Manuel de Saldanha e Albuquerque, the Count of Ega (in Goa), that all Portuguese properties in Lapa and nearby islands had been abandoned. It seems that exposure to devastating typhoons made permanent habitation of the islands near impossible. Additionally, due to the anti-Society of Jesus campaigns in Portugal, all the Jesuits had by this time been expelled from Macao and the surrounding islands in 1762. Yet looming Lapa could not be ignored. Primarily it remained an important source of fresh drinking water for Macao with Chinese sampans ferrying back and forth constantly bringing essential fresh water supplies across to the Portuguese colony which was perennially short of drinking water.

1874 – Lapa particularly features in many accounts of the great and destructive typhoon that hit southern China, Hong Kong, and Macao in September 1874 – the third worst in recorded history and, of course, at a time of significantly fewer defences against typhoons than later.[136] Much of Macao was quite simply annihilated by wind, flood, or subsequent fire – totally wiped off the map. The Praia Grande and many of its grand villas were wrecked. The Igreja de Santo Antóni (St Anthony's Church) was badly damaged and the two domes of the towers of the Sé Catedral da Natividade de Nossa Senhora (The Cathedral of the Nativity of Our Lady in the Sé parish) similarly destroyed. Whole houses and entire streets were decimated, an estimated 5,000 people died, and approximately 2,000 ships (including almost the entire Macanese fishing fleet and whole sampan clusters, and the families living on them) were sunk.[137] A certain Mr Ybele, apparently a Dutch trader, had single-handedly built a house on Lapa and was determined to stay there. He was shocked to find that a

135 Walter George Dickson, *Japan: Being a Sketch of the History, Government and Officers of the Empire,* (Edinburgh: W Blackwood & Sons, 1869), p.241.

136 The previous most severe typhoon had been on August 31, 1848, when it was recorded that 67 houses in Macao were entirely demolished and 100 lives lost.

137 The Cathedral of the Nativity of Our Lady was the first cathedral in Macao to be built in stone. Consecrated in 1850 repairs were made after the 1874 typhoon. However, the church we see today was completely rebuilt in concrete in 1937. Similarly St Anthony's was first built using bamboo and wood in the mid-sixteenth century, and later rebuilt in stone.

junk moored in the Porto Interior opposite had been entirely lifted up by the ferocious winds and flung through his front window. Surveying the surrounding island Mr Ybele recorded that, 'the hills of Lapa were strewn with upended junks.'[138]

St Anthony's Church, damaged by the 1874 typhoon

1888 – Lisbon and Peking signed a treaty in 1887 guaranteeing Portugal's rights over Macao – a mere 300 years after Macao's occupation by Portugal! It is generally agreed that Macao, Taipa, and Coloane were included in the treaty's notion of Portugal's "perpetual occupation and government" of Macao, but the border with the mainland of China was never mutually agreed in terms of a jointly satisfactory fixed boundary. And nobody involved specifically mentioned Dom João, Montanha, or Lapa. They remained largely uninhabited and unoccupied by either Chinese or Portuguese troops. Some rumours circulated that the Chinese were willing to lease a portion of Lapa, '…and some other uninhabited islands in the vicinity' (presumably Dom João and Montanha) to the Portuguese, but if it was discussed it never officially happened.

Lisbon seems to have assumed that the islands were part of their imperial domain, although the Chinese Imperial Maritime Customs

138 'The Typhoon at Macao – Astonishing Particulars (from the *Overland China Mail*)', *Bendigo Advertiser* (Victoria), November 25, 1874, p.3.

pretty much established and maintained a station (and guard house) on a hill overlooking much of Lapa, claiming it as an 1887 treaty right. This started out very basically as a matshed, a temporary structure made of bamboo poles and palm leaves, though over the years did become a more permanent structure.

1890 – For a while it seems that the islands enjoyed a period of calm. Montalto de Jesus writes that Lapa became quite the destination with several Portuguese in Macao building themselves summer homes, as well as Europeans in Macao regularly visiting by sampan for weekend picnic parties or to shoot quail and other wild fowl. The small ferries would land at Shek Kok Tsui, then opposite the *Camões Gardens.* Near the Chuk Sin Tung (alternatively Chook Seen Toong), or The Grotto of the Bamboo Fairy, a shelter had been built with stone tables for shaded picnics. Crucially, Lapa was also still supplying a good deal of fresh drinking water to Macao.

1896 – The historic lack of clarity over the islands persisted: who exactly controlled them and had the right to be on them. It all became something of a free-for-all in the late 1890s. The Chinese guard house and troops on Dom João were reported as, 'causing annoyance to Portuguese residents', and so Portugal dispatched troops to the island. Lisbon wanted China to vacate the territory and for Portugal to incorporate Dom João, Montanha, & Lapa into a greater "*Província da Macau*". A tense stand-off ensued. In May 1897 the *Boston Evening Transcript* of Massachusetts reported ominously that, 'The two battalions stood waiting to fly at each other's throats.'[139] The Viceroy of Canton and the Portuguese Plenipotentiary met for negotiations, and both agreed to remove their respective battalions and stand them down. It was, by all accounts, a showy retreat with both sides blowing whistles, firing off cannons, and with military musicians playing martial music. Noisy, but at least a conflict and any bloodshed had been avoided.

But then things got distinctly weirder. It was reported in, of all places, a Berlin newspaper, the *Vossiche Zeitung*, that China had 'ceded' the island of Lapa to Germany. *The Times* in London reported, '…40 or 50 German Marines are surveying the harbour and the roads of the island', and also that the German Imperial Navy cruiser *SMS Irene*, under the command

139 'Chinese Interference at Macao Ceases', *Boston Evening Transcript* (Massachusetts), May 20, 1897, p.12.

of Rear Admiral Paul Hoffmann had sailed from Hong Kong for Lapa.[140] It was certainly the case that the Germans were looking for a location for a coaling station for their newly formed East Asia Squadron to bolster their long dreamed of *Deutsches Kaiserreich* empire in the Far East. Rear Admiral Hoffmann appears to have favoured Lapa, or perhaps Quemoy (Kinmen, and now part of Taiwan) but, crucially before any occupation could take place (and possibly an international incident resulting from such an action) Hoffmann was replaced as Squadron Commander by Rear Admiral Alfred von Tirpitz, slightly later to become German Grand Admiral and Secretary of State of the German Imperial Naval Office (a position he would hold till mid-way through World War One when he fell out with the Kaiser over restrictions on submarine warfare). Von Tirpitz favoured northern China and so the Germans leased Kiautschou Bay (Jiaozhou Bay) in northern Shantung province with its administrative centre at Tsingtao and forgot about Macao. Lapa remained largely deserted again.

SMS Irene by James Scott Maxwell

1907 – Writing in 1905 the Canton-born scholar James Dyer Ball noted that 'the large island on the other side of the Inner Harbour is called Lapa. The Portuguese in the early days had some settlements on it;

140 'Germany and the Far East', *The Times* (London), March 10, 1896, p.5.

but it is now entirely in the hands of the Chinese.'[141] The Chinese indeed, or more specifically, Chinese pirates. Suggestions that sea bandits had established bases on Lapa began circulating around 1903. Though pirates had long called at the island as a port in storms, to replenish fresh water supplies, or to use Lapa as a temporary base to slip into and out of Macao for a bit of smuggling, they had never occupied it. But in 1907 it seemed a bandit build-up was occurring.

Portuguese Navy anti-piracy patrols engaged a force of an estimated 300 pirates just offshore of Lapa. The Portuguese were fired on by cannons mounted in the stern of the pirate junks which moored up and pointed back towards Macao's Porto Interior from Lapa. They could technically have shelled the city. The Portuguese also came under fire from a rain of 'stinkpots', locally made grenades with bamboo fuses nastily filled with sulphur, gunpowder, nails, and shot. The ferocity of the pirate defence was such that Lisbon decided to permanently send two cruisers, the *NRP Rainha Dona Amélia* (later renamed the *NRP República)* and *NRP Adamastor*, to Macao to boost the existing naval presence, as well as deciding to start construction of a naval air station at Taipa with planes as airborne pirate spotters.

The Portuguese also used the excuse of a leprosarium established on Dom João to send troops to the island claiming that the leper colony needed to be protected from pirates. As Macao and China's long alliance against piracy was still agreed the Chinese said little about this occupation. Macao had a number of leprosariums; in the 1740s, the King of Portugal Dom João V, had ordered serious steps be taken to study and contain leprosy in Portugal's overseas colonies. But China could not fail to notice that, with a leprosarium on Dom João and another on Montanha, these institutions also functioned as extensions of Portuguese colonialism to the islands allowing the Macao authorities to claim limited sovereignty over them and build garrisons supposedly to protect them.

1916 – China underwent a republican revolution only a year or so after Portugal did. Fighting continued in southern China with various factions vying for power. At times that fighting spilled over onto Lapa Island. In April 1916 residents of Macao were startled and the crew of the Portuguese gunboat *Pátria* scrambled after gunfire from Lapa hit houses

141 Dyer Ball, *Macao: The Holy City*, p.45.

in Macao and even pinged off the hull of the moored-up *Pátria*.[142] The Governor, José Carlos da Maia, was a navy man and a staunch supporter of Portugal's new republic, and China's. He had allowed Sun Yat-sen to use the colony as a base. In 1916 da Maia sent an army officer and 20 policemen to Lapa to assert Portuguese sovereignty. The Chinese responded by sending a hundred soldiers to Lapa and reinforcing the Portas da Cerco. The Portuguese retreated.[143]

1926 – Another ferocious typhoon swept through Macao destroying buildings and tossing junks about like matchsticks. It was one of the heaviest and most prolonged torrential rainfalls in the history of the Hong Kong Observatory's records. This time round the storm was so fierce that the Portuguese Navy's 1,200-ton cruiser *NRP República* was driven ashore onto Lapa as if it was a flimsy wooden egg-boat. After quite some effort the *República* was eventually re-floated. The pirate menace on Lapa had not, despite efforts by the Royal Navy's Piracy Suppression squads and continuing Portuguese Navy anti-pirate patrols, completely gone away. EG Lebas, a British official in the Chinese Maritime Customs service overseeing affairs at both Lapa and the adjacent port of Chung Shan (Zhongshan), reported in 1923 that the oil-press factories on Lapa Island which converted groundnuts into cooking oil had mostly shut operations rather than submit to extortion and continual raids from pirates.[144]

1938 – Throughout the early twentieth century China had not totally forgotten the Hengqins. Portuguese language newspapers in Macao reported that Generalissimo Chiang Kai-shek proposed reclaiming land

142 For many years the *Pátria* was the best-known Portuguese navy gunboat in Macao. She arrived at the Macao Naval Station in 1908 and stayed till 1930 (though left for some month in 1912 to suppress a revolt in Timor). In 1931 the 28-year-old *Pátria* was sold to the Chinese navy.

143 Da Maia was governor from 1914 to 1916. He was pulled out fairly quickly – so fast indeed that no new governor had been appointed and none arrived for two years. The rumours said the issue was around building a new harbour (something Macao had needed for a long time if it was to compete with Hong Kong for shipping). There were rows about the funding between Lisbon, Macao, and Portugal's African colonies that also wanted the investment. However, back home his career recovered, and he became Minister of the Navy and of the Colonies before being murdered in Lisbon in the October 1921 coup d'etat, the so-called "*Noite Sangrenta*" ("Bloody Night").

144 EG Lebas, Commissioner of Customs, Lappa and Chung Shan, *Lappa Trade Report for the Year 1923*, submitted March 10, 1924.

to unite the islands of Dom João and Montanha. Perhaps to head this initiative off at the pass, and taking advantage of China's war with Japan, while also claiming to be protecting the lepers, missionaries, and residents on the islands, the then Governor Artur Tamagnini de Sousa Barbosa saw a chance to extend the boundaries of Macao. De Sousa Barbosa was a man of many sides – he had visited the colony as a baby and attended St Joseph's Seminary School while his father served as Inspector of the Treasury. The family then returned to Portugal. Artur returned as an adult and was to be governor of Macao not once, but thrice, previously between 1918 and 1919, then again between 1926 and 1931, and finally reappointed in April 1937. He was quite the character, a diplomat-scholar, and with a noted poet for a wife – Maria Anna Acciaioli Tamagnini – and boasted one of the best moustache-beard combos ever to be seen in Macao.

Extending Portuguese colonial territory, furthering the *Império Colonial Português*, was likely, at the time, to go down well with the relatively new Second Portuguese Republic, more commonly known as the *Estado Novo*, in Lisbon. Headed up by Portugal's strongman Salazar, it was to be a 'corporatist authoritarian' government (but let's not split hairs and just call it fascist) that championed imperialism while also vocally stating Portugal's position of neutrality in World War Two. But protestations of impartiality were a constant thorn in relations between the new invaders of southern China, Japan, and the Portuguese authorities in Macao. Tension ratcheted up when Japan bombed Montanha while attacking and occupying southern China.

With troops infesting Kwangtung province up to the Hong Kong border, 600 Imperial Japanese Army soldiers were moved to Montanha, while others seized control of the barely defended Chinese Customs House on Lapa. This was all achieved by orchestrating a "provocation" next to the Portas do Cerco border gate area such that many in Macao thought a full-scale invasion imminent. The Portuguese sent an emissary to the Japanese military authorities in Shanghai who initially agreed to withdraw from Montanha and Lapa. However, several months later the Japanese reoccupied Montanha citing supposed Free China guerrilla activity.

1940 – Then in 1940 the Japanese reoccupied Lapa too, but not so easily. Their reconquest came only after a battle to the very last bullet with the Portuguese side led by police Captain Alberto Carlos Rodrigues

Ribeiro da Cunha, who was hailed as a genuine hero of Macao at the time. According to the Portuguese language press, 'numerous' Japanese were killed by Ribeiro da Cunha's men, while the Portuguese saw only two shot and wounded.

1945 – The defeated Japanese unconditionally surrendered and left the Hengqin islands. Portugal had hoped, back in 1938, that any post-war settlement in Asia would clearly award the islands to them in perpetuity. But this was not to be, and there were no widespread post-war territorial agreements in Asia similar to those seen in Europe. Nationalist China regained control of southern China and the Hengqins returned to the Chinese Nationalist Republic.

1949 – The winds of history swept across the islands of Dom João, Montanha, and Lapa once more as China became a People's Republic and the names eventually become officially Xiao Hengqin, Da Hengqin, and Wanzai. The New Zealand foreign correspondent Quentin Pope visited Macao in 1951 for the *Chicago Tribune*. He found a detachment of Portuguese troops comprised mostly of grumpy teenage draftees alongside two battalions of rather more impressive and battle-hardened soldiers from Portuguese Mozambique. Pope maintained that the Portuguese East African battalions had occupied Big and Small Hengqin, but that Wanzai, so close to Portuguese Macao that Pope could see the soldiers clearly across the small channel, was occupied by People's Liberation Army troops who could, Pope wrote, 'smash all of Macao flat with artillery fire.'[145]

1952 – A year later, in July 1952, shots were actually traded between Wanzai and Macao's Porto Interior after a Portuguese soldier allegedly, and seemingly accidentally, slightly overstepped the Macao-China border during a flag-lowering ceremony. Things quickly escalated and the People's Liberation Army began rushing troops to Wanzai. Two Portuguese soldiers were killed and seven wounded. The border between Macao and the Chinese mainland was closed and the Guia Lighthouse switched off its beam to prevent shipping from landing. Eventually calmer heads prevailed, shipping resumed, with the soldiers kept strictly to their respective sides of the border.

145 Quentin Pope, 'Make Hay As Red Sun Shines', *Chicago Tribune*, October 21, 1951, p.49 & Quentin Pope, 'Gambling and Gossip Macao's Chief Activities', *Chicago Tribune*, October 22, 1951, p.33.

1957 – The close proximity of Wanzai to Macao meant it was possible for swimmers to cross the short channel in order to leave China. A Canadian journalist wrote in 1960 of watching from the Porto Interior as refugees slid down the grassy banks of Wanzai and slipped into the water for the short swim. As the numbers making the crossing grew the Chinese side stationed a speedboat mid-channel to intercept swimmers. In the 1960s the Hengqin islands saw some agricultural development and the creation of several "model farms" by Maoist China which began the process of flattening the once majestic 'mountains of Lapa'.

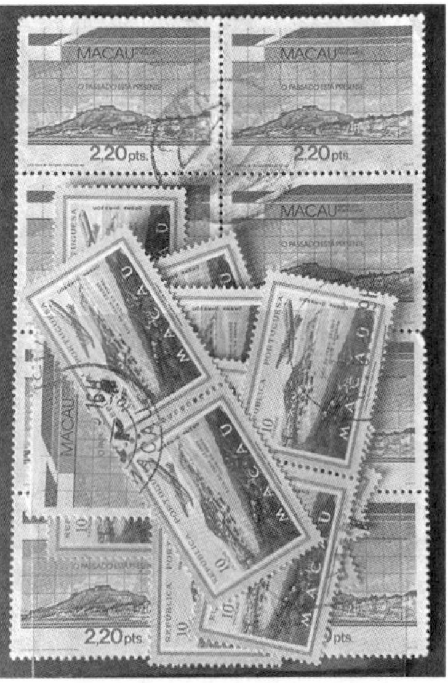

Lappa Island Macao stamps

And Then…

The 1980s saw quite fruitful co-operation between China and Portugal as the handover began to be discussed as well as the start of construction of the new international airport (eventually built on reclaimed land off Taipa). The role of the Hengqin islands as a staging post between Macao and Zhuhai became crucial as a way for Macao to expand and to connect to the mainland. Nowadays when visitors to Macao look across at Zhuhai they're looking at what was once Wanzai. When they travel across the *Ponte Flor de Lótus*, from the reclaimed land of Cotai, switching from left hand drive to the right they arrive on Hengqin Island. It's unlikely anyone passing through Hengqin these days thinks back to the green banks of the hills that once hosted picnics, sea-bathing parties, snipe hunting expeditions, pirates, and invading armies. But once there were islands.

Mr Markwick's English Tavern

Richard Markwick: Shopkeeper at Canton, Innkeeper at Macao (1836)

The Praia Grande, an engraving by Thomas Allom

Macao from the sea looks beautiful, with some most romantic spots. We arrived there about ten o'clock, took sedan chairs and went to our house, which we liked the looks of very much. The streets of Macao are narrow and irregular, but we have a garden in which I anticipate much pleasure.

– Harriet Low, *Diaries*, 1829

Richard Markwick – Shopkeeper at Canton[146]

Quite frankly the foreigner living in Macao in the 1830s didn't have much to do. According to the visiting British surgeon Charles Toogood Downing in 1836, there were no shops selling curios or artworks, 'no theatre or exhibition of any kind.' He could find only the zoological gardens to recommend with its birds of paradise from Borneo.[147] Harriet Low, a rare, and partly for that reason, much courted, single young woman from Salem, Massachusetts kept copious diaries in which she regularly refers to the boredom of dinner parties filled with nothing but chatter about the China Trade, Bengal vs Turkish opium, cargo prices, spice and tea costs, the politics of Europe and America, and the opaqueness of China.[148] And, of course, they bemoaned the punishing heat of Macao and the seasonal maladies of festering sores, prickly heat, the Canton gut rot, Happy Valley fever (malaria), the Macao flux, pus-filled styes, the Asian distemper. Most European households kept their windows closed against the noxious gases and miasmas they believed caused all their ailments.

Certainly there wasn't much to interest the younger male visitor either. The EIC Supercargoes – those representatives of the East India Company responsible for overseeing the arriving cargo and its sale – their crews and staff, the growing number of private "Country" traders, and the first Royal Navy ships to anchor in the Taipa Roads, all found Macao a bit lacking in diversions. Not much action for any sailors on the clippers who found themselves in town waiting to head to Canton, or to sail for Japan, Malacca, Bombay, or home to England. It was the same for the young Portuguese would-be *fidalgos* (nobles, or more likely wanna-be nobles) whom many observed strutting about in early nineteenth-century Macao with money in their pockets and little to spend it on. Macao's heady days of the red-light Rua de Felicidade's easily accessed brothels and of casinos would come later. In the 1830s things were a bit dull.

146 As Markwick is described in the official records contained in Hosea Ballou Morse, *The Chronicles of the East India Company Trading to China, 1635-1834, Vol IV,* (Oxford: The Clarendon Press, 1926), p.128.

147 Downing, *The Fan-Qui in China in 1836-7*, p.40.

148 Harriet Low Hillard, *Lights and Shadows of a Macao Life: The Journal of Harriet Low, a Travelling Spinster, Vol. 1,* (Woodinville, Washington: History Bank, 2002).

Nevertheless the trading community had little choice but to wait out their off-season in the Portuguese colony, sweating through the hot spring and typhoon-driven summer months. The "Indiamen"[149] and others were prevented from returning to Canton by order of the *Hoppo*, the Chinese official who controlled the port and access to their "Factories". They were barred until the China clippers began arriving again from Europe and India in the autumn. So how to pass the time between trading seasons was a question asked by both the traders themselves, and their families (who spent all year in Macao as foreign women were entirely banned from the Canton Factories). There was little to no interaction with the Chinese population and Macao was generally too small for much exploring aside from a few temples and the occasional picnics and snipe hunting trips to Lapa Island. The more curious investigated the so-called local *sim-sungs* (tea houses with music and opium), but most stuck close to their residences.

The Factories at Canton, Auguste Borget, 1842

Community organisations for the non-Portuguese – Protestant churches, charities, theatres, a club, a racecourse – were still to be created. Hong Kong was yet to become a British colony. The nearest alternative destinations were weeks of sailing away.

149 i.e. another generic term for those engaged in trade with India or the East.

Of course, there was reading (courtesy of the small EIC library established as early as 1806), painting, amateur-theatricals, and perhaps music. The predominant British private trader William Jardine reputedly had the only piano in Macao, though was, according to legend, a player of truly awful ability.[150] Some sort of distraction was required. Step forward Richard Markwick and his business partner Edward Lane…

It has often been claimed that Markwick and Lane's English Tavern and Hotel that opened for business on the eastern end of Macao's Praia Grande around 1830 was the first expat bar in Asia – or perhaps the second as Markwick had previously run a small establishment in the Canton Factories. It was known alternatively as simply Markwick's Tavern, the Macao Tavern, the Beach Hotel, or the English Tavern.

However, Markwick's Tavern was actually a successor to a small inn run earlier by an Englishman, John Budwell, that was open at least in 1807 (incidentally the year Robert Morrison, the Scottish Presbyterian missionary, arrived in Macao, though he probably didn't patronise Budwell's). We don't know much about Budwell or his establishment except that he provided drink and food, and, on the upper floors, a few rooms were available. Budwell also offered an informal legal service for ship captains new to the region, advising on Chinese customs regulations and the formalities of proceeding on from Macao up to Canton. The tavern was in an ideal location – on the busy Praia Grande, just two doors down from the Customs House.[151] When Budwell retired, Richard Markwick enthusiastically snapped up the spot. The location can be seen in the famous engraving by London artist Thomas Allom – *The Praia Grande* – from 1835.[152]

150 Richard Hughes, Hong Kong: *Borrowed Place – Borrowed Time*, (London: Andre Deutsch, 1968), p.89. This may or may not be true. George Chinnery's portrait *A Woman Seated at a Piano* shows a European woman next to a piano. The woman is thought to be Julia Baynes, who famously, in February 1830, accompanied her husband to Canton against Chinese regulations forbidding women to reside in the Factories. After some arguments she was allowed to remain. However, her husband was later dismissed by the EIC. Jane Daniell, wife of another China Trader, apparently also had a piano she lent to anyone who asked, including Harriet Low.

151 Approximately at the junction of the Praia Grande and Rua do Campo today.

152 Allom (1804 –1872) was a London architect, artist, and topographical illustrator who was a founding member of the Royal Institute of British Architects (RIBA). As an architect he is best remembered for his work laying out the Notting Hill district of London and contributions to the Houses of Parliament. He is also remembered for his

The long crescent of the Praia Grande, first developed in the 1600s, afforded a spectacular view, and was tree-lined for shade. It was fronted by stone buildings, 'a handsome row of houses' thought Toogood Downing, with wrought-iron gates and balcony railings, the traditional Portuguese blue and white glazed *azulejo* tiles set in the outside walls.[153] It gave the water frontage a Mediterranean aspect (if you ignored the sampans and junks), looking down on what was then known to English-speaking foreigners as Bishop's Bay and Taipan's Beach. In the 1830s the Praia included several houses owned by the EIC as well as the wealthy French opium and coolie labour trader Jean-Antoine Durand. Durand let the French painter Auguste Borget have a studio within his residence.[154] Visiting sometime later, the Australian journalist David G Falk remarked of the Praia Grande that with it 'Macao has put all its best goods in the shop window.'[155]

Markwick's Tavern became the major spot in 1830s Macao for those in need of a drink and some food.[156] Fifteen or more years later in the late 1840s as the new British Crown Colony of Hong Kong was founded after the First Opium War, taverns quickly became commonplace – entrepreneurs in Hong Kong were to open the Britannia, the Fortune of War, the Rainbow Inn, the Phoenix, the London, the Pilot Boat Inn

---

illustrations of China and Macao, published in the *China Illustrated* in 1845. Allom himself never visited the site instead drawing on the work of local amateur artist Warner Varnham who moved between Macao and Canton in the 1830s and 1840s working as a tea taster. As an amateur artist he sketched everyday scenes in Macao, Canton, Chusan (Zhoushan) Island, and the Philippines. He was most likely influenced in his approach and style by George Chinnery. Several of Varnham's drawings were adapted by Thomas Allom as illustrations for the Rev. GN Wright's *China: Its Scenery, Architecture, Social Habits etc.*, (London: Fisher, Son & Co., 1843).

153 Downing, *The Fan-Qui in China in 1836-7*, p.26.

154 Borget (1808–1877) went to Canton and Macao in September 1838 and stayed in the region for ten months. While in Canton, he met Chinnery, and they went on several sketching trips together. In July 1839 he visited Manila, Singapore, and Calcutta.

155 David G Falk, 'Sketches in China: A Chinese Monte Carlo', *The Marlborough Express* (New Zealand), November 10, 1900, p.4.

156 Rogério Miguel Puga, *The British Presence in Macau, 1635-1793*, (Hong Kong/ Macao: Hong Kong University Press/Royal Asiatic Society Books/Universidade de Macau, 2013), p.135, n.1.

and the Beehive, among others.[157] But these were all in a sense heirs of Markwick's English Tavern in Macao.

And Markwick did well. In the 1830s Macao was a thirsty market. There was a growing population of (all male) China Traders, adventurous so-called "Cathay Bucks" who'd pitched up to seek their fortunes in various, often undesirous and frankly illicit ways, as well as sailors eager for some shore time (as the Taipa Roads became a deep-water concourse for shipping awaiting the opportunity to sail up the delta to Canton). A ready clientele was forming. The later Macao-Hand Austin Coates, writing about a slightly earlier period in his Macao-set novel *City of Broken Promises*, thought loneliness was a big problem in those early days – 'Though the foreigners lived in China surrounded by teeming thousands of Chinese humanity, their lives were in some respects lonely and strange'.[158]

*

Records of Markwick's English Tavern are scant to non-existent. But there are a few recollections from travellers. Pretty much the entire, though small, English-speaking colony in Macao (Americans with the occasional Irishman or Scotsman for company) visited at some point and many, including the American Harriet Low as well as Charles Toogood Downing, and the sojourner throughout the Far East, Benjamin Lincoln "BL" Ball, all recalled Markwick's English Tavern in their memoirs of the period.[159]

Toogood Downing noted that 'the only English hotel in the place is large and kept by a man called Marquick, who has another still larger in Canton.'[160] In the *Topographical Plan of the City of Macao* from 1838, an "English inn" is mentioned next to the "*hopu*"(or more commonly *Hoppo*) – the anglicised name for the Chinese customs house – on the

157 This list of taverns in Hong Kong in 1847 from Vaudine England, *Fortune's Bazaar*, (London: Corsair, 2023), p.48.

158 Austin Coates, *City of Broken Promises*, (Hong Kong: Hong Kong University Press, 2009), originally published 1967, p.3.

159 BL Ball, *Rambles in Eastern Asia, Including China and Manila During Several Years Residence with Notes of the Voyage to China, Excursions in Manila, Hong-Kong, Canton, Shanghai, Ningpoo, Foochow and Macao*, (Boston: James French & Co., 1855).

160 Downing, *The Fan-Qui in China: in 1836-37*, p.31. *Fan-Qui* being an Anglo-Chinese term, literally "foreign devil".

Praia Grande. In 1840, in Robert Burford's *Description of a View of Macao in China* (overleaf), which details a panoramic image of the city drawn by the pre-eminent English panorama artist, two taverns are identified, "Sandford and Mark's Tavern" and "Edward's Tavern" in adjacent buildings next to the Customs House. Sandford, it seems, was one of Mark's (Markwick's) several partners in the Tavern along with Edward Lane.[161]

Apparently within the tavern was also a shop stocking European goods. Markwick was a shopkeeper in Canton too, but both his tavern and provisions store were new to Macao. Until the nineteenth century Macao did not really have shops catering specifically to foreigners. Wine, dried foodstuffs, the novel invention of canned goods, and various other items from Europe were purchased directly from the arriving Canton-bound ships or their local agents. Goods from Europe retailed at very high prices. Osmond Tiffany Jr., a decade later in newly established Hong Kong, wrote that 'the Europeans (in Hong Kong in the late 1840s) were supplied by several shops kept by English, and in which the wares of London are retailed at enormous profits.'[162] In his history of early Macao, Austin Coates explains that the arrival of goods was erratic and nobody could afford to miss buying when a shipment arrived and that this was why most European families in Macao lived largely on the first floor of their residences. The ground floor was kept sparse of furniture being devoted entirely to storage of foodstuffs and wines at certain times of the year when they got the chance to stock up.[163]

Osmond Tiffany, Jr., the son of a Baltimore merchant, visited Macao slightly later, in September 1844. Tiffany, Jr. too was a merchant though he sent back contributions from his travels to the *Atlantic Monthly* and *Knickerbocker Magazine*. He wrote that 'A man sick of the world, worn out and disgusted with himself and everyone else, would find Macao a home more suited to his palled tastes and jaded spirit than any other spot

161 Burford (1791-1861) was a noted English painter of panoramas. He famously opened the Panoramas gallery site in London's Leicester Square exhibiting 'a succession of panoramas of the chief places of interest.' Amongst the panoramas he exhibited were *Battle of Waterloo, Athens, Constantinople, Cairo, The Ruins of Pompeii, The Siege of Sebastopol, Venice, Rome* and *Macao*.

162 Osmond Tiffany, Jr., *The Canton Chinese, or the American's sojourn in the Celestial Empire*, (Boston: James Munroe & Co., 1849), p.260.

163 Coates, *A Macao Narrative*, p.43.

I could name.[164] Perhaps his 'worn out' and jaded men, 'sick of the world' and finding themselves in Macao might well have found a second home at the bar rail of Mr Markwick's Tavern.

*

Richard Markwick had been born in Cheshunt, Hertfordshire, just north of London, in December 1791. He originally came to Asia with the EIC and had been stationed in Canton as a steward on £100 a year. It appears that he resigned his position around 1825. Between 1826 and 1833 Markwick ran the European Bazaar and Hotel, an establishment adjacent to the foreign Factories. It was well known and frequently noted on maps of the Canton Factories.

In 1826, his first full year of business running the European Bazaar and Hotel, Markwick apparently made a decent profit. Not bad, given how numerically small the Canton trading community was. *The Chronicle of the East India Company Trading to China* covering those years shows a mere 45 British residents including the powerful and important Englishman of Huguenot origin Hollingworth Magniac, as well as the Scots William Jardine and his soon-to-be partner James Matheson, and their rivals the Englishmen Lancelot and Thomas Dent.

Along with the British were 19 Americans including the two men that ran a rival shop to Markwick's – Messrs French and Pitman.[165] Add to them four Dutchmen, two Swedes, two "Frenchmen" (both watchmakers and actually Swiss) and four Spaniards presumably trading between Canton and Manila, and you got approximately 76 European men in total.

The number was to increase steadily over the years, joined by over 40 Parsees who had come to reside and trade in Canton, Armenians, and others, but always remained small and claustrophobic. Just a few years later in 1829 the number had risen by over a dozen and included a newly arrived English portrait painter named George Chinnery. Another dozen men had arrived by 1831, including Markwick's younger brother Charles who seems to have made his way out East from Hertfordshire in order

164 Osmond Tiffany, Jr., *The Canton Chinese*, p.262.

165 Sadly Mr French, the American shopkeeper of 1826 Canton, is no known relation to Mr French, the author of this book.

1. South Bay
2. Fort of Bomparto
3. Penha Hill and Church
4. Gardens of Mrs. Paiva
5. Praya Grande
6. Mr. Plowden's residence
7. Captain Grant's
8. Mrs. Constantino's
9. Residence of Sig. Jorge
10. American Mission
11. St. Lorenço, below which is Beale's Garden
12. Mr. Daniell's and Mr. Innes'
13. Mr. Robertson's
14. Parsee's, Gent.
15. Mr. King's
16. New Company's Factory
17. Old ditto, ditto
18. Government House
19. St. Pedro
20. Edward's Tavern
21. Tan-kea, or Egg-House Boats
22. Mr. Dent's
23. Judges' House
24. Chinese Chop or Custom House
25. Sandford and Mark's Tavern
26. Edward's Tavern
27. Formerly Mr. Whiteman's
28. Capt. Elliott's
29. Capt. Elliott's Tender, "The Louisa"
30. The Lappa
31. St. José
32. St. Agostinho
33. Mr. Jardine's
34. Portuguese Professor
35. Senhor Gulartes
36. Dr. Morrison's
37. St. Paolo
38. Cathedral
39. Fort Monte
40. St. Clara
41. Via Sacra
42. Fort Guia
43. St. Francesco and Fort St. Francesco

44. Nine Islands
45. Canton Schooner
46. Peak Lintin
47. H. M. Brig Lyra
48. H. M. Ships, Volage and Hyacinth
49. H. M. Brig, Harrier
50. Junk
51. Cutter receiving Passengers and Goods
52. Typa-ka-brado
53. Marris none
54. Bay of Typa
55. Montanha
56. Lorchas
57. Don Juan Point
58. Mackareera
59. Cutter
60. Entrance to the Inner Harbour

to help his brother's business grow. Still perhaps profits were not so great and required a few creative "side hustles".

*

Markwick clearly dabbled in a range of businesses – promoting himself as an agent for the schooner *Sylph*, which plied the waters between Canton and Macao carrying passengers, supplies, post, and opium. The *Sylph* had originally been built for the Parsee merchant Rustomjee Cowasjee who had sold her to William Jardine. A smart buy by the Scotsman given that the best opium prices were achieved by those who got to Canton fastest. In 1833 the *Sylph* set a record by sailing from Calcutta to Macao in just 17 days and 17 hours. Markwick did well as the *Sylph's* agent in Canton.[166]

But not all these side hustles went according to plan. In 1830 the EIC's annual report noted that on the first day of July a boat belonging to Richard Markwick, 'former steward at the English Factory but now for some years past a tavern-keeper and store-keeper', was seized and found to contain 14 cases of silk piece goods and four cases of miscellaneous Chinese goods being taken from the Chinese-run Luenking shop in New China Street, on the border with the Factories and Canton city. It appears that the goods were being transferred to a ship at Lintin Island. The goods were valued at 5,000 dollars and their ownership was attributed to the Chinese shopkeeper Luenking and so were confiscated by the authorities. Markwick's boat was ordered destroyed as punishment. Clearly either Markwick, or Markwick in league with Luenking and the Chinese shopkeepers on New China Street adjacent to the Factories, had tried to circumvent the EIC's tax and customs regulations on cargoes and make themselves (and the receiving ship's captain) a quick profit.

Markwick had more luck with his newly launched fast boat service on the Pearl River between Canton and Macao. This boat-ferry business also functioned as a post office with Markwick's boats, crewed by Lascars (hired on from the *ghaut serang* Malay labour agents in Macao), taking letters and parcels between Canton and Macao in a day or so where in

166 The *Sylph* disappeared en route to Singapore in 1849 presumed captured and burned by Hainan Island-based pirates. Alternatively, she may have shipwrecked with the loss of all hands near Pedra Branca, an outlying island off Singapore.

the late 1700s it could still take several days to make the journey on most vessels.

Markwick was making good money from the European Bazaar, the *Sylph's* cargoes, and the postal boats. He decided it might be a profitable idea to have a hotel at each end of the Canton-Macao route. So Markwick found himself a partner, a Scotsman and another former EIC employee called Edward Lane, reputed to have originally come to China on a trading ship. Lane had been employed by the EIC as a butler (and also acted as Clerk of the Chapel at the Canton Factories). However, Lane, like Markwick when he was with the EIC, was what were termed by the EIC as Supercargoes, which meant that they derived a commission on the total sale of arriving cargo at Canton thereof. These commissions could significantly increase – treble or quadruple – their basic salaries. For instance, in one year it was recorded that Edward Lane earned a total of £417 on top of his basic butler's salary of £100 and then an additional £100 for taking on the Clerk of the Chapel duties – over £600 in total for the year.[167]

Together they pooled their money and formed a company called Markwick and Lane, took over the recently deceased Budwell's premises in Macao, and the English Tavern on the Praia Grande was opened.[168]

*

Markwick seems to have established himself pretty quickly in Macao. He soon married a Portuguese woman, Maria Quitéria Ângela Vidal. This wasn't Maria's first marriage, and she came complete with a family. She was just two years younger than Markwick and had previously been married to João António Baduel who, despite his name, had been born in Gloucester in about 1780 and so was approximately 13 years older than Maria. The couple had had six children in quick succession – Eufémia, Joana, Maria, João (junior), Ana and Carlota. All were healthy and all later married and had their own families in Macao. João died in 1820

167 Or approximately £62,000 in 2022. Not perhaps a stupendous amount but given purchasing power parity (PPP) quite significant.

168 Some details from Lindsay Ride, May Ride & Bernard Mellor, *An East India Company Cemetery: Protestant Burials in Macao,* (Hong Kong: Hong Kong University Press, 1955), p.104.

aged just 40 and, shortly afterwards, it appears Maria married Richard Markwick.

Here things get a little interesting and speculative. The records are unclear, but Baduel's original name may have been John Anthony Badwell, or Budwell, though after settling in Macao he appears to have rendered his name into a more Portuguese-friendly format as was a quite common custom for British settlers in Portugal and its colonies. So, as well as assuming Budwell's tavern it seems Markwick also married Budwell's widow and took on their six children.

Richard and Maria had their own child (Maria's seventh) in 1829, but the baby died immediately, even before they could officially name the child. A daughter, Leopoldina Ricarda Markwick was born in 1831, presumably named after the new King of the Belgians Leopold I, crowned in July 1831 (Leopoldina was a briefly fashionable name in Europe), and then with Ricarda as a feminisation of Richard. Leopoldina was followed by a boy, Richard (Junior) – Maria's ninth child. Both lived and later married and continued the family tree in Macao.[169]

Edward Lane died in 1831 and so Markwick and Lane had to be dissolved.[170] For a couple of years it seems Markwick tried to run all the businesses himself, but the hotels and taverns in Canton and Macao catering to the expanding clientele at both ends of the Pearl River estuary, as well as the agenting business with the *Sylph* and the mail boats, became a bit too much. New partners needed to be found, and a new company formed to run the businesses.

*

In May 1835 the *Canton Register* carried a NOTICE that Richard Markwick's businesses at Canton, Lintin Island, and Macao would now be carried out by Markwick in partnership with Robert Edwards, Henry Skinner (another former EIC steward and most likely the man who had

169 Information on Richard, Maria, João António Baduel and their combined children from Jorge Forjaz, *Familias Macaenses Vols-I-III*, (Macao: Fundação Oriente, Instituto Cultural de Macau, Instituto Português do Oriente, 1996).

170 Though shopkeeping was clearly in the blood – a relative of Lane's, Thomas Ash Lane, later got together with a man called Ninian Crawford in Hong Kong to open a store called Lane and Crawford, of course still in business. Patricia Lim, *Forgotten Souls: A Social History of the Hong Kong Cemetery* (Royal Asiatic Society Hong Kong Studies Series), (Hong Kong: Hong Kong University Press, 2011), p.185.

been Markwick's replacement when he had left the Company's employ), and his younger brother Charles Markwick.

We do know a little about the shopkeeper Robert Edwards, who seems to have been a Londoner by birth, and joined with Markwick after (it seems) having worked for the British trading house Magniac & Co. Markwick and Edwards's Canton premises were on a site leased from Magniac. Edwards had then been a partner with Markwick on the agenting of the *Sylph* – though he very publicly denied any role in the Luenking smuggling incident.[171] He was a keen freemason and sent back several treasures from China to the Grand Masters Lodge No. 1 in St James's, London, including a set of massive and elaborately decorated Chinese porcelain punchbowls from the Daoguang period (circa 1823-1827).[172]

With his new partners Markwick's Tavern on the Praia Grande stayed open for business.

Get a Round In

Who actually owned the building Markwick's Tavern occupied is not clear. In the early 1800s laws forbade any but Portuguese from owning Macao property, and this (though perhaps a little flexible elsewhere) applied strictly along the prestigious Praia Grande. Canny Portuguese early acquirers of Macao property formed a small, but wealthy, rentier class in the colony.

What was it actually like in Markwick's Tavern? A bar, a restaurant/dining room, billiards, some rentable bedrooms upstairs as back in Budwell's day. Perhaps akin to a mix of an English pub and a Portuguese *pousada* (inn). From what we know of other establishments in Macao at the time there was probably a hand-painted wooden sign outside. Inside the floors were probably formed of orange tiles, with polished wood doors, and blackwood chairs. Most shops had indoor plants as a basic cooling mechanism while swaying punka fans were essential to provide some relief from the extreme humidity. While, back in the early 1800s, Budwell had catered overwhelmingly to the maritime trade passing

171 Jardine Matheson Archive, Manuscripts/MS JM/F14.

172 EMP Williams and Bernard Davis, *A Revised History of the Lodge and List of Members 1756 to 1957,* (London, 1957, pp 78-79.

through, Markwick and Lane served a larger resident foreign population too, and this probably meant a little smartening up of the establishment's act compared to the earlier days.

New arrivals would immediately note the older fashions of those who had been in Macao for some time – wigs long out of style in London, suits of 30 years vintage. Presumably the busiest time for Markwick's was the spring and summer months when the Canton Factory community was banished to Macao while towards the end of the summer and early September the clippers and other craft would arrive and business slacken off as the Supercargoes were allowed to return. Charles Toogood Downing, who visited in 1836, observed that Markwick's (or "Marquick" as he misremembered him) was 'where most of the male visitors meet at the *table d'hôte*, and amuse themselves in the evening, by playing at billiards, after the Russian fashion.'[173]

The British doctor Archibald Ridgway visited Macao in the early 1840s. He sent back his impressions to London's *New Monthly Magazine.* His *Letters from Hong Kong and Macao* were rather disparaging of the facilities available to the traveller in Macao and pretty racist towards China and the Chinese in general. However, in one despatch in 1844 he described what appears to be Markwick's Tavern ('the best of them'). He never names the establishment though he locates it on the Praia Grande. There was a door that led to a large room 'half shop, half warehouse, which, in terms of variety of contents, bears a considerable resemblance to a store in a large English village: wines, pickles, hats, preserved meats, boots, hams and other delicacies.' In the bar area Ridgway was appalled (a state he often found himself in while travelling through Asia) to see tables crowded with 'black bottles and tumblers.' Markwick was still letting rooms as Budwell originally had – not just on the upper floors but also it appears in a new property they had taken over at 'another house in a lane a few yards from the beach.' Ridgway was predictably not happy and fancied the room had, until about five minutes prior, been a storeroom though he admits that the charge of 'one Spanish dollar' for a day and a night was reasonable.

173 By which he means Russian billiards or "Russian pyramid", a form of billiards played on a large table with narrow pockets. Toogood Downing, *The Fan-Qui in China: in 1836-37*, p.31.

Ridgway also gives us some sense of the bar-dining room area. A long communal table, more black bottles (probably Port wine) and cups, the bottles having Chinese labels, 'joss-stick holders for the convenience of smokers', 'rickety chairs', two 'worn out sofas' and a small 'coffee room' to one side. The walls were adorned with paintings in black frames of horse races. *Tiffin* was a rather English affair with pork chops, beefsteaks, Macao capon (local chicken), ham, hog knuckle, eggs and potatoes. Beverages included port, sherry, sack, gin, and rum toddies, as well as cups of chocolate, boiled lemon water, and tea for the more genteel. If there was one thing the Portuguese and British could agree on then it was the virtues of port wine (a development originating in Porto and the Douro Valley around the late 1600s). The extension of wine's longevity with the addition of brandy was God's gift to sailors and those far from home and to tavern owners in the East such as Richard Markwick. Additionally stocks of Madeira wine had been arriving in Macao since the mid-1700s at least.[174] Manila cigars were also sold. There were several screened-off rooms for private dining. Despite his complaints about the worn state of the furniture, some inveterate drunks about the place, and the heat, Ridgway stayed a fortnight.[175]

Markwick's was overwhelmingly a place for the British and only a few others, the Portuguese having their own clubs and establishments and preferring to promenade at sunset along the Praia Grande in the evening, dressed up and engaging in polite conversation, rather than drink. However, as Toogood Downing noted, Markwick's staff were Chinese men (no women) who spoke broken Portuguese and English, a hybrid of both, as well as China coast pidgin. They wore tunics of blue nankeen cloth, white knee-length trousers and hose with footwear, that Downing described as resembling clogs with inch-and-a-half-thick wooden soles. Downing recalled being asked if he was 'catchee dinner can?' to which he replied 'Can'.[176]

Fresh water for drinking and bathing was supplied by Chinese water carriers who fetched well water by *tam-kon*, a stout wooden pole carried

174 Jessica Hanser, *Mr Smith Goes to China: Three Scots in the Making of Britain's Global Empire*, (New Haven, Yale University Press, 2019), p.41.

175 Archibald R Ridgway, 'Letters from Hong Kong and Macao', *New Monthly Magazine*, Letter II, Vol. 70, 1844, pp.160-164.

176 Downing, *The Fan-Qui in China: in 1836-37*, pp.35-36.

across the shoulders to which, at each end, were attached buckets by pieces of rope to hold the precious, clean liquid.

*

Eventually life in southern China took its toll – or was it over-imbibing at his own tavern? Richard Markwick died (and here we have some very precise information) at 8am on Saturday, January 30, 1836, just shy of his 45th birthday and while his children – Leopoldina and Richard Jr – were still toddlers.[177] Maria was widowed for the second time. Apparently, the cause was a non-defined "lingering illness", which is annoyingly non-specific.[178] His death was formally announced in the EIC-sponsored publication, *The Asiatic Journal.* He was buried in the East India Company Cemetery, known as the *Cemitério Protestante*, or the Old Protestant Cemetery.

In July 1837 it was formally announced in the *Canton Courier* that 'the previous business of Markwick, Edwards & Co is closed.' Edwards left Macao to run a hotel adjacent to the American Factory in Canton.

*

Where Richard had been a slightly "wide" character, crossing his former employers and engaging in dubious practices at times, his brother Charles appears to have been keener to enter the more respectable foreign elite of the Canton-Hong Kong-Macao world. Charles scorned the tavern business, moving from Macao to Hong Kong after his older brother's death. He became one of the first property owners in Hong Kong, after the first land auction of 1842, and was then appointed government auctioneer and appraiser in 1846 with a sales room on Queen's Road. His business was to auction off goods acquired from those who had died in the colony intestate or bankrupt. This seems to have been a highly profitable enterprise, propelling him into the elite with the likes of William Jardine, James Matheson, the Dents, and the Parsee Rustomjee family.

177 Lindsey Ride, *An East India Company Cemetery: Protestant Burials in Macao,* (Hong Kong: Hong Kong University Press, 1996), p.186.

178 I can find no definitive date of death for Maria. She is not included in Ride, *An East India Company Cemetery,* as is Richard Markwick above because, I presume, she was Catholic.

The Hing Kee Hotel, Praia Grande

He was also one of the pioneers of freemasonry in Hong Kong (a practice endorsed by George Chinnery too who had joined up in Calcutta). Freemasonry established itself in the colony in 1845 and flourished from the 1850s onwards with Charles Markwick, and Richard Markwick's other former partner Robert Edwards, as prominent freemasons.[179]

After nearly 30 years shuttling between Canton, Hong Kong and Macao, Charles was among the oldest English residents in Hong Kong by the 1850s, though, despite his financial success, still disparaged by some as of the 'rougher type' – the English class system was never far away.[180] He might have lived out his days on the Peak in a comfortable retirement or perhaps planned a return to Hertfordshire. But neither was to be.

His wife Sarah Ann (and the daughter of another Hong Kong auctioneer) died in 1852 after they had been married for just two years. Charles Markwick was murdered in April 1857 aged 63. He was

179 Christopher Haffner, *The Craft in the East,* (Hong Kong: District Grand Lodge of Hong Kong and the Far East, 1977).

180 Patricia Lim, *Forgotten Souls: A Social History of the Hong Kong Cemetery* (Royal Asiatic Society Hong Kong Studies Series), (Hong Kong: Hong Kong University Press, 2011), p.185.

subsequently buried in the Colonial Cemetery at Hong Kong. Newspaper reports claimed that he had been sick with an unknown malady and confined to his bed for a fortnight when he was strangled by one of his Chinese servants, Ho Apo (described as a "door-coolie") who was attempting to rob him. His murderer was caught and hanged, after the British authorities tracked him down to his home village on the shores of Mirs Bay (also known as Tai Pang Wan) north of the Sai Kung peninsula (not then part of British Hong Kong) where he was being sheltered. The British threatened to bombard the place with cannon, which could have led to a serious diplomatic incident with the Chinese. However, fearing the destruction of the village, the local elders surrendered Ho Apo and also claimed the lavish reward (HK$500) offered for his capture.[181]

Charles Markwick's granite headstone in Hong Kong reads:

> 1ST APRIL 1857 / SACRED TO THE MEMORY / CHARLES MARKWICK / GOVERNMENT AUCTIONEER / AGED 62 / MANY YEARS RESIDENT IN CHINA

The British press, finding this an interesting story, tracked down Markwick's mother still alive in Cheshunt. The newspaper described her son as '…a swashbuckler, who owned riverboats, had a tavern, had a shop, was an auctioneer and a smuggler. His mother commented that "he was so rich he ate off beautifully embossed silver plates."'[182]

The Eternal Praia Grande

The Praia Grande may have lost Markwick's Tavern, but it remained a popular location for hotels, often with English connections. The English-run "first-class family hotel", the Royal, opened in the 1860s with 14 rooms and a long balcony advertising heavily in Hong Kong to sojourning families. The prolific Scottish photographer of China and

181 The case and trial is recounted briefly in James William Norton-Kyshe, *The History of the Laws and Courts of Hong Kong: Tracing Consular Jurisdiction in China and Japan and Including Parliamentary Debates: and the Rise, Progress, And Successive Changes In The Various Public Institutions of the Colony from the Earliest Period to the Present Time,* (London: T Fisher Unwin, 1898) and also *The Indian News and Chronicle of Eastern Affairs* of May 1857.

182 Lim, *Forgotten Souls,* pp.185-188.

the Far East, John Thomson, stayed there in the late 1860s enjoying the view of the bay from the balcony and perhaps the hotel's famous home-made ice cream. The British-run Oriental Hotel seems to have been built actually on the site of Markwick's Tavern, eradicating the old structures. The Oriental eventually passed into American hands and was developed as a holiday destination for Americans in Hong Kong or those passing through on American packet ships.

The British and Americans got some competition with the opening of the Hotel Macau at #65 Praia Grande in 1877 under Portuguese management – "We only provide the best quality wines, spirits and food. Moderate prices." The former US President Ulysses S Grant stayed at the Hotel Macau the year it opened when he was on his famous round-the-world trip.

Chinese interests opened the Hing Kee Hotel in 1878, close to the steamship pier. The establishment was owned by the (reputedly fluent Cantonese, Portuguese, and English-speaking) Chinese entrepreneur Pedro Leong Hing Kee, originally from Southeast Asia and who had a string of successful hotel, property, and shipping businesses in Hong Kong. The Hing Kee included a well-stocked and 'beautiful' bar according to the visiting American journalist Margherita Arlina Hamm in the 1890s.[183] There was also a billiard room – long a popular pastime among the young Portuguese clerks and junior traders in Macao. When the Portuguese poet Camilo Pessanha first arrived in Macao in 1894 to take up a teaching post, his first address was the Hing Kee. Pedro Leong Hing Kee demolished and entirely rebuilt the hotel in 1897.

The Praia Grande would continue to be the place to stay in Macao – the Boa Vista that opened in the 1870s would become the Bela Vista in 1936, one of Asia's grandest and best-known hotels. But by the time it first opened and dominated the crescent of the Praia Grande, Messrs Budwell, Markwick, Edwards, and Lane were long gone and long forgotten.

183 Hamm, *Manila and the Philippines*, p.56.

The Boa Vista Hotel, Praia Grande

Beware, There Be Pirates!

Tales of Portuguese Ruffians, Coloane Bandits, the Pirate Queen, and the Loss of the Miss Macao (1850s-1940s)

Piracies Limited by Bok, 1938

'On this morning a Portuguese and I were the only passengers on board. He was a sea captain, born and reared in Macao. Naturally, he knew all the ins and outs of the charming little Portuguese Colony. I ventured to ask him what he knew about pirates.
"Oh, plenty!"
"Now, what do you mean by plenty?" I urged him on.
"Oh, I know them all."'

– Aleko E Lilius, *I Sailed with Chinese Pirates* (1931)

Pirates Ahoy!

Piracy and Macao go together like London and fog, Manhattan and cockroaches, or China and tea. Piracy was the eternal curse of the China coast. Macao's waters had long been home to a multitude of pirates from as far afield as Japan. Wokou pirates, largely from the Ryukyu Islands, raided all down the South China coast and across to Macao throughout the 1500s.[184] In part the 1554 deal between Ming dynasty China and the Portuguese, which allowed the latter to settle in Macao and to trade in Canton, was agreed with a hopeful desire on the Chinese side that Portugal would assist them with pirate suppression along the Kwangtung coast. Which they did.

Famously a Portuguese fleet of three ships – the *Princesa Carlota*, the *Belisário* and the *Leão* – sailed from Macao to engage the Red Flag Fleet of the pirate queen Ching Shih (Zheng Yi Sao) in September 1809 in what became known as the Battle of the Tiger's Mouth. Ching Shih's fleet was substantial – reputedly composed of 280 junks, 2,000 guns, and over 25,000 men. The two fleets fought until January 1810 around the Bocca Tigris (now the Humen Strait). Ching Shih finally surrendered in February 1810 in exchange for a pardon and seemingly retired from piracy. But, of course, criminality abhors a vacuum and Ching Shih's fleet was soon replaced by more China coast pirate gangs.

Throughout the mid-nineteenth century the Portuguese commanders João da Silva Carvalho and João Eduardo Scarnichia, both long-time seamen in the waters around Macao, were capturing pirate junks off the coast, often working in cooperation with the Royal Navy out of Britain's new colony of Hong Kong.[185] A little while later renegade Portuguese

184 The Wokou (or alternatively "Wako"), "Japanese pirates", raided the coastlines of eastern and southern China and the Korean peninsula from the thirteenth to the seventeenth century. Important to note, as we come to discuss the multiethnicity of China coast piracy, the Wokou were not exclusively Japanese but included Koreans and renegade Chinese as well as perhaps Formosans (aboriginal Taiwanese) and other East Asian ethnicities. Wokou raiding peaked during the Ming Dynasty and the mid-sixteenth century. Chinese suppression efforts and clampdowns by the Japanese authorities saw the Wokou largely eradicated by the seventeenth century.

185 Scarnichia (1832-1888), who married into a Portuguese-Macao family, was appointed captain of the Port of Macau in 1861, and, in 1868, commander of the

– petty criminals, AWOL soldiers, deserting sailors, desperate Chinese fishermen and farmers, runaway slaves, and the odd adventurer – formed their own pirate fleets to raid the China coast.

By the twentieth century the British had assumed the key role of piracy suppression. Partially curbed in British-controlled waters, pirates and other bandits fled to Macao where Portugal stationed far fewer troops than the British garrisoned in Hong Kong. A crime wave inevitably broke out. Unable to secure any more troops for Macao during the Great War in Europe, the Macao Volunteer Corps was formed along the lines of similar citizen militias in Hong Kong, Singapore, and Shanghai.[186] After World War One the Royal Navy stepped up efforts, bringing in more gunboats and even submarines (Great War surplus deployed East) to combat the rise in seaborne banditry. Portugal was not to be left out – two warships were sent from Portuguese East Africa (Mozambique) by Lisbon to conduct anti-piracy patrols and augment the two cruisers already stationed at Taipa. Additionally, a naval air station was established at Taipa with spotter planes.

In response the pirates changed tack. Traditional junks were now too slow and too technically inferior to fight modern gunboats, submarines, and aircraft. They couldn't outrun or outgun them, it was more difficult to hide, subs could get close to them and into their lairs, like Bias Bay (Daya Bay), without being seen. So, in the 1920s, the infamous "passenger ploy" of pirates infiltrating coastal steamer ferries to rob passengers and cargoes came into vogue. The term "hijack" came slightly later, but that's what it was. Passenger Ploy hijackings regularly affected the Hong Kong to Macao ferries. Hong Kong passed legislation requiring coastal ferries to retain armed guards (invariably Sikhs), install cages to separate passengers, better protect the bridge and engine room, as well as institute better passenger searching before embarkation. The new measures didn't solve the problem. Confrontations between pirates and guards became deadly, passengers got caught in the crossfire, civilian ships were fired upon by navy piracy suppression vessels.

Macau Maritime Police.

186 Though never as high profile as the volunteer corps in Hong Kong and Shanghai the MVC grew to a force of about 400 men. They never actually engaged in combat, but did enjoy public marches in full uniform and lively band concerts.

In the mid-1920s the Ivy League graduate, wandering adventurer, and professional "vagabond" Richard Halliburton arrived in Hong Kong. He decided to try his luck at the Macao casinos. He was a long way from home, had US$500 and figured that if he could double or triple his stake at the fan-tan tables then he could keep on travelling for another year. One Sunday he boarded the *Sui An* bound for Macao with 300 Chinese and 70 European passengers. He arrived in Macao to hit the casinos knowing the return voyage of the *Sui An* was at 5pm. Halliburton gambled the day away, enjoying the gratis tea and local sweets supplied to discourage you from leaving the gaming tables. Comfortably ahead he pocketed his winnings and spent a couple of hours before departure seeing the sights of Macao. He then boarded the *Sui An* to return to Hong Kong.

Ten miles out of Macao, suddenly, from among the normal-seeming Chinese passengers in steerage, emerged what turned out to be a 60-strong band of pirates. Others, in slightly better attire, emerged from among the passengers in first- and second-class. This was the "passenger ploy". They waved revolvers about that had been hidden in women's skirts (exempt from searching by the rather prudish security guards) and concealed in secret compartments in baggage and started to relieve all the passengers – male and female, Chinese and European – of their wallets, purses, and valuables. Some armed Sikhs, hired in Hong Kong as guards, attempted to stop the pirates and were killed or beaten unconscious for their trouble and thrown overboard.

According to Halliburton the pirate gang was led by a young woman who ran to the bridge, found the captain, and without hesitation shot him dead. She then shot at the Chinese purser (who held the keys to the ship's strong room). The purser shot back and wounded the pirate queen in the shoulder, but by then her motley crew were already in full control of the *Sui An*. Halliburton, in first-class, lost his winnings, coat, hat, belt (with silver buckle), wristwatch, and a pack of Camel cigarettes to the brigands.

Eventually, sometime late that night off the coast of Kwangtung the pirates rendezvoused with their junks, transferred their stolen loot (approximately US$40,000 Halliburton estimated) as well as all the 'coats, hats, overcoats, assorted silverware, furniture, dishes, sundry supplies'.[187]

187 Richard Halliburton, *The Royal Road to Romance,* (New York: Garden City Books, 1925), pp.259-266, (Chapter XXXI).

Then the pirates, carrying their wounded queen departed and sailed away into the black night, probably for the notorious Bias Bay pirate enclave. The *Sui An* managed to limp home to Hong Kong arriving at noon on Monday to the enormous relief of the owners, as well as the passengers and their relatives. The ship had been posted missing at sea and feared lost. A three-hour voyage from Macao had lasted a rather dramatic 19 hours. Halliburton decided to put the whole experience down in his memoirs as a 'jolly adventure'.[188]

Chinese Pirates – German cigarette card, 1920s

Of course, despite anti-piracy efforts by Britain, Portugal, and China, as well as ever more sophisticated technology, manpower and co-ordination, sea piracy never really went away in Macao.[189] Pirates were mostly a nuisance, and just occasionally useful, as during World War Two

188 Ibid.

189 Piracy was seemingly the one issue that brought all the authorities in southern China together in common cause. In the 1920s Hong Kong colonial officials, Portuguese officials from Macao, and the Chief Inspector of the Canton Police all met fairly regularly to discuss the issue of piracy. As well as the Royal Navy deploying cruisers, submarines and minesweepers, Macao sending spotter planes and navy vessels, and China contributing some patrols and attempting to suppress, overland, places like Bias Bay and smugglers from Kwangtung towns like Shum Chun (Shenzhen). Hong Kong also had the Anti-Piracy Force, composed of mainly Sikhs, formed in 1914 and the Anti-Piracy Guard Contingent (funded by local shipping companies) founded in 1930 and which recruited a mix of Sikhs (from the Punjab), Chinese (from Weihaiwei) and former Tsarist "White" Russian soldiers (recruited in Shanghai).

when they helped smuggle cargoes of precious food and fuel supplies, as well as running much-needed contraband consumer goods into Macao. They also (usually for a fee, occasionally out of patriotism) moved people (allied nationals, British army soldiers escaping Hong Kong, Free French out of Indochina, Free Chinese to join the resistance) via Macao to Free China guerillas on the mainland who moved them across country to the wartime capital of Chungking or Yunnan-fu where planes came and went from British India. Wartime pirate junks sailed with a chest of flags – British, French, Japanese, Portuguese, Nationalist Chinese, Dutch. They simply hoisted whatever was deemed required at the time.

In the 1950s gold – the trading, smuggling, smelting, and stealing of it – became an obsession and a big business in Macao. Technology moved on too. Pirates moved to raiding planes as well as ferries and tramp cargo ships as precious cargoes moved from the sea up into the air. One of the first ever recorded plane hijackings by pirates was recorded near Macao (see below). With seismic political changes in China, cross-border gun, gold, consumer goods and people smuggling, all boomed. Ship's captains would look at their charts in the sixteenth century and see "THERE BE PIRATES" warnings. By the latter half of the twentieth century they were still keeping a constant watch.

Macao Ruffians

Despite well over three and a half centuries of rancour between Portugal and the Ming and Qing dynasties (and subsequently Republican China and the People's Republic after 1949) over the former's rights to Macao, there was one area where the two sides did, to an extent, agree and cooperate – piracy eradication. Pirates (or often *ladrone*, or thief, in Portuguese) were a scourge affecting both nations' trade. Pirate attacks peaked around 1801, leading to hope that the issue had been contained, but then surged back again in the chaos and confusion of the two mid-nineteenth-century Opium Wars. Pirates didn't allow small matters like a war or two between Britain and China slow them down. They saw treasure to be had and those fighting piracy distracted and weakened. They consequently kept right on attacking opium hulks and clippers during the conflicts despite there being a record number of foreign gunboats in southern Chinese waters. Jules Itier, a French customs inspector, amateur daguerreotypist, and travel writer in China, noted French opium ships anchored in the Taipa Roads maintaining round-the-clock watches with their cannons loaded on both sides ready to fend off potential pirate attacks from the sea or from land.[190]

In the mid-nineteenth century Portuguese *ladrones* also took to piracy. Dubbed "Portuguese Ruffians" by the London *Times* correspondent George Wingrove Cooke, this motley band of Europeans and assorted others were often ex-policemen, AWOL *soldados* or sailor-deserters along with Manilamen from the Philippines, impoverished Chinese coastal dwellers, and escaped African slaves brought to Macao from Brazil before taking the opportunity to escape.[191] This multi-racial European-led pirate band sailed in captured Chinese *lorchas*. They were well armed, well supplied, able seamen, and had good contacts in littoral communities both in Macao and along the China coast.[192]

In the 1850s pirates – both the traditional Chinese gangs and the "Portuguese Ruffians" – were making life difficult in the waters between

190 Jules Itier, *Journal d'un voyage en Chine en 1843, 1844, 1845, 1846,* (Paris: Dauvin et Fontaine, 1848). Itier travelled to China in the 1840s as part of a diplomatic mission sent by King Louis-Philippe (the "Citizen King"). He visited Macao briefly in 1844, interestingly the only photographer of significance to overlap with the artist George Chinnery.

191 Though little work has been on it to my knowledge it has also been suggested that some of these "Ruffians" may have been formerly Transported criminals from Britain and Ireland, and even some Hong Kong Chinese after the colony's foundation. Though rumours of convicts escaping the Australian penal colonies and making it to China abounded it is unlikely any did (excepting some who perhaps smuggled themselves out on ships). However, both Shanghai and Hong Kong noted "Returned from Transportation" (i.e. sentence concluded and having gained the all-important Certificate of Freedom) as arriving in the mid-nineteenth century.

192 Large decked Chinese ships of between 20 and 40 tons incorporating Portuguese design elements – Portuguese style hulls and Chinese rigging. Many Europeans in Macao also sailed *lorchas* as cargo boats after they were seized from pirates – the Portuguese Ruffians acquired some and sailed them while this is, of course, the back story of Dirk Struan, *tai-pan* of the Noble House in James Clavell's historic epic novel of the founding of Hong Kong. Struan captures a pirate *lorcha* that forms the basis of his Noble House trading fleet. James Clavell, *Tai-Pan*, (London: Michael Joseph, 1966). Multi-racial pirate gangs in southern China don't get mentioned much these days in the histories though they do crop up in various fictional forms, not least the mixed bunch of pirates who raid Tyler Brock's clipper *White Witch* for its cargo of silver bullion off Hong Kong in the aforementioned novel *Tai-Pan*.

Hong Kong and Macao. In 1858 the steamer *Wing Sun* departed Macao for Hong Kong. While just off the so-called Nine Islands the ship was raided by pirates who overpowered the crew and robbed the passengers.[193] Just one in a large number of hijackings and sea-stormings at the time. In response a British pirate suppression fleet sailed from Hong Kong in search of pirate junks off Macao. Twelve junks were destroyed, averaging eight guns each, and a village in Macao that was thought to be sheltering pirates was looted. These suppression campaigns carried on pretty much continuously over the coming decades.

Yet pirate gangs became ever bolder. Portuguese Ruffians effectively took control of much of the roughly 400 miles of coastline between Ningpo and Foochow, north of the Taiwan Straits. They extorted fishing boats and raided the cargoes of junks sailing between the two port cities and on towards Shanghai. And all without any reprisals from Qing naval junks or Portuguese warships which seemed never to be in the right area. The Ruffians were receiving good intel from somewhere.

But the Ruffians eventually became too notorious and too violent – laying waste to coastal villages, carrying off local women, murdering objecting husbands, fathers, and brothers, burning crops. Chinese officials thought the suppression of this gang should be led by Portugal, but the Portuguese Consul in Ningpo appeared distinctly disinterested, denying they were his problem. The only person who seemed willing to deal with them was a Cantonese pirate chief called Ah Pak (or alternatively A'Pak or Apack) who was willing to sell his services as a pirate turned pirate-suppressor.

Ah Pak had been losing out in the piracy game along the Ningpo-Foochow coast to these interlopers and wanted rid of them. Chinese government and Kwangtung coast organised crime could perhaps, in this instance, work together. In June 1857 Ah Pak was officially made a mandarin (third class) and his pirate fleet co-opted into the Qing Navy. Ah Pak's brigand mob was actually pretty multinational too, including many Cantonese, as well as English, American and French navy deserters.

193 *The Treaty Ports of China and Japan: A Complete Guide to the Open Ports of Those Countries, Together with Peking, Yedo, Hongkong and Macao* by Wm Fred. Myers, NB Denys and Chas. King, (London and Hongkong: Trűbner and Co./Shortrede and Co., 1867), p.76.

A showdown was inevitable. Ah Pak, with his brother (recorded in British records as Aliun Kay) formed a fleet of about 20 junks with 500 men. The Portuguese Ruffians seemed disorganised, their *lorchas* scattered along the coast. The Ruffians enjoyed casual raiding, but not so much hard fighting. Many deserted and disappeared inland, melting into Kwangtung, Foochow, and Chekiang provinces while most retreated to the villages around the port city of Ningpo, the city where eventually the two gangs would meet.

Overwhelmed and surprised, the bulk of the Portuguese Ruffians retreated to a Ningpo graveyard intending to regroup and launch a counterattack. However, Ah Pak's men pursued them with fowling pieces, swords, muskets, pistols, and bayonets. Many of the Ruffians were reportedly shot or stabbed with spears. Getting slightly out of control, Ah Pak's men then started sacking the Portuguese Consul's house, which was deemed a step too far. A French naval frigate arrived to put an end to the fighting. However, by then the Ruffians had been massacred. The foreign piracy scourge was at an end. Ah Pak resigned his commission and went back to his pirating ways without much competition. The Qing Navy returned to half-heartedly chasing him, and the Portuguese stayed largely south of the Taiwan Strait.[194]

*

Portuguese Ruffians, escaped African slaves, and navy deserters aside it wasn't difficult to see why Macao and so many southern Chinese coastal fishing communities produced legions of pirates. Fishing was hard, dangerous work that didn't offer much in terms of either prospects or money. Coastal communities lived almost exclusively on a diet of fish and rice, many families were lost at sea in storms or saw their livelihoods smashed on the rocks in typhoons. And of course the fishermen were

194 This account of the "Ningpo Massacre" largely from George Wingrove Cooke, *China: Being "The Times" Special Correspondence from China in the Years 1857-1858*, (London: G Routledge, 1859), pp.129-134. Cooke coined the term "Ningpo Massacre" for the events – 40 dead on the Portuguese Ruffian side; two Cantonese and an Englishman on Ah Pak's team. He felt the Portuguese authorities in Ningpo and Macao had been very lax for not reining in their errant nationals. There is also a collection of various eye-witness accounts contained in *Correspondence of His Most Faithful Majesty's [Portuguese] Consul with the English, French, and American Consuls Before and After the Ningpo Massacre*, (Hong Kong, 1857).

preyed on by pirates – extorting them and stealing their catch, or any money they got paid for it. It was all too tempting to swap sides.

In the 1920s Macao had a community of approximately 1,800 fishing boats providing some sort of livelihood to about 40,000 people – approximately 30 per cent of the colony's population. Add in customs and immigration staff, dockers and stevedores, boat builders, pilots, ship-to-shore lighters, cargo ship crews, lighthouse attendants, ship chandlers and dry dock workers, the *ghaut serangs* and crewing companies, ferry steamer and pleasure boat crews (and the anti-piracy guards they had to carry), those that temporarily lodged sailors, fed and watered them in taverns or at the seaman's mission, did their laundry, serviced them as prostitutes, and some estimates say fully half of Macao's Chinese population was employed in one part of the maritime economy or another in the 1920s.[195] There were bound to be a few local pirates too.

Pirates of Coloane

If many in Macao had chosen to think of piracy as something that happened at a certain remove – massacres in Ningpo, hijacked coastal and river steamers, Kwangtung villages raiders – events in 1910 brought home the pirates in their midst. Seventeen Chinese schoolchildren and a cook were kidnapped along the China coast and transported to the Coloane base of a band of pirates who called themselves the Society of Perfect Justice (*Ang Ngui T'ong*). The Coloane pirate leaders, Leong Tai-chan and Leong Ngui-vá, then demanded a significant ransom amount and stated that they would kill the children if the money didn't turn up.

Urged on by Macanese and Chinese businessmen the Portuguese authorities felt compelled (though not overly enthusiastically) to do something about these local bandits, especially when it was claimed that another random 50 or 60 people were being held captive in Coloane. Apparently they had been there some time and nobody had claimed any responsibility for them. But the Portuguese authorities dragged their feet. Perhaps a dozen or more Portuguese kids might have elicited a different response; a kidnapping in central Macao possibly received more attention, but these were Chinese nationals largely from poor coastal Kwangtung

195 Geoffrey Gunn, *Encountering Macau: A Portuguese City-State on the Periphery of China, 1557-1999*, (London: Routledge, 1996).

villages and nobody in the Chinese government was very interested in them either.

Additionally, in 1910 Coloane was still contested territory – a ferry ride away, somewhat remote, and little known to Portuguese colonial society. It was not formally part of Macao, technically Chinese territory, and the hostages Chinese subjects. However, the Portuguese had long claimed Coloane as integral to their enclave, randomly stationed a few police and soldiers there, collected taxes, and provided street lights to bolster their territorial claim. Surely criminality in the area was really their problem to deal with if their assertion of ownership was a serious one?

The capture of a female pirate during the 1910 incidents

On July 12, 1910, Governor Eduardo Augusto Marques (who served little over a year from September 1909 to December 1910) declared martial law on the two islands of Taipa and Coloane. A small force of 45 Portuguese soldiers arrived in Coloane Village to find it deserted and resembling a ghost town. The troops fanned out into the nearby hillsides to hunt the pirates. In the ensuing skirmishes one Portuguese soldier was killed. Then, a day later on July 13, Marques ordered more Portuguese troops to Coloane.

Two hundred men, plus the gunboat *NRP Macau*, duly headed out. Governor Marques ordered the troops to use whatever force was needed to put an end to the disturbances and restore law and order. The *Macau* subsequently bombarded Coloane Village. Then the soldiers attacked with full force, using explosives and firing at will. They killed three pirates and captured many more – estimates of approximately 300 are mentioned, including some women. The kidnapped Chinese children were all rescued and sent to the Hospital de São Rafael.[196] However, the Governor's order to use 'whatever force is needed' unfortunately led to several hundred dead villagers. Over 350 pirates were thought to have escaped.

Coloane after the bombing, 1910

More warships arrived the next day (July 14) – including the gunboat *NRP Pátria* and the cruiser *NRP Dom Amélia*, while a further nine Chinese warships anchored off the coast of Coloane offering support to the Portuguese (the common cause of piracy suppression taking precedence over territorial disputes once again). Coloane remained under martial law for the next month or so, occupied by Portuguese soldiers, and watched over by gunboats. The pirate chiefs and their wives were handed over to the Chinese authorities and sent to Canton for trial. Eight pirates found to have committed crimes in Macao were tried, convicted, and sentenced

196 Now the Portuguese Consulate on the Rua de Pedro Nolasco da Silva.

to 28 years' penal servitude in Mozambique. By the end of the operation the Portuguese had only lost two men and seen three wounded.

The troops returned to central Macao to parade past Governor Marques, cheered by the public, while parents of the kidnapped children held banners aloft praising their courage. Later a statue commemorating the routing of the pirates and the rescue of the hostages was erected on the then Largo St Francis Xavier, close by the Chapel of St Francis Xavier, on what became the Largo Eduardo Marques in Coloane.[197] It remains there today.

*

The question left was who were these pirates in Coloane? And the answer to that went to the heart of piracy all across the South China Seas. They were rarely the dedicated cut-throat brigands of popular legend and Hollywood B-movies, but rather, as we have seen, members of small-scale farming (or in the case of Coloane, mostly fishing) communities who, when times were hard, turned to a little piracy, smuggling or kidnapping. Rather than a dedicated way of life, it was an occasional economic survival strategy. But did the Portuguese fully appreciate this? Portuguese soldiers fired at random in Coloane. How to tell die-hard pirate from local fisherman or woman? And indeed was there a difference? It seems the troops didn't much care.

Territorially Governor Marques made the most of the events. Portugal vociferously pushed its claim to Coloane against persistent Chinese objections. But now they insisted that Taipa and Coloane's formal incorporation into Macao was essential for reasons of pirate suppression. It was to be a winning argument.

Hunting the Pirate Queen

At the end of the 1920s the adventurous Finnish-American journalist Aleko Lilius came to Macao to hunt the "Pirate Queen" of Macao, Lai

197 Eduardo Augusto Marques, Governor of Macao September 1909-December 1910. Marques was a monarchist and so opposed the October 5, 1910, revolution that aimed to overthrow the monarchy and install the First Portuguese Republic. He reluctantly supported the outcome but was soon replaced by a pro-Republican Commander in the Portuguese Navy, Álvaro de Melo Machado (who is perhaps best known for having started the Boy Scout movement in Macao in 1911).

Choi San ("Mountain of Wealth") whose twelve junk flotilla plied the waters between Macao and the West River.[198] Whether this Pirate Queen was the same one Halliburton had encountered and seen wounded on the *Sui An* a few years before we don't know. Halliburton never got a chance to ask her name.[199]

Thrilling for sure, inspirational to some, but Lilius is never quite to be trusted.[200] He claims in his bestselling 1930 book *I Sailed with Chinese Pirates* to have first heard tell of Lai Choi San 'from an American who had sailed these waters.'[201] Certainly the public and press lapped it up. In 1931 the *New York Times* reviewed the book:

Aleko Lilius

> 'A meeting with a mysterious woman pirate chief, Lai Choi San, with several thousand ruthless buccaneers under command, is described in the volume *I Sailed With Chinese Pirates*… while traveling in the Orient Aleko E Lilius, according to the publishers, succeeded in winning the confidence of this unusual woman, and he accompanied her and some of her desperadoes on one of their expeditions on a junk equipped with cannon. Mr Lilius's publishers describe him as the only white man who has ever sailed with these pirates…'[202]

But there's not much evidence of Lai Choi San's actual existence. Lilius enjoyed writing novels and screenplays (often under his pseudonym

198 The Xi River or Si-Kiang, the western tributary of the Pearl River.

199 Lilius does suggest it may have been Lai Choi San, though as with most of his claims, without any verifiable evidence. Aleko E Lilius, *I Sailed With Chinese Pirates,* (New York: D Appleton & Co., 1931), p.14.

200 Certainly to comic strip artist Milton Caniff whose long-running *Terry and the Pirates* strip was inspired by reading about Lai Choi San, probably in Lilius's book. Additionally, Arthur Ransome, whose Swallows and Amazons novel *Missee Lee* (London: Jonathan Cape, 1941) includes a China Seas Pirate Queen.

201 Who remains anonymous. Lilius, *I Sailed With Chinese Pirates*, p.26.

202 'Chinese Pirates', *The New York Times*, November 15, 1931, p10.

"Bok"), as well as serialised long reads for the American newspapers, that mixed up his non-fiction with fiction, the verifiable with the fabulous.[203] The photographs he included in his book don't ultimately prove much more than a woman was aboard a pirate vessel – certainly not an unknown phenomenon in southern China. Lilius claims Lai Choi San inherited the pirate flotilla from her father who had been given refuge in Macao by the Portuguese authorities on the understanding he'd leave the local fishing fleet alone. A rather unlikely backstory. She was apparently phenomenally rich and owned property in Macao. But throughout *I Sailed with Chinese Pirates* he mostly chases her ghost, invariably just missing her as she flits between Macao, Bias Bay, and Canton. Ultimately, she is an exciting fiction more than a historical reality.

The pirate reputed to be Lai Choi San (centre)

Finally, one could argue that the portrait of Macao that Lilius presented the western reading public in *I Sailed with Chinese Pirates*, as well as his "Bok" novels and newspaper articles, is deliberately dated. Lilius, it seems, prefers an older, indeed by 1931 quite considerably older, Macao. The academic Philippe Forêt has spoken of, '…the trope of a "charming bay", understood as the aesthetic fusion of geographical confusion (Macao as an imitation of Naples or Lisbon, 'Latin American' says Lilius) and historical denial (the eighteenth-century landscape present in twentieth-century Macao).'[204]

203 For more on Lilius's "recycling" of his tales through his non-fiction and then his pseudonymous fiction as "Bok" see Paul French, 'Who was "Bok"?', *The Journal of the Royal Asiatic Society of China,* Vol.79, No.1, 2019, pp.293-299.

204 Philippe Forêt, *Globalizing Macau: The Emotional Costs of Modernity* (1910-1930), Chapter 6 of Wu Fulong (ed), *Globalization and the Chinese City*, (London: Routledge, 2006), pp.108-124. Lilius, *I Sailed with Chinese Pirates*, p.73.

Lilius presents us with an Orientalized Macao, presented as if frozen in time and traditions, unaware of and untouched by modernity. He introduces Lai Choi San in her out of date pirate junk with rather out-of-date weaponry – harking back to an age before advanced anti-piracy hunts involving fast cruisers, the Passenger Ploy, spotter planes, and submarines... and long before Lilius ever sailed in Macao's waters.

The Age of the Catalina and Flying Piracy

After World War Two the favoured target of the pirates became the amphibious Catalina flying boats. Catalinas had been developed by the Americans during World War Two to island hop and supply outlying islands in the Pacific. Post-war many were decommissioned and sold off to small entrepreneurial cargo transport firms in Macao and southern China. In the late 1950s Taiwan's China Airlines was initially formed with the acquisition of two Catalinas. For a time Catalinas were synonymous with Macao – constantly flying in from Saigon and Hanoi, out to Bias Bay and Junk Bay (Tseung Kwan O) in the Hong Kong New Territories. Carrying? Who knows what? Gold, guns, drugs, people…

The Catalina was perfect for the terrain – it could land anywhere. It had originally been designed for long haul resupply with large fuel tanks. Now wealthy passengers and rich cargoes could quite simply fly over the pirates in safety. Catalina air freighters (formally the Consolidated Aircraft Company Model 28) pop up in popular culture of the time – filled with contraband 400-ounce gold bars in the 1951 Hollywood B-movie *Smuggler's Island*, or dope in Francis Van Wyck Mason's 1957 novel *The Gracious Lily Affair*.[205] They flagged as Macanese, Filipino, Indochinese, Thai, Hong Kong. They could fly low, under radar, and land on water,

205 *Smuggler's Island*, Universal Studios, 1951; Van Wyck Mason, *The Gracious Lily Affair* (Colonel Hugh North series #13), (New York: Doubleday & Co., 1957). Incidentally Macao also makes an appearance in Mason's *The Hong Kong Airbase Murders* (Colonel Hugh North series #11), (New York: Doubleday, Doran & Co., 1937). Shanghai, Rangoon, and Singapore also pop up in the once very popular series.

deposit or pick up their cargoes and be back up in the air again within minutes. They were cheap to run and could fly at night.

But they were not without risk. The fledgling Hong Kong airline Cathay Pacific (founded 1946) purchased two Catalina seaplanes in 1947. On July 16, 1948, one of those planes, the *Miss Macao*, was the first ever commercial flight to be hijacked – though in 1948 the crime was still termed piracy. It seems four hijackers booked passage on the *Miss Macao* among the 23 passengers and four crew aboard scheduled to fly the short hop from Macao to Hong Kong. They had received intelligence that the plane was carrying a cargo of 3,000 *taels* (or 113kg) of gold bullion.

It was possible. Catalinas were used to ferry gold around Southeast Asia, the Philippines, Taiwan and between Hong Kong and Macao. The pirates knew this. It was believed they had spies in all the Hong Kong and Macao banks, the major *hongs*, in both customs departments, and all along the wharves and godowns of both colonies. It was reported that the Hong Kong authorities believed the pirate spies were targeting the new airlines flying cargo into and out of the colony.[206]

During the flight a pirate pulled a gun and put it to the pilot's head. The pirate's aim was to force the Catalina to land somewhere remote, rob the passengers, and then hold them for ransom. It was, in essence, an in-flight version of the old 1920s Passenger Ploy.

But, perhaps intentionally, perhaps due to a sudden dip in air pressure, the gun fired and blew out the back of the pilot's skull. A pirate trained to fly Catalinas took the controls. But just as on the Hong Kong-Macao ferries a quarter century previously the pirates met with fierce resistance. A gun battle broke out in close quarters, the Catalina went into a steep dive and crashed into the sea. All the crew and 22 passengers died.[207]

The sole survivor, a Chinese man named Huang Yu (or sometimes reported as Wong Yu) had survived by jumping out the emergency exit just before the plane hit the water and exploded. Gruesomely rescue boats had to search for the dead bodies using large fishing nets. Huang

206 'Pirates Now Use Bazookas', *Sydney Morning Herald*, July 3, 1949, p.36.

207 Marco Lobo, *Everyday is Mine: The Life of Pedro José Lobo*, (Macao: Instituto Internacional, 2020), pp.161-163.

Yu was picked up by one of the junks and taken to Macao with two broken legs.[208]

At first the Portuguese police in Macao assumed a terrible accident. But eventually Huang Yu confessed to being a pirate and outlined the whole plan and its disastrous outcome. The pirates had believed the plane contained gold bars, had wanted to force it to land on water and rendezvous with two pirate junks. The whole caper had gone terribly and tragically wrong.

The Miss Macao

Still, plane hijackings became a new front in the war on piracy. A Curtiss C-46 Commando cargo plane loaded with Chinese banknotes was hijacked en route to Chungking in 1949. Shortly after a Douglas C-47 Skytrain loaded with silver bullion was hijacked over Taiwan and disappeared, never to be found. The newspapers speculated that the pirates had taken over the controls and landed the plane at 'one of 50 aerodromes built by the Japanese for use during the Pacific War.'[209]

Pirates Forever

The go-go years of the early Chinese reform era saw high-powered speedboats – often with four to five outboard engines, with a combined horsepower of 1,200 to 1,500 and a speed of more than 100kms per hour – racing between Hong Kong and Macao to southern China. In the

208 '25 Die When Plane Falls in China Sea', *Honolulu Star-Bulletin*, July 17, 1948, p.7.

209 'Pirates Now Use Bazookas', *Sydney Morning Herald,* July 3, 1949, p.36.

1970s and 1980s, as the novelist Daniel Carney observed, 'Heroin is the new gold of Macau.'[210] They skimmed the surface of the South China Sea loaded down with luxury cars stolen in either territory to provide Mercedes and BMWs to China's new wealthy. People, drugs, medicines, infant formula, gold, silver, flat screen TVs, refrigerators… anything and everything continued to be moved illicitly by sea. The Hong Kong Marine Police invested in equally high-powered speedboats while helicopters tracked the smuggler's fast *dai fei* (aka *tai fei*) boats. The PRC side tracked smugglers with their fast *hoi kung* patrol boats.

Pirates and smugglers of course morphed into and became interchangeable with traditional organised crime. Macao's pre-handover scourge of triad violence. In 2000, Chinese and international newspaper readers were introduced to a convicted gang of Chinese pirates paraded before their execution in the Guangdong city of Shanwei. They had hijacked a Hong Kong cargo ship, killed the crew, and sold the ship for cash. They admitted to having committed at least two earlier ship hijackings in the South China Seas. They were seen on TV aboard a truck being taken to be shot – drunk on rice wine, smoking cigarettes, and singing Ricky Martin's World Cup song *The Cup of Life* – "go, go, go, olé, olé, olé."[211] But for the song, they could have been from 150 years before – violent, unrepentant and, among their number, an Indonesian, showing that South China piracy was still international.

They were executed. But piracy continues to be a threat. Indeed, it can be argued that regional piracy is still closely linked to the coastal economy and the fishing industry. Falling fish stocks (either as a result of climate change, over-fishing or both) threatens the livelihoods of many. Bo Jiang, an assistant professor in the faculty of social sciences at the University of Macau, told *The Guardian* newspaper in 2023, 'There are a lot of fishermen in nearby waters who are known as "standby pirates".'[212] Bo was referring to the wider Southeast Asian region while the Australian think tank The Lowy Institute has observed a spike in piracy following the Covid-19 pandemic noting that 'socio-economic pressures and poor

210 Daniel Carney, *Macau*, (London: Corgi, 1985), p.25.

211 John Gittings, 'Tipsy Pirates Go Down Singing', *The Guardian*, January 30, 2000.

212 Karen MacVeigh, 'Impact of warmer seas on fish stocks leads to rise in pirate attacks', *The Guardian*, May 11, 2023.

economic conditions in coastal communities can motivate unemployed shipyard workers, seafarers, and fishers into piracy.'[213]

Perhaps, then, maps should still contain the legendary warning: *Beware, There Be Pirates!*

213 Jade Lindley and Dhiyaul Aulia Huda, 'The surprising link between piracy and Covid-19', *The Interpreter,* The Lowy Institute, October 2, 2023.

Rebellion: The Almost Republic of Macao (1929-1930)

ARTILLERYMEN ON PORTUGUESE ISLAND REVOLT

By United Press

Hong Kong.—A revolt of Portuguese artillerymen, who seized the entire garrison on the Portuguese island of Macao, lying outside the harbor of Canton, China, was reported here today.

Wisconsin News Record, December 24, 1929

Salt-laden sea, how much of all your salt
Is tears of Portugal!
For us to cross you, how many sons have kept
Vigil in vain, and mothers wept!
Lived as old maids how many brides-to-be
Till death, that you might be ours, sea!
Was it worth while? It is worth while, all,
If the soul is not small.
Whoever means to sail beyond the Cape
Must double sorrow – no escape.
Peril and abyss has God to the sea given
And yet made it the mirror of heaven.

– Fernando Pessoa, *Portuguese Ocean* (1934)[214]

214 Translated by Jonathan Griffin, Fernando Pessoa, *Selected Poems*, (London: Penguin, 1982). 'Portuguese Ocean' is part of Pessoa's *Mensagem* (*"Message"*), a collection of 44 poems published in 1934.

Revolt in Macao

It had been agreed upon. The action decided, the secret signals predetermined. Portuguese men had met in taverns and bordellos, *pensão* billiard halls, and small cafés in Macao's old town, down at the foot of the ancient ruin of St Paul's Church.[215] Others had conspiratorially whispered at night after lights out in their barracks, given each other knowing nods in the mess and on the parade ground. They were stationed in the large square Fortaleza de Nossa Senhora do Monte de São Paulo (or the Monte Fort, built 1675) in Santo António; the Edifício da Capitania dos Portos (or the so-called Moorish Barracks) in São Lourenço;[216] in the smaller Mong-Há (or Monga) Fort bound by the Rua Francisco Xavier Pereira, in the Colina de Mong-Há; and the Fortaleza de Santiago, commonly the Barra (or Bar) Fort, at the entrance to the Porto Interior. They had argued the details, the justice of their claim, the rightness of their cause, their hopes, and aspirations. But now all those resolved to act had concurred, the plans had been finalised. There was no going back.

The view from the Monte Fort

215 Sources at the time often refer to the historic centre of Macao then as the "old town", or alternatively as the "Portuguese Quarter", "European Quarter", or occasionally the "Christian Quarter".

216 This Moorish inspired building was designed in 1871 by the Italian architect Cassuto to accommodate about 200 Indian policemen from Goa who were sent to Macao by the Portuguese. It was built in 1874. The building is now used by the Maritime Authorities in Macao. "Moorish" was also a local term for the Indian (Goan invariably) policemen recruited to work in Macao by the Portuguese.

On Sunday December 22, 1929, the signal was given and the largest ever revolt by artillerymen of the Portuguese Army stationed in Macao commenced. However, despite the planning, from the start things went awry. The four forts containing garrisoned men were supposed to rise up simultaneously and arrest their commanding officers. In the event only one fort followed through as originally planned. In that fort, the Monte Fort, close by the ruins of St Paul's, approximately 70 men under the command of a sergeant revolted and successfully took control of their garrison barracks. The soldiers then ejected all the officers from the fort and placed all the non-commissioned officers (NCOs) under detention.

Despite the slightly more chaotic nature of the rebellion than planned, the Portuguese authorities on the island and the governor, Artur Tamagnini de Sousa Barbosa, were taken by surprise, and shocked by the revolt. It was true that there had been rumbles of discontent for some time, but they had not been expecting a full mutiny. Perhaps they should have paid more attention to the news from Portugal. By 1929 military uprisings had become surprisingly common at home – a *coup d'état* in 1926, a revolt by the military in Porto in 1927, and other uprisings effectively killed the 1910 republic and ushered in a conservative dictatorship that would later formalise as Salazar's *Estado Novo* in 1932. Many of these rebels were eventually deported to the Azores or Portugal's colonies.[217]

By dawn on Tuesday December 24, Christmas Eve or *Noite de Natal*, slightly less than 48 hours after the initial uprising, the army rallied those of their troops who remained loyal. They warned the mutineers to free the captured NCOs and to immediately surrender or face the consequences, which they assured the rebels would be severe. The men in the Monte Fort, despite being massively outnumbered and outgunned, as well as let down by the majority of their fellow would-be mutineers at the other forts, initially opted to continue their protest.

*

However, their resolve soon crumpled. Faced with the partial failure of the rebellion many of the men in the Monte Fort soon began to lose heart and decided to surrender with only a few diehard rebels voting to hold out. Their former comrades-in-arms, not wanting to massacre anyone,

217 The majority of these to Portugal's African colonies in what are now Angola, Mozambique, Guinea-Bissau, São Tomé, and Cape Verde rather than to Macao.

gave the holdouts until seven the following morning to surrender. They chose not to. The loyal troops were then ordered to unleash a ferocious bombardment by cannons upon the fort and the men remaining inside. It was of such intensity, and the odds so unevenly stacked, that the mutineers remaining in the Monte Fort, realising they were now on a suicide mission, surrendered unconditionally. Had they not and had the Governor insisted on maintaining the bombardment the Monte Fort would have been totally destroyed.

The city was reported to be quieter than usual that Christmas Day. Macao's citizenry stayed inside, shuttered their windows, barred their doors. Loyal troops patrolled the streets. Macao was effectively under martial law. Where possible essential food and provision businesses, as well as water sellers, stayed open to trade within both the Chinese and Portuguese portions of the town, but people stayed off the streets. Non-essential businesses, educational establishments, and banks all closed.

Though there were rumblings that would break out into revolt some years later, both in Portugal and throughout the colonies concerning the economic policies of the *Ditadura Nacional* (the National Dictatorship government of 1926-1933), the soldier's protest had been primarily about poor pay and bad living conditions specifically at the Macao garrison.

The *soldados* had a good point. Pay and conditions had been a simmering point of discontent for some time – many of the men felt themselves effectively *degredados* – akin to exiled convicts!

The Monte Fort in particular was unsanitary, rodent infested, and unbearably hot pretty much all year round. No wonder – it was ancient. It had been built by the Jesuits between 1617 and 1626 to defend the College of the Mother of God against pirates. The Jesuits later transferred control of the fort to the colonial government. The barracks and associated storehouses were designed to allow the fort to survive a two-year siege, but not in any comfort, and with little upgrading since the time of the Jesuits. The fort's cannons had only been fired once, during the aborted attempt by the Dutch to invade Macao in 1622.[218] Little in the way of

218 The Battle of Macau in 1622 is the only major engagement ever fought between two European powers in China. It was part of the wider Dutch-Portuguese War, really a fight between the Dutch East India Company and Portugal. The Dutch sailed from Batavia (Jakarta) in the Dutch East Indies. The Portuguese were outnumbered, their forts ill-prepared and ammunition low. However, they managed to repel the Dutch on June 24 after a three-day battle. It was constantly celebrated by the Portuguese in Macao

refurbishments or improvements had been done since then. Its main role in 1929 was simply as a barracks from which soldiers could patrol the old city and along the ancient city wall of Macao.

A Second Revolt

It seems that Governor Barbosa felt that suppressing the mutiny was enough. There were no immediate courts martial, floggings or executions. He seems to have hoped the problem would just go away, and normality resume; the cause appeared hopeless. He resisted formal punishments as he was not keen to create martyrs. It's not clear what he could do about soldiers' pay, though he could perhaps divert municipal funds to upgrading the barracks. Still, some soldiers continued to conspire, discontent simmered, and the next uprising didn't take long to emerge.

Colonial troops and policemen stationed in Macao, 1920s

On Thursday December 26, 1929, just a few days after the first uprising, another group of Portuguese soldiers stationed in Macao mutinied. Once more the complaint was low pay and poor living conditions. However, again troops remaining loyal to Lisbon and the Governor put down the rebellion with the threat of cannon fire. This time the insurgents were arrested and imprisoned in a fort with the assumed ringleaders confined in the brig of a Portuguese Navy gunboat then at anchor in the harbour.

---

and was in fact a yearly public holiday, the annual City Day holiday, until the handover in 1999. For those craving more on Macao's cannons, defences and forts I recommend Richard J Garrett, *The Defences of Macao: Forts, Ships and Weapons Over 450 Years*, (Hong Kong: Hong Kong University Press, 2010).

Though not all the forts involved in the planned mutiny had ultimately participated, many individual artillerymen had. So the mutineers were initially imprisoned and watched over by their own former comrades. But the governor could not be sure how many of the troop-guards secretly sympathised with the troop-mutineers, or quite how, depending on what punishments were handed out, the rest of the soldiers would respond if their comrades were punished too harshly. The somewhat damp squib of a revolt could conceivably be re-energised and resurge more powerfully, this time with the cannons turned on the Governor's mansion or the *Leal Senado*. So, Governor Barbosa took no chances. On New Year's Day 1930 he ordered additional troops to be sent immediately to Macao from Mozambique in Portuguese East Africa.[219] The situation calmed; Governor Barbosa found time to enjoy his traditional new year Bolo-rei (king cake) and hope the storm had passed.

*

Barbosa was, in 1929, three years into his second term of office as Governor of Macao. A civil servant, a civilian colonial administrator (as opposed to many other governors who came from the Portuguese army or navy), Barbosa had first been appointed Governor of Macao in October 1918, though he had served barely a year before being replaced by Henrique Monteiro Correia da Silva, who came from a more traditional naval background. Correia da Silva served for just over three years before being replaced by Rodrigo José Rodrigues, whose background was as a military doctor and who had previously served in the Portuguese territories of Cabo Verde (Cape Verde) and Goa. Rodrigues was then moved to Geneva to become Portugal's chief representative to the League of Nations and Barbosa was brought back to Macao for a second term of office.

Between Rodrigues and Barbosa's second term of office there was a brief period when the Governorship was temporarily held by Manuel Firmino de Almeida Maia Magalhães, a local cavalry officer and placeholder while Barbosa returned from Lisbon.[220] Perhaps things would have been

219 This was extra troops. At any given time there were invariably a number of soldiers originally from Portuguese East Africa, usually based in Laurenço Marques (Maputo), stationed in Macao alongside Portuguese regulars.

220 After his service in Macao, he served and then became director of the Army's Cartographic Services. In 1931 he was arrested together with a group of officers

different if the rebellions had occurred during the tenures of the Navy man Rodrigues or the army man Magalhães rather than the civilian Barbosa.

Governor Artur Tamagnini de Sousa Barbosa and his wife Maria Anna

Barbosa arrived back in Macao just before Christmas 1926, accompanied by his wife, the Portuguese poet Maria Anna de Magalhães Colaço Acciaioli Tamagnini. The two had met in 1916 when Barbosa was hired to tutor Maria. Despite a 20-year age gap they fell in love and married. On their first tour of duty to Macao Maria had come to appreciate the place, spending her time studying the French language and French literature, and also learning Cantonese. The couple had five children.

In 1926 when they returned Barbosa was 46, Maria 26. They were a striking pair. Maria was short and pretty with a warm and winning smile, a little Bohemian, artistic. Barbosa was tall, barrel chested, erudite, and well-educated. He sported a monocle in his right eye that offset his dyed black bushy goatee beard and carefully waxed handlebar moustache.

The couple liked Macao and the South China coast. They had been keen to return. Maria had written her best-known poetry collection *Lin-Tchi-Fá: Flor de lotus* (*Lin-Tchi-Fá: The Lotus Flower*) which paints a poetic descriptive portrait of a Chinese woman.[221] She was also a feminist, champion of women's rights, and of local female suffrage in Macao (therefore, as a poet, feminist and suffragette, not the usual wife of a Portuguese governor of Macao). An active philanthropist, she established an asylum for beggars. Reading her work now we can see, as Lusophone literary scholars have argued, that Maria walked the line between

involved in the Madeira Revolt, an army uprising against the *Ditadura Nacional*, which the regime feared would spread to the continent. He died the following year.

221 Maria Anna Acciaioli Tamagnini, *Lin-Tchi-Fá: Flor de Lotus – Poesias do Extreme Orient*, (Lisbon: Coimbra Editora, 1925).

providing the Portuguese audience back home with a story of the exotic Orient and trying to cater to those readers with a greater sensibility by telling of a woman's search for happiness through self-actualization.[222]

Though Barbosa was not a military or naval man he did preside over a substantial military build-up in Macao during his second term. Piracy was a perennial and persistent issue in the surrounding waters and interfered with Macao's trade with southern China and Hong Kong.

The British Royal Navy was on regular anti-piracy patrols out of Hong Kong so Barbosa felt that the Portuguese Navy should increase its presence and more determinedly show the flag too. Consequently, the cruisers *NRP República* and *NRP Adamastor* joined the warships in the harbour.[223] The Glasgow-built *NRP Macau* and the Lisbon-built *NRP Pátria* were already based there after long service in East Africa, though were due to be decommissioned soon. *NRP República* was a former Royal Navy World War One-era minesweeper. The Italian-built *NRP Adamastor* had seen action in Portuguese East Africa in World War One, had a crew of 237, and had in the past been used as a pirate hunter around the Dutch East Indies based out of Portuguese Timor. At the same time the

Aviação Naval Portuguesa, Taipa, 1929

222 For instance, Theses, Ellen Thompson, *Maria Anna Acciaioli Tamagnini: O quadro da mulher feliz (Maria Anna Acciaioli Tamagnini: The Picture of the Happy Woman,* (Provo, Utah: Brigham Young University Press, 2009).

223 NRP = Navio da Repùblica Portuguesa. *NRP República* was a familiar vessel in Chinese waters. In 1927 the Portuguese consul general in Shanghai, Francisco de Paula Brito Jnr, requested a consignment of troops be sent to Shanghai to offer protection to Portuguese citizens in the bloody disturbances that took place that year in the International Settlement and French Concession. The soldiers arrived aboard the *NRP República*. There had been a steady movement of people from Macao to Shanghai seeking better economic opportunities throughout the 1910s and 1920s. In 1927 approximately 73 per cent of the community was Chinese or mixed-heritage Macanese and the remaining 27 per cent European Portuguese. The Portuguese historian Moisés Silva Fernandes has written that by 1927 Shanghai 'had become more Macanese than Macau or Hong Kong.' See Antonio Caerio, *Xangai, 1927: O Dia Em Que Portugal Entrou Na China* (in Portuguese), Calouste Gulbenkian Foundation, 2021.

Aviação Naval Portuguesa (Portuguese Naval Aviation) branch opened its first Asian station on Taipa. Known officially as Centro de Aviação Naval de Macau (CAN Macao) it was home to a small squadron of British-made Fairey III seaplanes tasked with supporting the naval vessels undertaking pirate suppression.

So, by 1929 there were more Portuguese troops stationed in Macao than ever previously. The barracks and forts were full to bursting, the parsimonious pay rates for soldiers determined by Lisbon and out of Barbosa's hands. Tempers were simmering over. And not just in the military.

Civilian Revolt

If the first few months of 1930 appeared to be a period of renewed calm, then beneath the surface Governor Barbosa was missing something big. The first the wider world knew of any further trouble in Macao was in early April when it was announced that three Portuguese citizens, all civilians, were to be charged with High Treason. It appeared that the trio had called for an end to Lisbon's sovereignty over Macao and championed the colony's secession and independence printing their demands in a number of Chinese language newspapers. Further to that, these seditious articles called upon the Chinese residents of Macao to rise up against their Portuguese colonial masters, declare a "Republic of Macao", and appeal to the League of Nations in Geneva to recognise their new state and anti-colonial struggle.[224] Although it wasn't quite so straightforward – letters between the three conspirators seized in police raids on their houses seemed to indicate that the plan was to stir up significant anti-colonial feeling such that the Governor would feel threatened enough to pay the trio to stop agitating. Arguably this was all more a blackmail scam than a noble anti-colonial struggle.

224 Barbosa and the Portuguese authorities would have been especially alarmed by the call to Chinese in Macao to rise up. Several years before, in 1927, there had been a minor crisis in the colony after it was reported in Hong Kong newspapers (and ultimately in British and North American papers, as well as in Portugal) that a movement had been started in southern China to reclaim Macao. The Portuguese refused to acknowledge the demand while the British in Hong Kong said that it was inappropriate at a time of such severe political disturbances in mainland China. 'New Movement (London, Associated Press)', *The Montreal Star*, August 19, 1927, p.6.

Extortion perhaps? Mischief making. Easy for Barbosa and the colonial regime to ignore expect that the three conspirators were not nobodies. Damiao Rodrigues was a notary (*notário*) of long standing in the colony.[225] José Maria Rodrigues Almeida was Secretary of Macao's Municipal Council (the *Leal Senado*). Isidoro (Isidore) Graça was a well-known local figure in the Portuguese community. All three were allegedly born and bred in Macao, though had Portuguese citizenship.

The *Leal Senado* heard the case against the three men and voted to immediately expel them all from the colony. As employees of the Macao government Damiao Rodrigues was ordered to be sent to Portuguese Timor for 14 months while José Maria Rodrigues Almeida was to be sent there for eight months. It seems Graça had decided to avoid the sentencing and had already decamped swiftly for Hong Kong in a classic midnight flit. In absentia Graça was simply declared expelled and told never to return to Macao.

Damiao Rodrigues certainly wasn't happy with the decisions of the *Leal Senado* and argued vociferously against the idea that the call for a Republic of Macao was just an elaborate attempt to extort Governor Barbosa. He appealed to the *Leal Senado* through the pages of *The China Truth*, a Hong Kong newspaper. But nothing came of his appeals – Barbosa and the administration simply ignored him.

External Pressures

It would seem that Barbosa had managed to suppress two attempted military mutinies and also foiled an attempt at establishing a republic independent of Lisbon in Macao. He left office for the second time in March 1931 succeeded by the also impressively handlebar moustachioed Joaquim Anselmo de Mata Oliveira who had been a Portuguese Member of Parliament during the Constitutional Monarchy (1834-1910) and, back in 1909, the Commanding Officer (*Primeiro-Tenente*[226]) of the gunboat *NRP Macau*, then patrolling the waters between Hong Kong and Macao.

Still, it's worth looking at the wider pressures being exerted on Governor Barbosa at the time of the insurrections. Aside from the continuing

225 Fully a *Notario Publico de Comarca* (County) of Macao.

226 First Lieutenant.

political and social turmoil back in Portugal in the preceding years – the overthrow of the First Republic, a military regime, a counter-coup, and various rebellions – 1929 was really the start of quite concerted pressure being placed on Macao by Japan. That pressure was to increase over the next decade in the run up towards Japan's invasion of Manchuria in 1931 and the supposed attempt by Tokyo to buy Macao in 1935 (see chapter 8), before the full invasion of China and then the fall of Hong Kong during World War Two.

In 1929 Portugal had controversially granted Japan fishing rights in Macao's waters. Fishing was a contentious issue in Macao which, in 1929 had over 2,000 fishing junks registered in its waters, and many smaller craft engaged in the trade occasionally and surreptitiously, all of which made the Porto Interior very picturesque. But these were all working boats. Fishing was Macao's largest industry and employer. Including canning and exports, fishing was (according to the Portuguese government in Lisbon) valued at US$5 million a year in 1929 (approximately US$90 million in 2024 money).[227]

Having attainted these rights despite opposition from Macanese fishermen Tokyo began to push further, this time for the right to anchor a gunboat in Macao's harbour. The Japanese also lobbied to acquire a water supply concession, and to establish a seaplane base.[228] Similar pressure was being exerted by Tokyo on the Portuguese colonial authorities in Timor. Fishing, many argued, was the thin end of the wedge in what was a long-term attempt to annex Macao from Portugal.

The fear that Tokyo would opt to disregard Portuguese neutrality in World War Two and invade was very real (and realised in Timor). In 1929-1930 this was not a negligible fear given Japan's pressures throughout the region, notably The Twenty-One Demands on China during the Great War, that culminated in 1931 with the annexation of Manchuria as well

---

227 'Islanders Form Company to Develop Water System in Portugal's China Port', *The Honolulu Advertiser,* March 3, 1929, p.1 & p.3.

228 America was also active, and in some cases more successful than Japan, in the same areas of interest. Pan American Airlines did establish an airport base for their China Clipper seaplane service while, as early as 1929, the American-Luso Investment Company was formed with a capitalisation of US$100,000 with the intention of building a modern water treatment plant in Macao. For more on seaplane machinations in the region see Chapter 8: *Did Japan Try to Buy Macao?*

as a staged attack on Shanghai in 1932.[229] Diplomatic tensions were high, the colony feeling vulnerable and its ability to defend itself seen as paramount. The distractions of a military rebellion, combined with civilian conspiracies to declare a republic were the stuff of nightmares for the Governor and Lisbon.

Governor Joaquim Anselmo de Mata Oliveira

Barbosa was recalled home in 1931 and replaced by Oliveira, a naval man. It seemed Lisbon preferred a military hand on the tiller. However, with a few relatively short-lived governors in between, Barbosa was to return once more, for a third time, in 1937. His third tour was far more difficult than the first two. The Japanese pressure on Macao was building at the same time as Japan invaded all of China. Additionally Barbosa was reeling from personal tragedy. Maria had died in Lisbon, just before her 33rd birthday, while giving birth to her fifth child (who survived). Barbosa arrived a widower to remain in Macao until 1940 constantly arguing with the Japanese to respect Portuguese neutrality in Macao. Barbosa died in the Palacete de Santa Sancha (then the newly built governor's residence) in July 1940.[230]

*

Ultimately the attempted army rebellions in Macao, the apparent desire to establish a republic, free of the Portuguese state and Lisbon, all ignominiously failed. It seems that the inscription placed over the entrance to the Town Hall in 1654 by order of the Governor, João de Sousa Pereira – *Não há outra mais leal* ("There is None More Loyal")

229 A set of demands made on China by Tokyo during World War One and after Japan's occupation of Tsingtao and Shantung province that, if acceded to, would have greatly extended Japanese control of China in both land, political and commercial terms.

230 Now the state guest house of the Chief Executive of Macao. It remains the best example in Macao of the Portuguese Pombaline architectural style, more commonly found in Lisbon during the rebuilding of the city after the 1755 earthquake.

– held true. Most rank-and-file *soldados* did not ultimately rally to the mutiny, nor did ordinary citizens choose to hear the call of independence in any great numbers.

The English historian of Portuguese maritime and colonial history Charles Boxer noted the work of Carlos Estorninho, a Portuguese scholar of Macao, who wrote in the 1960s that, 'Macao is the only one of Portugal's overseas possessions which has not contributed to any of the so-called independence movements which exist, on however small a scale, in all of the others.' The events of 1929 and 1930, the garrison uprisings, and the attempt to declare a Republic of Macao, though both failures, would seem to somewhat disprove Estorninho's claim though Macao ultimately remained true to its colonial master.[231]

231 Estorninho quoted in Charles R Boxer, *Portuguese Society in the Tropics: The Municipal Councils of Goa, Macao, Bahia, and Luanda, 1510-1800*, (Madison & Milwaukee: University of Wisconsin Press, 1965), p.71. The original work quoted by Boxer is Carlos Estorninho, *Macau e os Macaenses, Divagações e achegas historicas,* (Lisbon: Rotary Club de Lisboa, 1962), p.15.

Macao: City of Sin

Hendrik de Leeuw
(1934)

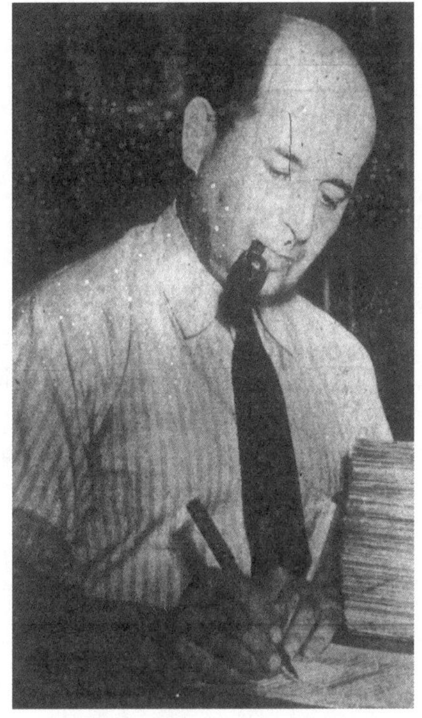

Hendrik de Leeuw, 1941

'Macao: A tableau of decay…'
– Hendrik de Leeuw, *Cities of Sin* (1938)

Sin Seeker

The "city of sin" label has stuck with Macao for a long time now. Recycled endlessly through sensationalist journalism, gratuitous pulp fictions, blatantly Orientalist novels, hyped-up travelogues and, of course, the movies. University of Macau historian Jingzhen Xie noted that with references such as '"paradise of vice," "gambling," "brothels,", "opium dens," and "devils," a strikingly lamentable image of Macao' persists: the colony had 'a glorious past' but occupies 'a sinful present.'[232]

It seems to have been there almost from the start. In the 1740s a Franciscan monk described the colony as infected with 'lechery, robbery, treachery, gambling, drunkenness and other vices.'[233] In the 1860s the French traveller Ludovic de Beauvoir took one look at the casinos and fan-tan houses and declared, '*Macao est le Monaco du Céleste Empire*' (Macao is the Monaco of the Celestial Empire), noting the wealthy Chinese from Hainan, Kwangtung, and Fukien who came to Macao to gamble.[234] This was perhaps the first Macao-Monaco comparison in print, but the "Monte Carlo of the East" trope was to be a long running one. Fast forward to 1939 and we're still in Auden's 'City of Indulgence' with all the deadly sins on display.[235]

The clichés ran deep, confirming and perpetuating persistent stereotypes. In Eileen Chang's (Zhang Ailing) novella *Aloeswood Incense: The First Brazier*, the heroine Ge Weilong is fatally attracted to the wealthy Eurasian playboy George Qiao though, as her aunt Madame Liang cruelly says, 'Qiao, you little half breed, your father may have bootlicked till the British gave him a garter, but your mother's a Portuguese whore from who knows where, a poker-chip girl from the Macao casinos.'[236]

232 Jingzhen Xie, *The French in Macao*, p.36.

233 Donald Pittis and Susan J Henders, *Macao: Mysterious Decay and Romance,* (Hong Kong: Oxford University Press, 1997). p.33.

234 Ludovic de Beauvoir, *Java, Siam, Canton. Voyage Autour Du Monde*, (Paris: Henri Plon, Imprimeur-Éditeur, 1870).

235 From WH Auden's sonnet, *Macao*, contained in *Journey to a War* (with Christopher Isherwood) – 'This city of indulgence need not fear/ The major sins by which the heart is killed/And governments and men are torn to pieces.'

236 In the novella a Shanghainese young woman, Ge Weilong, visits her estranged aunt, Madame Liang, who has married an old wealthy man for his money. Madame Liang "pimps" Weilong, marrying her to George, a Eurasian playboy, but actually

Alongside this sinful reputation went one of lassitude, a sense that ethics were somehow lacking, that, despite all the Catholicism, there was something seriously morally askew in Macao. Observing from Hong Kong the British thought Macao a generally poorly administered and underutilised colony by Lisbon. Often wondering if anything at all – besides fan-tan, smuggling, a little casual piracy, and a general sense of torpor, occurred over there. The well-travelled English writer, and wife of a Chinese Maritime Customs Service officer, Stella Benson visited in the early 1920s and wrote for the Hong Kong-based newspaper the *South China Morning Post*: 'The city of Macao is old, but it seems older than its years. Here, I think, you have China victorious. Portugal lies drugged and asleep in the arms of China.'[237]

Benson continued to emphasise the commonly expressed sense of lethargy in the colony (invariably in comparison to seemingly dynamic Hong Kong and to a lesser extent cacophonous Canton), she was scathing about its aesthetics and architecture: 'The empty shell of taste is there, the coloured plaster walls, the low corrugated convents, the churches full of a vulgar and ardent daylight… the city seems almost wholly Chinese at heart.' She concluded her essay on Macao with a nod to the wider colonial presence: 'Only when the shadows of the big African soldiers cross the door does it seem as if Portugal opened an indolent eye.'[238]

Macao appeared perhaps more overtly sinful than other notorious cities of sin – Amsterdam, Shanghai, Las Vegas, Manila. Nobody expected much else of a playboy city like Shanghai or high roller Vegas, but Macao was somehow sly in its sin, mainly because of its official Catholicism setting such a high moral bar. But Macao was part-garrison town, overwhelmingly male (at least among the foreign population), with

---

tricking her into prostitution so as to sustain the fake marriage. *Aloeswood Incense: The First Brazier* was first published in the journal *Violet* (1943, Vol.2). The story has been adapted for film by the Hong Kong director Ann Hui as *Love After Love* (2020), and is also included in the collection, *Love in a Fallen City and Other Stories*, (New York: Penguin, 2007). Chang has only a few other Macao references in her work. In *The Book of Change* she notes, 'Sister Dominic being Portuguese from Macao spoke Cantonese but not Mandarin', (Hong Kong: Hong Kong University Press, 2010), p.94.

237 Originally written for the *South China Morning Post,* but also contained in Benson's collection of travel writing, *The Little World*, (London: Macmillan, 1925), p.44-45.

238 Ibid.

streets of (legal) welcoming bordellos, state-sanctioned opium shops, and similarly permitted high revenue generating gambling alongside the numerous convents, religious orders, churches, and church-run schools.

Brown Girls and Fan-tan – Hendrik de Leeuw's Macao

There is probably no more sensationalist account of Macao in the interwar years than Hendrik de Leeuw's voluble chapter on the place in his bestselling 1938 travel book (thanks no doubt to its titillating title) *Cities of Sin*. Before he reached Macao, De Leeuw had visited Yokohama, Hong Kong, and Shanghai – three cities with, in 1930, firmly established reputations for sin and debauchery. Arriving in Macao De Leeuw hit on the chapter title 'Brown Girls and Fan-tan'.

De Leeuw's account hits the ground running in a torrent of racism. Of Macao he declares in his opening paragraph, 'It is evil of itself. Its perversions, its strange lusts, its fever of gaming, all those deeds that slay and break thousands of girls in those shadowy dens – all these rise out of the soul of a bastard people, a lascivious creature that runs riot with all the bloods of the East and the West'.[239]

De Leeuw contextualised his account of Macao in a discussion of the popular subject of the White Slave Traffic. And, of course, in order to determine the extent and severity of the White Slave Trade in Macao De Leeuw must, as he has done in the cities he has visited previously (and will do after Macao in Port Said and then finally Singapore), stop in at a brothel and see what's going on.

He consistently claimed that his work, trawling the world's bordellos, brothels, and supposed White Slave Markets was done to 'substantiate the sordid findings of the League of Nations's Special Committee on

239 Hendrik de Leeuw, *Cities of Sin*, (New York: Modern Age Books, 1938), p.146.

White Slavery and Prostitution'.[240] The League's work on this subject had begun in 1921 with the Protocol to the International Convention for the Suppression of Traffic in Women and Children. Then, in 1930, the League's Advisory Committee on the Traffic of Women and Children had recommended the formation of a Sub-Committee to 'study the laws and regulations tending to the more effectual punishment of *souteneurs*, and especially the nature of the penalties that should be imposed for that purpose.'[241] The sub-committee was subsequently appointed, met in Paris in December 1930, and presented a report to the Advisory Committee.[242]

The League of Nations Advisory Committee on the Traffic of Women and Children

However, all this journalistic justification from De Leeuw was just a veneer, his purported links to the League of Nations were ostensibly to avoid accusations of prurience and possible censorship or boycotting by respectable bookshops. It's hard to think, reading De Leeuw's accounts of his travels through 1920s and 1930s Macao and across Asia in search of prostitutes, pimps, bordellos, their madams, and customers, that he was not writing with an eye to the mass market and best-seller lists. However, his protestations of serious enquiry and support for the League

240 De Leeuw, *Cities of Sin*, Introduction.

241 *Souteneur* being a French word for a pimp and commonly used in the interwar period, presumably to avoid offending more delicate English-language ears.

242 'Convention for the Suppression of the Trafficking in Persons and of the Exploitation of the Prostitution of Others, 1950', United Nations Audiovisual Library of International Law, Uploaded 2013.

did help circumvent various national censorship bodies and probably put publishers' nerves at rest.

So, whether ultimately sensationalist or serious, did De Leeuw know what he was talking about?

*

Hendrik de Leeuw was born in 1891 in Amsterdam. Around 1912 he emigrated to the United States and became a naturalised citizen in 1923. Between leaving the Netherlands and finally becoming American he travelled widely, largely in Asia, as a representative of the Firestone Tire and Rubber Company. His adventures formed the basis of his first travel books, his "Crossroads" series spanning a quarter of a century – which from the start accentuated the sensational and the lurid. *Crossroads of the Java Sea* (1931) was followed by *Crossroads of the Caribbean Sea* (1935), *Crossroads of the Buccaneers* (1937), *Crossroads of the Zuider Zee* (1938), and *Crossroads of the Mediterranean (1956).* He liked to rewrite for different audiences. Children could fire their imaginations with his book *Java Jungle Tales* (1933) while adults could fire theirs somewhat differently with *Cities of Sin.* His first foray into sin was so successful he later followed it up with *Sinful Cities of the Western World* (1951). After sex came drugs and De Leeuw wrote *Flower of Joy* (1944) about his encounters with narcotics around the world. Quite what De Leeuw's wife Bess thought of all this is not clear.

In *Cities of Sin* De Leeuw is vague as to the dates he is in the various locations he visits, including Macao. However, in the introduction he notes that his visits preceded the League Special Committee's report by several years. So we can estimate that he is writing of experiences from, approximately, 1925 to 1929, given that the League report appeared in 1930.

Into the 'Plague Spot'

Having managed to avoid the 'swarm of beggars and rickshaw coolies' at the ferry terminal De Leeuw stayed at the Boa Vista (slightly later renamed the Bela Vista) Hotel above the Bom Parto Fort and the Praia Grande. He was well looked after, watered, and fed excellently as befitted the hotel's reputation.[243] Though he was rather alarmed (perhaps having become overly accustomed to American segregationist practices) at the preponderance of different ethnicities staying at the establishment – 'swarthy bearded men of a mixture of races.' De Leeuw is constantly remarking on the variety of ethnicities he encounters in Macao and the social mixing – 'a motley population' of Chinese, "Mestizas", Japanese, Filipino, Timorese, Goan Indians, black Africans, and Malays….' He is not complimentary about this facet of Macao life. Throughout his visit De Leeuw expresses his ideas about different types of Chinese – the 'crafty Cantonese', the more worthy Fukien men, the 'clannish' types of Ningpo and Chusan, and perhaps most bizarrely, the 'uncaring men of northern China'…[244]

Given his interests he might have cared to take a closer look at his fellow guests. In his novel of Macao life set in the 1930s, *The Bewitching Braid*, Macanese author Henrique de Senna Fernandes (who knew the city intimately and whose family had been in Macao for many generations) suggests English women would come across from Hong Kong for the weekend looking for romance in Macao and usually stayed at the Bela Vista.[245] However, De Leeuw rarely commented on the assignations and liaisons going on in polite society – the affairs and "dirty weekends" in Macao of Hong Kong's colonial elite (*á la* Han Suyin's *A Many Splendoured Thing*[246]) – and seems to have considered illicit sex a thing to be found only in brothels.

He decides that he must go in search of sin, begin his 'investigations' and find the 'plague spots' of Macao. He wanders the city, starting in the early evening – visiting the crowded Men Seng general stores and the Bazaar (or market) on the Rua dos Mercadores and Rua das Estalagens. Chinese and European bargain hunters jostle together amid numerous stalls, puppet theatre shows, hair-braiders, knife-grinders, story tellers, impromptu Cantonese opera performances, jugglers, acrobats, and crowds

243 De Leeuw, *Cities of Sin*, p.148.

244 De Leeuw, *Cities of Sin,* p.146.

245 Fernandes, *The Bewitching Braid*, p.28.

246 In which semi-autobiographical novel Han Suyin is taken to Macao by her married lover foreign correspondent Mark Elliot (in real life the married British journalist Ian Morrison – son of the famous *Times* Peking correspondent George Morrison) supposedly on assignment in the colony. Han Suyin, *A Many Splendoured Thing,* (London: Jonathan Cape, 1952).

gathered around tables watching games of *clu-clu* (named for the noise of the three dice being shaken). From there to the Largo do Pagoe do Patane, the old Patane Night Watchhouse on the Rua da Palmeira, and the Tou Tei Temple. He sees young Portuguese clerks gather for endless games of billiards and glasses of beer at *pensão* style boarding house-hotels like the Aurora Portuguesa on the Rua do Campo, a thoroughfare lined with a number of *pensão*, some large villa-mansions, and shady evergreens.[247]

It is never entirely clear if De Leeuw is always aware of what is going on around him – even the nefarious activities of the sin city he is seeking out. There were licensed opium shops in Macao, but also illegal dealers, often disguised as itinerant musicians concealing the drugs in their instruments and moving from bar-to-bar, restaurant-to-restaurant, house-to-house.[248] He is almost wholly focussed on the sex trade and pays no more than a glancing aside to the colony's extensive gambling industry – fan-tan, mahjong, *baigepiao*, roulette and (as was also so popular in Canton and Shanghai) a variety of local numbers lotteries, including *vaeseng*, *pacapio* and *Shanpiao*. Gambling had grown in Macao, in large part because it was banned in mainland China and colonial Hong Kong. Gambling existed in the treaty ports, notably the Shanghai International Settlement and French Concession, and in the mid-1930s would come to Kwangtung and especially the border town of Shum Chun when the innovative and entrepreneurial governor of the province, Chen Jitang, looking to boost his municipal coffers permitted large casinos that severely dented Macao's revenues from Hong Kong day-trippers for a few years.

De Leeuw seems to see prostitutes wherever he goes. Travelling by rickshaw through some alleys he notes 'substantial houses' that have an 'evil air' about them. He takes these for bordellos, but it is far from clear that these are quite the dens of vice he presumes – given he simply mentions women wearing lipstick looking from windows as children play in the streets.

247 The night watch sounded the time and reminded householders to take precautions against fire and theft. It provided a night watch patrol system in the neighbourhood. The Patane Night Watchhouse on Rua da Palmeira is now the only remaining example in Macao. The Aurora Portuguesa hotel (once at #45 Rua do Campo) was only one of many smaller *pensão* that maintained billiard tables and tap rooms on their ground levels. In World War Two the Aurora Portuguesa would become well known as a hostel for European Jewish refugees in Macao.

248 This seems to have been more to avoid tax than criminal sanction.

ONE OF THE TWELVE GAMBLING HOUSES RUN BY THE FAN-TAN SYNDICATE IN MACAO.

A fan-tan house De Leeuw claimed to have visited

He eventually does find the address he is looking for where he seems to have arranged some sort of introduction to the owner, a Portuguese Eurasian with 'slate-grey eyes' who is described as being covered in 'sweat like grease'.[249] Naturally he has found the notorious red-light street of the Rua de Felicidade (aka the Street of Happiness – a narrow street and adjoining alleys of two-storey nineteenth-century houses).[250] Very few interwar sensationalist writers about Macao failed to find Rua de Felicidade. De Leeuw is surprised to be shown into the man's office, equipped with a writing desk, punka fans, and a telephone. The man is apparently a dealer in opium and trafficked women. De Leeuw believes he can sense the man is a murderer – 'he smelled of blood, of lives taken for the sake of gold.'[251] Though if they have something terrible to hide they don't make much effort to conceal it. De Leeuw is taken on a tour of the house by the owner's second-in-command, Wong.

249 De Leeuw, *Cities of Sin*, p.150.

250 Readers who have never been to Macao may still be familiar with the Rua de Felicidade. It served, along with Rua do Bocage and Avenida de Almeida Ribeiro, as one of the exterior locations for the Obi Wan Club (in actuality the 1949-built *Pensão*/Hotel Sun Sun) which spectacularly opens the movie *Indiana Jones and the Temple of Doom* (1984). However, some confusion may arise in the viewer's mind as the Obi Wan Club is supposedly in 1930s Shanghai and not Macao.

251 De Leeuw, *Cities of Sin*, p.153.

De Leeuw sees some fan-tan played, some wine drunk, and some mixed-race women sitting about or gambling. Some in western, some in Chinese dress. He detects the fumes of opium and tobacco in the air. There do appear to be prostitutes. De Leeuw believes the youngest to be perhaps fifteen and the woman to be Chinese, or maybe Javanese.

De Leeuw then encounters a woman whom he initially believes to be a white European prostitute – she has black hair, but fair skin and blue eyes. She claims to be half-Chinese, to have a Dutch father. She has spent time in brothels in Hong Kong, consigned there by her Chinese mother who later disappeared into the backstreets of the British colony while her European father rejected her. She apparently only consorted with white clients in Hong Kong and had come to Macao as a Eurasian's mistress. He had then hooked her on opium and forced her to prostitute herself. She had finally met and fallen in love with a Dutchman, had a child by him before the man left her forcing her to become a prostitute once again. It is pure B-movie backstory.

Rua da Felicidade in the early 1900s

De Leeuw visits several other brothels along Rua de Felicidade. Some mix gambling with prostitution, others not. One house is run by a Portuguese woman and appears to cater specifically to European lesbians. Outside on the street he sees other women working the pavements, smoking opium, catering to the sailor trade.

De Leeuw's considered opinion of Macao was that, more than any other Sin City he had visited, it combined the prostitution systems of the East and of the West. De Leeuw believes though that while the Portuguese authorities have 'licensed houses of prostitution' they have done nothing to outlaw the trafficking of women to these houses, and in particular the recruitment of children within them. This is slightly disingenuous as De Leeuw admits the Portuguese have a law in Macao against the 'promotion, facilitation or corruption of children' although he does not consider it is being enforced. The Macao laws allowed prostitution for women over 21 but De Leeuw dismisses this and argues that the Portuguese do nothing to stop the trafficking of women and children despite not having actually encountered any of either – nobody in his preceding description of Rua de Felicidade claims to have been trafficked nor admits to being underage (despite his vague guess at one woman's age as 15).

The Register of Prostitutes

De Leeuw admits that houses of prostitution appeared to be generally well regulated in Macao. As of 1925 all working women were compelled to enter their names as prostitutes in an official police Register of Prostitutes. The registered women were then divided into two classes – those working out of a bordello establishment and those working out of their own homes. Licensed women were forbidden from living close to any schools, churches, or public parks.[252] Women licensed at home must notify the police if they move house. They are forbidden from continuing to work if diagnosed with a sexual disease, though no medical care is provided by the authorities if this is the case. De Leeuw rightly points out that this lack of support means women are extremely reluctant to admit to any afflictions that could lead to a loss of income.

If any registered woman wished to leave the profession and enter another, for example become a maid or seamstress (these apparently being the major alternative career paths), then if she can provide evidence of employment her name will be struck from the prostitute list. Similarly so women marrying, leaving Macao, or being claimed and supported by parents. Additionally, if a man takes a registered woman as a mistress then he can write a declaration of this fact and pay a fee of $6 to have her name removed from the Register. All minors (i.e. those under 16) are

252 De Leeuw does not give any specific on the definition of 'near' which seems hard to enforce in the close-knit streets of Macao's "old town" at the time.

forbidden from entering licensed houses or any clubs, taverns, or hotels where gambling occurs, as well as all cinemas and theatres.

Additionally the Register records three types of licensed brothel in Macao. The first is a licensed house in which the prostitutes live with the madam/proprietor; the second is houses in which the women have their own domicile; and the third, a *maison de passe*, is a building which women visit to conduct their trade but do not reside in. All houses are subject to inspection for illegally working women and hygiene. None can legally sell wine and spirits. And finally, a woman cannot be the madam of a licensed house without the consent of her husband.

However, while the houses were well regulated, how the women who worked in them came to be in their profession was not regulated at all. Trafficking was rife. De Leeuw suggests that these laws were regularly and routinely circumvented, broken by traffickers, procurers, and pimps.

*

As evidence of this De Leeuw claims to have visited a brothel, run by a 'Slavic' European woman, that specialised in young and underage prostitutes. It was a place where several murders had occurred, according to De Leeuw, including that of a black sailor, as well as a number of suicides by young women in the establishment. De Leeuw believes the police 'drew a veil over the incidents', suggesting they were corrupt and in league with the Madam.[253] Inside he claimed to have seen approximately eight young Portuguese girls 'in tight-fitting dresses that revealed the maturing lines of their breasts and hips.'[254] He suggests that they were all under the influence of a narcotic of some sort. De Leeuw describes himself sitting there, near the girls, smoking while clients came in and out with them during the evening.

De Leeuw asserts in *Cities of Sin* that for a 'large sum' the madam of the house allowed him to interview one of the underage girls.[255] She maintains that she and her sister had come to Macao from Lisbon though had originally been born in the wine growing regions of the Douro Valley near Porto. Their parents had died and so the daughters, 13 and 14 years old at the time, went to Lisbon. Neither of the girls had much formal

253 De Leeuw, *Cities of Sin*, p.176.
254 De Leeuw, *Cities of Sin*, p.178.
255 De Leeuw, *Cities of Sin*, p.180.

education. A friend of their deceased father's found the older a job with a dress maker. Her younger sister accompanied her to work. It seems the younger girl was raped at the dress makers. One of the rapists was caught by the police and imprisoned. The other escaped.

Sometime later the older girl was approached by a *souteneur* in a coffee house. He was well dressed and appeared wealthy, tipping the waiters with a gold coin. He offered both sisters the chance to travel to Macao where government jobs would be waiting for them in the colonies. The girls agreed and the older girl also agreed to marry the man. A priest was found, and the ceremony occurred. That night the man took her virginity. The next day they sailed from Porto for Port Said. In Egypt the man claimed he had received a telegram and had to rush back to Lisbon on urgent business. He introduced the girls to a helpful and friendly man and woman whom, he said, had agreed to accompany his now wife and sister-in-law on from Port Said to Macao.

The girls were taken to a house outside Port Said where they were forced to smoke opium and, it is suggested, were raped. Their fate became clear. There were no government jobs awaiting them, the Lisbon priest had been a fake. Their travel documents were forged to account for single young women travelling from Portugal to Macao. Their lives as prostitutes had begun. According to De Leeuw the girl concluded her story thus concerning her arrival in Macao:

'When we arrived at this establishment, there were a dozen devils waiting for us. They did not let us alone all night. We made much gold. He (their pimp from Port Said) had us registered and licensed on the ground that we had willingly practised prostitution and would not stop. We bought ourselves away from him. My sister is dead and I soon shall be, although when I sometimes have nothing to do I am a little happy.'[256]

*

It is hard to know if this story, and others from Macao and elsewhere that De Leeuw relates in *Cities of Sin*, is entirely or partially true, or simply invented. There are inconsistencies with his previous description of the Register of Prostitutes and the apparent ability to register underage girls. Perhaps there is a mingling of truth and fiction, or maybe De Leeuw

256 De Leeuw, *Cities of Sin*, p.190.

heard all manner of tales and rumours and elaborated on them for his readership.

There are verifiable facts – the Rua de Felicidade was a centre of prostitution, there was a Register of Prostitutes, we do know that there was trafficking of young European women east to Hong Kong, Shanghai, Rangoon, Yokohama, Singapore, Macao and elsewhere. But we also know De Leeuw is an author with an agenda – he wants to shock his reader, as well as to convince them that White Slavery is a real and concerning phenomenon, that the authorities should do more. Naturally *Cities of Sin* alarmed many readers. What the reaction of the Portuguese authorities in Macao was is not known. Whether these people – the greasy opium trafficker, the Slavic Madam, the Eurasian opium addict prostitute, the underage Portuguese prostitutes – were real, composites or fictional remains unknown.

It is clear though that De Leeuw comes across, both in his chapter on Macao and throughout *Cities of Sin,* as obsessed with race and miscegenation, constantly referring to black and racially mixed people in derogatory ways, to the Portuguese as somehow morally inferior to northern Europeans, and suggesting they are all weaker morally that white Americans. Presumably this played well to his predominant readership – segregation-era America. What is undisputed is that it played firmly into the principal narrative around Macao at the time.

Orientalogue

De Leeuw sold a lot of books between the wars, he was a big name on the US lecture circuit and appeared regularly on the radio. In 1932 he broadcast on WOR-710 The Voice of New York on *Macao: The Monte Carlo of the Orient* in a series of radio talks he gave rather clumsily entitled *Orientalogue*, which included some now politically incorrect talks such as *The Half-Caste's Lament* and *Malayan Poison.*

When World War Two came along De Leeuw remained in the USA lecturing and broadcasting in support of the anti-Japanese cause in Asia, as well as writing articles for the *New York Herald Tribune* and *New York Cavalcade*. He joined the Netherlands section of the Office of War Information in 1942. After the war he picked up his travel pen again and resumed his risqué titles – in the 1950s *American Morals: A Survey and a Report*, presumably read by anyone looking for examples of lack of morals, and *Women, the Dominant Sex.* Then in the 1960s, *Conquest of the Air* and *From Flying Horse to Man in the Moon; A History of Flight from its Earliest Beginnings to the Conquest of Space.*

In the 1950s he lived mostly in New York, on Remsen Street in Brooklyn Heights. He still wrote frequently, often controversially (admittedly more to modern readers' changing sensibilities than previously). In 1958 he penned an 'exposé' for the *Chicago Tribune* – 'What Else Do Women Want? A Male Asks This Question and Follows With Another: Has Victory in the Sex War Brought Unhappiness?'[257] De Leeuw asserted that many millions of American women were dissatisfied with being females – it does not read as a particularly progressive piece. Hendrik de Leeuw died in America in 1977 at 86.

De Leeuw is, understandably, not much read these days – a strange curiosity at best, you rarely see his books in second hand or antiquarian bookshops or even online much. He always claimed a semi-scientific, quasi-investigative journalistic element to his work, though to our twenty-first-century minds it is difficult to see him as anything than prurient, slipping round the censors and the easily outraged by arguing his travels were revealing of a great evil. Maybe so. But his work, particularly in the chapter in *Cities of Sin,* does offer us something of a traveller's insight into the underbelly of Macao life in the late 1920s. While it is highly sensationalist and completely unverifiable, there are probably elements of truth to be discerned. The denizens of the underworld – the prostitutes, pimps, madams, procurers, dope dealers, white slavers – naturally kept their stories to themselves and so De Leeuw survives as one of the only eye-witnesses we have to this aspect of Macao – so often hyped, but not entirely invented.

257 *Chicago Tribune*, March 9, 1958, p.114

Did Japan Try to Buy Macao?

A Tale of Competing Empires, Japanese Expansionism and … Seaplanes (1935)

The Pan Am China Clipper over Macao, 1937

Japan May Buy Macao

London: May 14 (Associated Press) – A Hong Kong dispatch to the Daily Express said today that Japan has offered Portugal £20,000,000 (about $100,000,000) for Macao, a Portuguese seaport in China.

Hard Times, Tough Choices

In May 1935, newspapers in America and Europe reported that Japan had made Portugal an amazing and seemingly unbelievable offer – one hundred million American dollars for their colony of Macao.[258] It seemed too fantastical – surely countries couldn't start trading colonies for cash? But Japan was land and resource hungry, in expansionist mode whether by annexation, occupation or acquisition and Lisbon was not in great financial shape in the 1930s. Macao wasn't a colonial goldmine, nor was Portugal by the third decade of the twentieth century much of a trading nation, nor a major naval power projecting military prowess and in need of far-flung ports. Japan was on an upswing, Portugal on a downslide. And so just maybe Lisbon might like an injection in its state coffers courtesy of Tokyo. But there was more to the offer than just Japanese imperial reach.

JAPAN WOULD BUY MACAO

Island Empire Covets Fine South China Seaport Owned by Portugal

Berkshire Eagle, July 11, 1935

Those with long memories in Macao had a sense of déjà vu when the news broke that Japan was attempting to buy the colony. It had been rumoured before. During the Great War, 18 years previously, Reuters had

258 'Japan May Buy Macao', via Associated Press, *The Courier Journal* (Lexington, Kentucky), May 15, 1935, p.19.

reported, 'Macao Sold – Purchased by Japan'.[259] It was speculated that, having seized Tsingtao from the Germans at the start of the war, Japan was now looking to expand. If an offer was ever made, and Japan and Lisbon both denied it, it was between two countries on the same side in the war. The British assumed that it was a fake news story and an obvious attempt to create trouble between allies.[260] And that was the end of that – barely more than half a dozen stories worldwide. Eighteen years later the apparently renewed offer from Tokyo to Lisbon to buy Macao generated a lot more press and the situation was very different.

Whether or not Tokyo tried to buy Macao in 1935 is in fact a story of a sleepy old colony suddenly becoming a key target for the new trans-Pacific air services, as well as a locus of Japanese-American-British-Chinese rivalry. If Manchuria in the 1930s was militarily 'the cockpit of Asia' (a key scene of geo-political rivalry), was Macao potentially a commercial 'cockpit' for the region? Did Tokyo really try and buy Macao? Was there ever actually a serious offer, or is this all a 1930s case of Fake News, some crafty false flag operation by (take your pick) Tokyo, London, Nanking, Washington, colonial officials in Hong Kong, or even perhaps Lisbon trying to put the idea in Tokyo's collective head? And if a serious offer was ever made, why did it never happen?

Loss-Making Macao

In 1934 times were hard for the Portuguese who ran Macao. The colony's often questionable economy was hurting financially. In the surrounding waters the Royal Navy was successfully suppressing piracy and smuggling. Officially good news, but not so great for Macao's illicit cash flows. Formerly fan-tan house concessions had brought in a significant US$5,000 a day for the Portuguese administration. That was about US$100,000 a day in 2024 money, approximately US$37 million annually – peanuts by the standards of today's casino economy in Macao, but a large chunk of the Portuguese administration's budget back then.

To make matters worse Macao was suffering from competition with mainland China. A good portion of the gambling revenue in Macao

259 This was reported widely as Reuters was a wire service; for instance, 'Macao Sold – Purchased by Japan', *The Sun* (New Zealand), March 20, 1917.

260 'An Official Denial – Enemy Intrigue', *The Sun* (New Zealand), March 30, 1917.

had always come from visitors from Kwangtung and Hong Kong but in the early 1930s the Nationalist Government in the province was promoting its own gambling houses in the border town of Shum Chun, easily accessible from Canton, a short train ride on the Kowloon-Canton Railway (KCR) from the colony across the border.[261] The development of Shum Chun as a gambling centre was the brainchild of military man-turned provincial governor Chen Jitang, often referred to as the 'Celestial King of the South'.[262] To begin with only fan-tan was played but soon, with so many westerners arriving from Hong Kong, roulette, chemin-der-fer, dice and slot machines were added to the menu. It was claimed that Chen Jitang's administration charged the casino operators approximately US$1,000 a day to be allowed to open. Another thousand a day went on operating costs, but each casino netted an annual profit of over two million US$ – approximately US$46 million in 2024 terms. Shum Chun dented Macao's casino business severely even though the combination of political change, clampdowns on vice and the Japanese invasion ruined Shum Chun by 1936 and 1937.[263]

Still, the damage was done. The government was only getting a fraction of its old gambling revenues as the pirates and smugglers were arrested, beheaded, or otherwise stayed away from Macao and the punters flocked to Shum Chun. What is more, the ever-reliable cash cow of opium sales, a colonial government monopoly that had long fuelled Lisbon's treasury, was not yielding its old gains as opium smoking was in decline and the lack of visitors contributed to reduced sales and consumption. Worried that Macao would become a serious drain on Portugal's not overly fecund coffers, Lisbon ordered its officials in its south China colony to urgently find some new sources of revenue.

261 Today the old town of Shum Chun (alternatively Shumchun, Shen Chuen or Shen Zhen) lies forgotten beneath the new mega-city of Shenzhen.

262 Chen Jitang (1890-1954) joined the Chinese Revolutionary Alliance in 1908 and eventually rose to Commander of the Fourth Route Army in 1928. He governed Kwangtung Province from 1929-1936. During World War Two he was a member of the National Government, Supreme National Defence Commission and Strategic Commission, and then Governor of Hainan Island before leaving for Taiwan in 1950.

263 For more on Shum Chun's brief rise to stardom and then collapse see Paul French, 'Myth Busting: Shenzhen's Sleazy Past as Short-Lived Gangster and Gambling Hub Shum Chun', *South China Morning Post Weekend Magazine*, January 17, 2021.

With the economies of narcotics, gambling, smuggling and piracy in decline there was some serious head scratching in Macao's finance ministry. Hong Kong had long eclipsed Macao as a trading port. The traditional local industries of fishing, firecrackers, and incense, as well as tea and tobacco processing, were all far too small-scale. Options for bringing in new industries were limited with a population of less than 200,000 people and no natural resources.

But there was one big potential source of profit. A new idea that didn't require a large workforce or much local money for investment. It was an idea that was not only lucrative for Macao and Lisbon, but one that could put the colony back on the map as an important hub once again – the possibility of trans-Pacific aviation flights.

The Macao Clipper

New York-based Pan-American Airways (Pan Am) was desperate to start a Pacific Clipper seaplane service from the west coast of America to its seaplane base on Oahu, Hawaii, and from there on to southern China via Guam, Midway Island, Wake Island, Manila, and possibly other stopover destinations that would include China, probably Canton, and perhaps end at Hong Kong. Here the Pan Am clipper would connect with British Imperial Airways developing routes to Hong Kong from London and on

Air Service To China In Clipper Ships To Shrink World Time-Map, Aid Trade

Before long, passengers can climb aboard one of the big flying clipper ships of Pan-American Airways (as they are shown doing above) in San Francisco and in less than a week disembark at Macao, China, 9000 miles distant—a three-week steamer trip. The first trans-Pacific ai mail flight is scheduled some time after November 22. The map show the far-flung system of Pan-American which spans 40,000 miles.

Round-the-world flying boat service

to Australia. John D Wong, an expert on the development of aviation services in the region, says:

'As a new technology, commercial aviation promised to rewire global traffic flows in the first half of the twentieth century. In the 1930s, the British Empire extended its aerial reach to the Hong Kong outpost through the expanding network of Imperial Airways (British Airways' predecessor). At the same time, American and Chinese interests (Pan Am and its joint venture in Republican China) strove to assert their power by expanding their flight network in Asia. On this budding route map, Hong Kong appeared as a "puddle-jumping stop" along the world's burgeoning skyways.'[264]

The Martin M-130 China Clipper

The plane maker Glenn L Martin Company (now merged into Lockheed Martin) had built three Martin M-130 flying boats at its Baltimore factory – the *Hawaii Clipper*, the *Philippines Clipper* and the *China Clipper*, named after the old nineteenth-century East India Company sailing clippers that raced across the Pacific bringing tea to America.[265] The M-130 made its debut in the skies in 1934 – an incredible looking all-metal flying aircraft with streamlined aerodynamics and engines powerful enough to fly passengers and cargo (overwhelmingly mail) from the western United States to China. Crucially, the M-130 could take off and land on water which meant rapidly expanding the trans-Pacific route while getting around both the political hassle and cost of building landing strips Pan Am could not control.

Central to the whole endeavour was the United States Post Office (USPO) who were determined to get a trans-Pacific service crossing from

264 Paul French, 'Q&A with John D Wong, author of *Hong Kong Takes Flight*', China-Britain Business Council *Focus* Magazine (online), October 2022.

265 As a side note, when Nixon went to China in the 1970s the Americans painted on the side of the B747's fuselage what they thought was the translation of China Clipper in Mandarin – though it actually translated more accurately as 'China Scissors', which remains the common Chinese translation today.

San Francisco via Hawaii, Guam, and the Philippines to China as soon as possible and was willing and able to significantly subsidise its development. The USPO was already working with Pan Am and had awarded the airline its airmail delivery contract. To start with Pan Am and the USPO had extended air services to New Zealand and Australia, via a stopover in American Samoa. They were hoping postal services would grow into additional freight revenue and then eventually passengers. The professorial-looking Harllee Branch was put in charge of the trans-Pacific project by the US Postmaster General who had publicly stated that he would fly a letter from California to Hawaii, and then on to any Asian or Australasian destination, in a day and a half, as opposed to the three weeks it then took. And wherever the destination the stamp would cost no more than a single American dollar. Branch was determined to meet this challenge.

Harllee Branch of the United States Post Office

But there was competition. The Japanese desperately wanted to start a Tokyo to Canton service via Shanghai. Japan already had significant investments and business interests in the International Settlement as well as a sizeable Japanese expat population of roughly 25,000, while Tokyo was keen to expand its influence down into southern China.[266] However, it was 1934 – the Japanese had recently invaded and annexed Manchuria and renamed it the State of Manchukuo with the young Puyi installed as the new puppet Emperor. Add to that the ferocious fighting in Shanghai between Japanese and Chinese soldiers in 1932, the so-called "Shanghai Incident", and diplomatic relations between Nationalist China and Japan were somewhere between seriously cold and frozen solid.

Consequently it was no surprise that the Nanking government refused Japanese Air Transport (JAT), then Japan's national airline, any landing rights on Chinese soil. But Nationalist China, still relatively weak in the

266 The statistic of 'roughly 25,000' was given by the Japanese Residents' Association of Shanghai in 1934.

face of Great Power politics, was forced to play a delicate balancing game. Nanking also felt compelled to refuse permission for Pan Am planes to stop and refuel at Canton, so as not to further annoy Tokyo by obviously favouring the United States of America.

And so the USPO/Pan Am, and JAT, both started looking closely at Macao. Each country began negotiations with the local authorities, and by extension Lisbon, with a view to acquiring landing rights and possibly building an air terminal. The race to secure enough landing and refuelling sites reliably to operate a trans-Pacific air service was on. Macao, whose original trade advantage back in the days of the spice trade and then the Canton trade had been largely forgotten by 1934, suddenly found itself geographically ideally situated once again.

Imperialism by Air Route

JAT had established a subsidiary, the Manchurian Aviation Company (MAC), in 1931, after its invasion and annexation of China's most north-eastern region. The idea was to consolidate its new enclave and be able to service the largely land-locked territory by air. MAC offered regular services from Tokyo and Kobe to Japanese-occupied Korea, and on to Mukden, Harbin, and the puppet state's new capital at Changchun (which the Japanese called Hsinking). JAT were also looking at developing a route from Tokyo to the island of Taiwan, then also Japanese-occupied.

Imperial Japan was advancing its expansion plans using air routes in northern China with little resistance. But, to the British at least, talk of routes down to Canton and their possible encroachment into southern China was a very different proposition. While Hsinking was 1,600 miles from where the British were firmly entrenched in Hong Kong, Canton was just 80 miles away. Of course, Tokyo knew that Great Britain would never sell a Crown Colony to Japan but was willing to gamble that Portugal just might if the offer was right. And they had good reason to think this not just looking at Macao's stagnant economy but also when they looked at Portugal's politics and economy at the time.

The interwar period was proving tough for Lisbon. The First Portuguese Republic, founded in 1910, had collapsed in a military-led coup d'etat in 1926 after nine presidents and 44 prime ministers! So began the *Ditadura Nacional* (National Dictatorship), that in 1933 became the so-called *Estado Novo* (New State), lasting until 1974 and the Carnation Revolution that finally restored democracy to Portugal. Throughout the First Republic, and the subsequent military coup, the country's financial situation was highly precarious. As described above Macao wasn't making much, if any, money for Lisbon in the 1920s and early 1930s, and offered nothing much more than its handy geographical position. Its glory days for Portugal were long gone and now even its heyday as a centre of piracy and smuggling seemed over.

So it seems Japan decided 'nothing ventured, nothing gained' and offered Portugal US$100 million for Macao. This was well over a billion US dollars in today's money, but still quite a bargain considering the estimate of US$1.1 trillion Donald Trump reputedly offered Denmark to sell him Greenland in 2019!

The story was initially broken by an anonymous Hong Kong stringer for the London *Daily Express*, who also claimed that an official delegation was on its way from Tokyo to Lisbon to talk money, contracts, and Ts&Cs.[267] Though, it must be said, no official confirmation of either the offer being made, or of it being received, was forthcoming from either Tokyo or Lisbon and quite how the intrepid stringer got this tale remains a mystery.

Still, the rumour understandably excited much interest in London. British-inclined editorialists universally thought it a bad idea. A plan that nakedly revealed Japan's ambitions in southern China, which London definitely considered its private sphere of influence, was always going to set alarm bells ringing throughout Whitehall. Coming after the invasion of Manchuria, where the League of Nations had appeared impotent to stop the Japanese Army, and Shanghai in 1932, where a multi-national response had been required to get Tokyo to back off, trying to buy up Macao was seen as a step too far and had to be prevented.

Pan Am and the USPO were not happy about the Japanese offer to purchase Macao either. Their M-130 flying boats, which the press and public all simply called the "China Clippers", had successfully flown and passed the necessary tests to begin trans-Pacific services. The USPO was reportedly preparing to issue a new stamp with the plane on it to celebrate the service's launch.

267 Japan May Buy Macao', via Associated Press, *The Courier Journal* (Lexington, Kentucky), May 15, 1935, p.19.

JAT and its offshoot, MAC, were heavily subsidized by the Japanese government which helped them advance their plans with new land-based airports. JAT had built and opened Haneda Airport in Tokyo, about ten miles outside the city on Tokyo Bay, with flights to Taiwan, Korea and Hsinking. The airlines used a mix of Japanese Nakajima Aircraft Company AT-2's and German Fokker Super Universals. Nakajima then purchased a production licence for America's Douglas DC-2 and built half a dozen of them. The DC-2 had powerful engines and carried 14 sleeper passengers but was not a seaplane. Unlike Pan Am's China Clippers, the JAT DC-2 would need a runway.

But both airlines had a shared problem. Pan Am could fly from San Francisco to Manila with stops at American-controlled Hawaii, Midway Island, Wake Island and Guam. But after that? JAT could fly from Japan into their new Manchukuo state in northern China, to Shanghai in Eastern China, and down as far as their colony Taiwan. But after that? Tortuously slow talks were ongoing with the British to eventually reach Hong Kong, but how to reach Canton and into the key southern China market? Macao had become a valuable prize. Japan's offer to buy Macao outright from Portugal appeared an opening gambit – US$100 million for a landing strip essentially.

Invoking the Lisbon Protocol

But Tokyo was to be frustrated. It turned out that the main legal fly in the ointment everyone had forgotten about was Nationalist China. The Portuguese had settled in Macao in 1557. But it wasn't until March 1887, with the signing of the Lisbon Protocol that Macao became a formal Portuguese colony. In 1935 this treaty was nearly half a century old, but its basic provisions still held. These were, firstly, that China recognised the "perpetual occupation and government of Macao" by Portugal. However, secondly, and now very importantly, the Lisbon Protocol required Lisbon to agree never to surrender Macao to a third party without Chinese government agreement. It was crystal clear – Lisbon could not sell Macao to Japan without Nanking agreeing. And that was something that was never going to happen. A legal condition in a protocol signed sixteen years before the Wright Brothers took off at Kitty Hawk was enough to stymie Japan's dreams of a Macao landing strip.

Some British commentators did raise the question of how much either Lisbon or Tokyo would actually care about honouring the clause in 1935. China looked weak – Japanese encroachments in the north, the foreign-controlled treaty ports along the coast, warlords still running around causing trouble from Hubei to Turkestan. Cash-strapped Lisbon, with US$100 million being dangled before it, could decide that falling out with Nationalist China was a price worth paying to get a major payday and rid itself of a costly colony. Japan, having already invaded Manchuria and clearly eyeing all northern China, might not give a damn about the provisions of the Lisbon Protocol, indeed any hostile reaction by Nanking to breaking it could be portrayed as a "provocation" in Japan providing excuses for further annexations of Chinese territory. And, if Portugal decided to take the cash, what could China do? Invade a Japanese-occupied Macao giving Tokyo just the excuse it needed to attack southern China? Appeal to a League of Nations that had done nothing to kick Japan out of Manchuria? Invade Portugal, 6,500 miles away on another continent?

The key difference between Manchuria and Macao, of course, was the close proximity of the Portuguese colony to the British Empire in Hong Kong. Some Hong Kong and Fleet Street newspapers reported that London, traditionally an old ally of Portugal, had immediately told Lisbon in the strongest terms not to even think of accepting Japan's cash.

However, it's tricky to untangle definitively what actually happened in the spring and summer of 1935. Did Japan ever seriously make an offer? Did Portugal seriously consider it? Did the British tell the Portuguese to resist? Was this all just the drunken fever dream of some hard-up Hong Kong stringer hitting on the idea of starting a rumour that would run for a few days? Was it all an hilarious wheeze cooked up after a few too many G&Ts at the bar of the Hongkong Hotel on Pedder Street where the hacks all gathered to drink and gossip? Or did someone, perhaps the *Kempeitai* Japanese military intelligence looking to spread misinformation, or the *Juntong*, Nationalist Chinese intelligence, looking to draw attention to Japanese intentions in southern China, play a trick on some susceptible young innocent journalist, feeding him a yarn to see if he'd report it back to London?[268] It wouldn't have been the first time.

Either way a week later, on May 15, the Portuguese Ministry for the Colonies in Lisbon vehemently and publicly denied Macao was up for sale – "Not one yard of Portuguese territory is for sale to Japan, or any other nation. Neither is any Portuguese territory to be ceded under any circumstances."[269] End of! Seemingly. Although, interestingly, there was no denial that any Japanese offer had ever been made.

And, perhaps, tellingly, quite a few newspapers pointed out that the Ministry for the Colonies had specifically said that no Portuguese territory was for sale to Japan, 'or any other nation'. Did perhaps London warn Lisbon off any sale to Tokyo, and then make its own counteroffer? London could presumably afford to top Tokyo's initial bid. Some commentators suggested that Japan might attempt a naval blockade of Macao given that the Portuguese naval presence in the South China Sea was minimal. But again, it was rumoured London had let it be known that the Royal Navy's three squadron-strong Far East Fleet would not allow that to happen.

Curiouser and Curiouser

Then things got curiouser. A week or so later, on May 28, 1935, the Portuguese made another vehement denial that they were selling any territory, the colony of Macao being mentioned specifically this time. However, the denial came not from Lisbon, but rather from the Portuguese Embassy in Berlin. This was, so the Portuguese said, due to rampant and alarmist speculation about a potential Lisbon-Tokyo deal over Macao appearing in all the major German newspapers.

And so the story didn't quite go away. It was still being trotted out in both the United States and European newspapers well into July that year, as well as in Hong Kong's *South China Morning Post* and *The Straits Times* in Singapore. Some newspapers in America expressed the opinion that

268 At the time the *Kempeitai* was the most active of Japan's various intelligence agencies in China. The *Juntong*, formed in 1927 was headed by China's infamous spymaster Dai Li and known formally as The National Bureau of Investigation and Statistics (Military Commission).

269 'Portuguese Won't Permit Sale of Colony to Japan', *The Daily News* (New York, New York), May 17, 1935, Brooklyn Section, p.7.

Lisbon's fulsome denials might just be a gambit to talk up the price a bit, perhaps to get Tokyo and London into an auction.

By the end of the summer of 1935 it seems Tokyo had changed tack. The outright purchase idea appears to have disappeared – if there ever was an offer it had apparently been rescinded. It was reported that a Japanese envoy had now approached the colonial government of Macao with the idea of creating a "Japanese Settlement", essentially a village, close to the Chinese mainland and the town of Chungshan. It would be a place for Japanese merchants to live, build homes, offices and godowns to trade from. Quite how this was envisaged as working was not clear, perhaps something like a mini-Japanese concession such as existed in the treaty ports of Shanghai and Tientsin. The Portuguese authorities in Macao were reported to be considering the request.

The Macao Clipper

But perhaps Japan's loss of interest in the outright purchase idea was due to another deal that had been offered to Lisbon and accepted.

Pan Am had managed to reach an agreement with the Macao authorities in September 1935. The Nanking government was still adamant in its refusal of landing rights to either Japan or the US so Pan Am dealt exclusively with Macao, who gave them a sea-landing spot right at the entrance of the Pearl River Delta. Passengers and post could disembark the Pan Am *China Clipper* and then take the regular ferries to Hong Kong and Canton. Macao became as much a strategically useful hub to Pan Am in late 1935 as it had been to the Portuguese fleet in the sixteenth century. As an added bonus for Portugal a sea-landing port was virtually cost-free and did nothing to drain either Lisbon or Macao's straitened coffers.

Pan Am Manila to Macao inaugural flight illustration

With landing rights assured Pan Am immediately started negotiations with the Macao authorities to build a radio-telegraphic and radio-chronometric station – essentially a much-need investment in the colony. The USPO's delighted and hard-working Harllee Branch was reported to be planning a San Francisco-Honolulu-Manila-China line ending at Macao and operated by the Pan Am China Clippers as soon as possible.

And, in November 1935, the service launched. A China Clipper with 18 sleeper passengers and a lot of mail took off from San Francisco Bay on a late afternoon. Seventeen hours later it arrived in Honolulu in the morning sunshine. Refuelled, the Clipper took off again and spent a night at each Pacific Island location – Midway, Wake and Guam – before arriving in Manila Bay. Then a half day's flight from the Philippines to Macao and the ferry connection to Canton where passengers could connect to flights to Shanghai, Nanking and Peking or train services to Hong Kong. The whole 19,000-mile journey would have taken three weeks by boat.

SAN FRANCISCO
U. S. A.-Hawaii-Guam-Philippines

Orient Exp.			Pan American Airways Co. (PAAP)	Orient Exp.	
(z)	PM			AM	(z)
Wed.	3 00	....	Lv SAN FRANCISCO, (Alameda),Cal.,...(PST) Ar	10 30	Tues.
Thur.	8 30	....	Ar HONOLULU, (Pearl Harbor), H. I...(HLT) Lv	N12 00	Mon.
Fri.	6 30	....	Lv HONOLULU, (Pearl Harbor), H. I...(HLT) Ar	5 30	Sun.
	3 00	....	Ar MIDWAY ISLAND................(MLT) Lv	6 00	
Sat.	6 00	....	Lv MIDWAY ISLAND................(MLT) Ar	5 00	Sat.
			(International Date Line)		
Sun.	3 00	....	Ar WAKE ISLANDS....................165° Lv	6 00	Sun.
Mon.	6 00	....	Lv WAKE ISLANDS...................165° Ar	7 00	Sat.
	5 00	....	Ar GUAM ISLAND....................150° Lv	6 00	
Tues.	6 00	....	Lv GUAM ISLAND....................150° Ar	6 30	Fri.
(z)	5 00	....	Ar MANILA (Cavite), P. I................120° Lv	•4 00	(z)
(x)					(x)
Wed.	8 30	....	Lv MANILA, (Cavite), P. I..............120° Ar	1 45	Thur.
	1 50	....	Ar MACAO.......................... " Lv	- -	
	3 05	....	Ar HONG KONG...................... " Lv	8 30	

•—Departure from Manila subject to advancement to previous afternoon as occasion demands.
All times are approximate other than at San Francisco westbound and at Honolulu eastbound.

Pan Am's China Clipper schedule

At the same time Pan Am was launching other Clipper services down into Latin America, as far as Buenos Aires. Meanwhile Britain's Imperial Airways, Germany's Lufthansa, as well as airlines from France and

Holland, were all launching trans-Atlantic services and pushing their networks further east to connect to their Asian empires. Britain was distinctly less interested in the Trans-Pacific routes preferring, like the French with Air France (though Pan Am was also in negotiation with the French for a Clipper link at Hanoi in French-controlled Indochina), to develop connections between its imperial possessions, for instance the 1930s developments of services between Hong Kong (from Kai Tak Airport) to Penang and Singapore.

A Frederich Schiff-designed advert for BOAC's flying boat service to Hong Kong

So Macao appeared to have established itself as the far Pacific end of the line. As regional aviation expert John D Wong has noted, while Macao by 1935 could obviously not hope to compete with Hong Kong as a shipping hub, due to its shallow draft and basic dock facilities, it could perhaps compete and win as an air hub.[270]

Harllee Branch got to launch his China Clipper stamp; the first one was posted to President Roosevelt from Manila. The Pan Am Clipper fleet was joined in 1937 by a Sikorsky S-42 flying boat that had a slightly larger fuel capacity. But it wasn't all smooth flying. For reasons that have never been ultimately determined the *Hawaii Clipper* disappeared somewhere between Guam and Manila in July 1938 with the loss of nine crew and six passengers.

Undaunted the Japanese airlines continued to expand too – more flights into Japanese-occupied Korea and Manchukuo, as well as new services to

270 John D Wong, *Hong Kong Takes Flight: Commercial Aviation and the Making of a Global Hub, 1930s-1998*, (Cambridge, Massachusetts: Harvard University Asia Center, 2022), p.29.

the Sakhalin Islands, Saipan, and Palau in the Western Pacific using converted military flying boats. Now renamed Imperial Japanese Airlines (IJA) they ran several trial long-haul flights to Iran and even as far as Italy in 1939, but then the invasion of China and the demands of war overtook civilian air route development.

USPO 25-cent China Clipper stamp

Special Japanese-only "villages" never did appear in Macao. Any talk of Japan having any level of overt influence in Macao had died a death by the end of 1935.

Historical Inevitability?

Japan didn't stop thinking about Macao. Tokyo was convinced Britain was planning to establish permanent air and naval bases in the territory.[271] Probably Japan decided that its long-term expansionist strategy in Asia wouldn't ultimately require them having to pay Lisbon US$100 million. Arguably Japan had always had another plan for China: military occupation. Eventually they simply took most of the country by force. Manchuria had just been the start. By the end of 1941 they had conquered southern China and Hong Kong. They didn't need Macao, which remained quietly neutral along with its colonial master Portugal throughout World War Two.

And Macao was outmanoeuvred in the trans-Pacific business too. The less than ideal 60-mile ferry connection between Macao and Canton was a wrinkle in the route that annoyed Pan Am. There seemed no way around steamer links (and potential piracy, theft of mails, inconvenience for passengers etc) to both Canton and Hong Kong. After interventions from Pan Am's founder Juan Trippe, Britain did eventually permit both Pan Am and the fledgling China National Aviation Corporation (CNAC)

271 Japanese newspapers continually claimed Britain was poised to establish bases in Macao according to Glyn Stone, *The Oldest Ally: Britain and the Portuguese Connection 1936-1941,* (Suffolk, England: The Royal Historical Society/The Boydell Press, 1994), p.64.

landing rights at Kai Tak.[272] CNAC was able to offer more convenient onward flights into China as far as Chungking, Shanghai, and Peking, rails services into southern China courtesy of the Kowloon-Canton Railway, and coastal steamers to destinations such as Foochow, Amoy, Tientsin, Shanghai, and others. Macao with no commercial airfield, obviously no rail links, and a far smaller coastal steamer fleet simply could not compete.

It was also the case, argues aviation historian John D Wong, that the colonial authorities in Hong Kong were nervous about Macao getting the jump on them as the major 'air junction' with China and wrote to London arguing for a deal to be done with Pan Am. Subsequently representatives of Imperial Airways also began talks with Juan Trippe and Pan Am.[273] Still locked out of Canton and mainland China, Pan Am smoothed things over with Lisbon by describing Macao as 'the Chinese base for the new Clipper venture.'[274] Despite this a formal seaplane base never was constructed in Macao even as in 1938 Pan Am and the Lisbon government completed the city's Aeroporto Marítimo at Cabo Ruivo. Clippers flew from New York to Lisbon via Bermuda throughout World War Two. In Asia though it had been a different story.

Now history remembers the "Hong Kong Clipper" rather than the more short-lived but pioneering "Macao Clipper". And so Macao was once again supplanted by Hong Kong while the idea of Tokyo paying US$100 million to Lisbon to buy the colony was consigned to the many "what ifs" of history.

272 CNAC was formed in 1930 and mostly headquartered in Shanghai. Passenger and mail routes connected Shanghai to Canton, Hankow, Chengtu, Kunming, Chungking, Kiating, Kweilin and other destinations. During World War Two the airline moved its fleet to India to support operations over "The Hump". The airline ceased operations in 1952.

273 Wong, *Hong Kong Takes Flight*, p.29.

274 Wong, *Hong Kong Takes Flight*, p.37.

Gambling Hell! – Maurice Dekobra's Vision of Macao

Maurice Dekobra
(1938)

Maurice Dekobra in 1932

Alors une autre image de Macao vint se présenter à mon esprit. Son image la plus moderne, la plus brutale, inspirée par les titres de tant de romans et de films d'aventure. Macao – nid de contrabadniers, royaume d l'opium, paradis de la débauche, enfer du jeu. macao, bordel, repaire de la drogue et tripot fantastique…

Then another image of Macao came to my mind. Its most modern, most brutal image, inspired by the titles of so many adventure novels and films. Macao – nest of smugglers, kingdom of opium, paradise of debauchery, gambling hell. Macao, bordello, drug lair and fantastic gambling den…

– Joseph "Jef" Kessel, *Hong-Kong et Macao* (1957)

Dekobrisme

French author Maurice Dekobra was one of the world's best-selling novelists between the wars. He made a lot of money and spent much of it on travel. His mid-1930s visit to China led to a number of books including a novel about Macao. *Macao, l'enfer du jeu (Macao, Gambling Hell)* was not Dekobra's most widely read or praised novel, though it is generally well crafted and a good read. However, in 1939, a year after publication, it was adapted as a film.[275] As the Nazis occupied Paris that film, which had been completed but was yet to be released in cinemas, became controversial. The controversy was more due to one of its stars than its content. Bizarrely this led to a reshoot, meaning that we have two movie versions of *Macao, l'enfer du jeu* – the original 1939 movie and a later 1942 substantial reshoot.

Dekobra, his interactions with China that saw him publicly spat with well-known literary figures of the day including the writers Lin Yutang and Lu Xun, as well as the controversies around the movie version of *Macao, l'enfer du jeu*, make it well worthwhile retelling his trip.

*

Maurice Dekobra was born Ernest-Maurice Tessier in 1885. He was trilingual in French, German, and English and began working as a journalist in Paris at 19. In World War One his English-language skills meant he was attached as a liaison officer with troops of the British Indian Army fighting in France. Later, in 1917 when America entered the war, he was transferred to become a liaison officer attached to the US Army. Tessier had first been published shortly before World War One, but his literary star really began to rise in 1920s France. He adopted the pen name Dekobra, derived from "*deux* (or two) cobras". Later he even more imaginatively claimed that he was inspired to adopt the *nom-de-plume* after watching a snake charmer in Morocco. His novels often involved travel – a lifetime passion of his – and all have a strong sense of place. He started out largely writing about areas of his native Paris and then, when

275 Maurice Dekobra, *Macao, l'enfer du jeu*, (Paris: Baudinière, 1938). Sometimes published as *Macao, enfer du jeu*. There is no English-language translation I am aware of.

his funds allowed, began to travel extensively. This lifestyle accelerated after 1925 and the success of his internationally bestselling novel *La Madone des Sleepings*.[276]

In the 1930s Dekobra was credited with being the inventor of a new type of fiction, the so-called "cosmopolitan novel", an emerging genre he combined with his own sense of what in France was called *l'exotique de charme* (a sense of exotic charm). Then he also mixed in elements of travel journalism (he was a great admirer of Mark Twain), often incorporating his own personal wanderlust, to lend his novels an added sense of authenticity.[277] In their paper *Imagining Adventure in Middlebrow Fiction: Cosmopolitan Novels by Maurice Dekobra and Johan Fabricius*, the Dutch academics Pieter Verstraeten & Karen Van Hove note that 'Dekobra's books, however, are cosmopolitan in yet another sense. Their main characters are cast as members of a high society that is depicted as profoundly international.'[278] In France the term *dekobrisme* was coined, inspired by his fictional style, to indicate such cosmopolitan, internationally centred novels; *Macao, l'enfer du jeu* would conform to his, by then tried and tested, style.

In photographs Dekobra always seems to have a quizzical, enquiring look about him. And he wanted to go everywhere and see everything. In the early 1930s, successful and flush with royalties from *La Madone des Sleepings*, he decided to visit Asia and write about the East, China, and Macao. At the time he was reported to be the highest-paid writer in the world, earning over a million and a half French francs a year on his translation rights alone.[279] And so he began to journey eastwards, first class with the Messageries-Maritimes line from Marseille. Fired up by his relationships in the war he visited India, then moved on further east to Japan and finally China.

276 *La Madone des Sleepings*, (Paris: Librairie Baudinière, 1925). Published in English as *The Madonna of the Sleeping Cars*, (New York: Dell, 1927)

277 Dekobra cites his admiration for Twain in 'My Debt to Books', *Books Abroad*, Summer, 1938, Vol. 12, No. 3 (Summer, 1938), pp. 292-296.

278 'Imagining Adventure in Middlebrow Fiction: Cosmopolitan Novels by Maurice Dekobra and Johan Fabricius', Pieter Verstraeten & Karen Van Hove, *RELIEF* 9 (1), 2015. Fabricius (1899-1981) was a Dutch author who combined journalism with travel writing. He was born in Java, Dutch East Indies, and though he moved to Holland at age fourteen he returned regularly to the region all his life.

279 *The Pittsburgh Press*, October 3, 1935, p.2.

A film poster for Macao l'enfer du jeu

Chinese Girls on Toast

Dekobra sojourned in Shanghai from November 1933. While there he engaged in an amusing "spat" in the pages of *The China Critic*, a Chinese-owned and edited English-language weekly newspaper in the city. The urbane writer, humourist (and many more things besides) Lin Yutang wrote an open letter to Dekobra in December 1933. He recalls a meal they had enjoyed on the International Settlement's Foochow Road. He intimates that Dekobra is in some trouble with the Shanghailander community for praising the beauty of Chinese women and the quality of Chinese cuisine simultaneously – something, Lin asserts, no foreigner in Shanghai would ever do! Lin suggests that a certain "Miss Pan" has organised a boycott against Dekobra in Peking claiming that the French writer must have meant these comments in sarcastic jest. Lin's short *feuilleton* is joking that foreigners never said good things about China or its people. Lin is also mocking the fads among Chinese women for European and American ideals of beauty.

> 'What with all this white superiority, and what with nudist pictures and Mae West and Greta Garbo, the Chinese college girls are all but dying to have blonde curly hair and blue eyes. It never occurs to Miss Pan that a Chinese girl with straight black hair and slim willowy figure could bewitch a European.'[280]

Dekobra, playing along, responded to Lin in the subsequent issue of *The China Critic*, writing a letter entitled *Chinese Girls on Toast.* He accuses Lin of fabricating the angry, boycott-leading (and probably fictional) Miss Pan and declares that he will continue to appreciate the beauty of Chinese women whatever their opinions of him. Dekobra declares himself 'a friend of China' but that,

> 'Let us advise them [Chinese women] not to dye their hair! The world is crowded with ten cent dolls, with platinum blondes turned out at the rate of 1,200 a day like Mr Ford's car… Chinese ladies need not change their colour neither of their eyes nor of their hair to win their battles on the field of love.'[281]

Gaining some column inches with some throwaway remarks in the European and American media Dekobra suggested that Chinese men

280 Lin Yutang, 'An Open Letter to M Dekobra', *The China Critic*, Vol. V1, No. 51, December 21, 1933, pp.1237-1238.
281 Maurice Dekobra, 'Chinese Girls on Toast', *The China Critic*, Vol. VII No. 8, January 18, 1934, p.69.

needed to show more devotion to their women, who he called 'attractive panthers', 'full of fighting spirit, quick at repartee and very ready to challenge their menfolk.' He also commented that Chinese men find it undignified to show jealousy, though 'jealousy is necessary to true love.'[282]

Following the back-and-forth banter between Lin Yutang and Dekobra on the Frenchman's appreciation of Chinese female beauty and cuisine, was no lesser a figure than the writer Lu Xun who also decided to weigh in. While appreciating that any anger over Dekobra's comments in China was akin to a storm in a teacup, Lu Xun did take issue with the idea of the travelling novelist and by extension the fashion for *dekobrisme*.

> 'Nowadays, foreign writers come to China almost every year. As soon as they arrive, they invariably stir up some trouble. First it was Bernard Shaw, then Dekobra.'[283]

Lu Xun complains about stereotypical representations of non-western locations in foreign movies and the depictions of foreign women and sex (his views on the movie version of *Macao, l'enfer du jeu* would undoubtedly have been highly negative).[284] He concludes that foreign literature is suffering the same malaise, relying on colonial narratives and pejorative representations,

> '...turning to the grotesque and the erotic to satisfy their customers – this is how travel adventures came about...Yet if you were to ask them bluntly about the places they visited, they would simply laugh it off as a joke. They actually don't know these places and have no need to. Dekobra is simply one of these people.'

282 'Jealousy Held Vital to Love', *The Daily Reporter* (Greenfield, Indiana), August 29, 1934, p.2.

283 Lu Xun, 'The Glory to Come', first published in *Shen Bao*, January 11, 1934, under the pseudonym Zhang Chenglu. Contained in Lu Xun, *Jottings Under Lamplight*, (Cambridge, Massachusetts: Harvard University Press, 2017), pp.278-279. This translation by Eileen J Cheng. Shaw had visited in 1933.

284 Sadly Lu Xun died in 1936 and so never got to read *Macao, l'enfer du jeu* or see the movie adaptation.

So, bearing Lu Xun's criticisms in mind, let's turn to *Macao, l'enfer du jeu...*

*

Dekobra developed something of a China fixation in the mid-1930s writing two books involving the country – the oddly titled *Confucius en pull-over: Ou le Beau Voyage en Chine* (1934), an account of his travels East, and a novel *Madame Joli-Supplice* (1934), translated into English as *His Chinese Concubine.*[285] In the latter a Shanghai man, Ho Chung, marries a naïve French shopgirl while in Paris. Returning to Shanghai's French Concession he confesses he is actually a communist sympathiser from a wealthy family, and also that he has a Chinese fiancée, chosen by his father, waiting for him. It's a novel of social manners, cultural confusions, some cheap gags around Chinese names, and a lot of stereotypes.

Madame Joli-Supplice is, to be fair, not a great novel by any standards, but it does betray a knowledge of Shanghai – the Little Club, the Del Monte, the Great Eastern Hotel, the Paramount ballroom, the streets of Frenchtown. It all feels a little rushed and it has been suggested that Dekobra, always hyper-aware of publishing and audience trends, was keen to publish an Asian-set novel given the recent success of André Malraux's *La Condition Humaine (Man's Fate)* which had found great success upon publication in 1933 and won the prestigious Prix Goncourt for that year.[286]

285 *Confucius en pull-over ou le beau voyage en chine*, (Paris: Editions Baudinière, 1934); *Madame Joli-Supplice*, (Paris: Editions Baudinière, 1935); *His Chinese Concubine* (translated by Neal Wainwright), (London: T Werner Laurie, 1935). Those seeking evidence that Graham Greene was influenced by Dekobra may like to note that in Greene's 1936 novel *A Gun for Sale* he refers to Dekobra's *His Chinese Concubine* published in English translation the previous year.

286 To my knowledge Malraux wrote nothing specific about Macao. However, he did visit with his wife Clara (née Goldschmidt) in 1925 as a break from searching out a Hong Kong printer for *L'Indochine*, his newspaper that championed Vietnamese independence. Malraux's biographer, the French journalist and historian Jean Lacouture wrote: 'They discovered the ambiguous charms of Macao, melting into the enormous crowds – followed the whole time by diligent little spies (in the pay of the French), who became less and less discreet as time went on and who, in the end, actually offered their services as guides.' They soon left Macao and sailed back to Saigon. Jean Lacouture, *André Malraux*, (London: Andre Deutsch, 1975), p.104.

Then Dekobra wrote *Macao, l'enfer du jeu* and a French film studio decided to adapt it as a movie.

A Tale of Two Movies

The Austrian-American director, screenwriter, actor, and producer Erich von Stroheim had become a star in the silent era. His career was transitioning successfully into the talkies though repeated clashes with Hollywood studio bosses over budget and workers' rights meant he became effectively blacklisted – a little too much trouble, a little too left-wing. Being offered no decent quality films to either act in or direct in Hollywood he had become a well-respected character actor in French cinema. The French film studio Demofilm hired von Stroheim to act in, write and direct a movie – *La Dame blanche* – but it was a difficult development process and Demofilm cancelled the production. Even after appearing in a couple of films solely as an actor von Stroheim still owed Demofilm money from *La Dame blanche*. Demofilm suggested that if he appeared in their latest project, an adaptation of Dekobra's *Macao, L'enfer du jeu* they would wipe the debt clean. Von Stroheim agreed.[287]

Erich von Stroheim as arms dealer Werner von Krall

287 *Macao L'enfer du jeu, (Gambling Hell),* 1939, Demo Films (later released on DVD by Gaumont France).

To paraphrase Dekobra's plot: the city of Canton has been attacked by Japan and is at war. An arms-dealing adventurer who captains his own ship, Krall (played by von Stroheim), rescues a dancer Mireille (Mireille Balin) from a firing squad. She, trapped in bombed Canton and dressed like she is about to enter a Paris nightclub, is accused of espionage. Together they travel to Macao (Mireille would prefer Marseille but settles for Macao), by now a wartime centre of gambling, smuggling, and intrigue. Their aim is to obtain a cache of weapons from a local underworld kingpin (Sessue Hayakawa) and owner of the Eldorado casino. There is a subplot where the casino boss's Eurasian daughter is shown enthralled to a Frenchman who is subsequently beaten up and thrown in a river. Krall rescues him and Mireille cares for him. The casino boss will not sell Krall the weapons except for cash.

Mireille Balin

Von Stroheim plays the international arms dealer well, with his rather raffish band of shipmates alongside. Hayakawa transitions from a gentle father to a mob boss effortlessly and Balin is a good "China Coaster" – perhaps not Dietrich in *Shanghai Express* (see Chapter 13 on *Josef von Sternberg's Fantastical Macao of the Mind*) but pretty good with her lost, wandering, out of work yet looking a million dollars look.[288]

288 Like Dietrich, Balin had played wandering "coaster" roles before. As Dietrich had begun to create her Shanghai Lil in *Morocco* (1930) with Gary Cooper so Balin had

Mireille Balin and Sessue Hayakawa

Sessue Hayakawa runs the Eldorado which has a rather elaborate early form of CCTV that neatly shows the various gaming tables. The Eldorado is a precursor to Josef von Sternberg's Mother Gin Sling's in his 1941 movie *The Shanghai Gesture*. Both are quite similar to actual venues in Macao in the 1930s. The English artist and aristocrat Francis Rose who sojourned in China and visited the Portuguese colony wrote 'In Macao gambling houses the balconies of each floor were for different classes: there were floors for drunken sailors and toughs of all nations, where they could bring their prostitutes and pimps, of which this town had a fantastic number. There were balconies above with separate gilded cubicles called private rooms for the very rich. The carved open-work partitions made them look like filigree opera boxes or cages of exotic birds. Tables and chairs filled these carpeted spaces and the occupants could lean over the velvet covered rails to watch what was happening below, shout their bets and lower gilded baskets. The bets went according to the floor: from the top stages thousands of pounds might drop while only silver and "quids" were likely to fall from the lower balconies. I remember sending down a thousand pounds and a Chinese warlord next door to me lowered five thousand while a crowd of prostitutes were

been to the Algiers casbah in the hit French movie *Pépé le Moko* (1937) with Jean Gabin – both locations that could easily be Dekobra territory.

fighting and screaming over ten shillings. There was a different entrance to each floor from the street.'[289]

*

Director Jean Delannoy began shooting *Macao, L'enfer du jeu* in 1939, shortly before the fall of France to the Nazis. The sets were constructed at Victorine Studios in Nice by the Russian émigré production designer and art director (as well as an accomplished watercolourist) Serge Piménoff with cinematography by Nicholas Hayer. There, on the Riviera, they recreated Macao's casinos and streets fantastically, complete with the louche mix of gamblers, adventurers, gun runners, and dope smugglers that populated them. Chinese and Indochinese workers in France were recruited in Paris and sent by train to Nice to work as extras on the movie. The scenes aboard the boat, supposedly in Macao, were also shot on the Riviera aboard a boat mounted on a scaffold in a swamp. The noise of frogs was ridiculously loud. Dynamite was exploded every so often to shock the frogs into silence so they could film. It was a major production with a script by the journalist Pierre-Gilles Veber and playwright Roger Vitrac accompanied by music from the composer Georges Auric (one of *Les Six,* a group of artists associated with Jean Cocteau and Erik Satie).

Now two versions of the film exist – the first, pre-war version filmed in 1939 and 1940, starred Erich von Stroheim as Krall. Von Stroheim, from a Viennese Jewish family, had dodged military service and emigrated to America in 1909. He was an outspoken opponent of Nazism and the scenes (a good percentage of the movie) in which he appeared were redacted after the Nazi Occupation and reshot, at Cité Elgé (aka the Studios des Buttes-Chaumont) in Paris. The actor Pierre Renoir (son of the painter, older brother of the film director, both called Jean) was cast to replace von Stroheim. This was particularly galling to the Austrian actor as he had once been close to the director Jean Renoir, starring in his film *Le Grande Illusion*

Pierre Renoir, 1943

289 Francis Rose, *Saying Life: The Memoirs of Sir Francis Rose*, (London: Cassell, 1961), p. 270.

(1937) as a German World War One flying ace (despite von Stroheim apparently having forgotten most of his German language).[290]

The reshoot meant recalling the Parisian starlet of the day Mireille Balin and Sessue Hayakawa. The Pierre Renoir version was released in France in 1942 during the Occupation and then, in 1945 after Libération, the original von Stroheim version was eventually released.

A Macao casino as imagined by the Victorine Studios in Nice

That the film ever got released – even reshot – is amazing. It got some international screenings – as *Gambling Hell* in English (and, for reasons not immediately apparent, *Mask of Korea* in some markets). While von Stroheim was the major problem for the Nazi administration in Paris and their Vichy collaborationist allies, it was also the case that they could have objected on many other grounds. Pierre-Gilles Veber was a well-known Leftist journalist and Jewish, Roger Vitrac had been prominent in the French surrealist movement (never a favourite art form of the Nazis), while Georges Auric was a well-known fellow-traveller of the French Communist Party. Sessue Hayakawa had been born in Japan, become a major Asian star in the early years of Hollywood and was, by the 1930s, working all over Europe as well. He found himself trapped in France by the Nazi invasion, unable to work, forced to try and make a living selling his watercolour paintings while also joining the French resistance.

290 Jean Renoir, *My Life and My Films,* (London: Collins, 1974).

Just about the only person involved with clean hands – as far as the Germans were concerned – was Mireille Balin, considered one of the major stars of France's 1930s cinema. She was later discredited by her fraternization with the Nazis and her romantic involvement with a Wehrmacht officer (at the end of war she was imprisoned for a time for collaboration and then "retired" in 1947).

Pierre Renoir also had an extraordinary wartime career. Approximately the same age as von Stroheim he agreed to replace him knowing von Stroheim was being forced out for being a Jewish anti-Nazi. Several years later in 1945 he was cast at short notice in Marcel Carné's *Les Enfants du Paradis* replacing Robert Le Vigan, a vocal fascist and Nazi collaborator who had to go swiftly into hiding upon the Liberation.[291]

The Portuguese film historian and former director of the Cinemateca Portuguesa (Portuguese Film Archives) in Lisbon, Luís de Pina, looked at representations of Portugal's empire (Malacca, São Tomé, and especially Macao, on film in the 1930s in his essay *Macau: Em Busca do Retrato Perdido* (*Macau: In Search of the Lost Portrait)*. De Pina notes that *Macao, L'enfer du jeu*, which was entitled *Labaredas* (*Flames)* in Portuguese, did not get a release in Portugal until 1947 and the fact that the setting was Macao was strangely not really mentioned in the press. De Pina interviewed Alberto Armando Pereira of Aliança Filmes, the distribution company, who 'hinted that censorship had cut from the full-length film the most characteristic scenes of the Portuguese presence in the colony.' De Pina concludes that it was simply impossible in Salazar's Portugal to show a film that portrayed a Portuguese colony in a bad light – even if by a French author and film studio describing fictional events from over a decade before.[292]

291 Le Vigan was soon caught and sentenced to ten years forced labour in 1946. Released on parole after three years he fled to fascist Spain, and from there to Argentina where he reportedly died in poverty in 1972. Strangely Pierre Renoir was not considered a collaborator.

292 From Luís de Pina, *Macau: Em busca do retrato perdido*, in ANDRADE, José Navarro de, coord., "Macau – Hong Kong", (Lisbon: Catálogo, Cinemateca Portuguesa, 1991), pp.7-21. Incidentally, de Pina notes that when Josef von Sternberg/Nicholas Ray's *Macao* (1951) came out several years later the Portuguese censors objected, banned it and the film was not shown officially in Portugal until 1982. Dekobra was used to censorship by this point – the 1937 French movie adaptation by Max Ophüls of his Japan-set novel *Yoshiwara* (he had visited Japan on the same trip as China) was banned

A Macao street as imagined by the Victorine Studios

*

After returning from his trip to the Far East the worsening situation in France and Europe meant Dekobra decided to relocate to the United States in 1939. He remained there until the end of the war. Asia didn't leave him completely though and he published his novel *Lune de Miel à Shanghai (Shanghai Honeymoon)* in 1943, a rather lurid for the times tale set in 1930s Shanghai.[293] It isn't one of Dekobra's best novels, but it does evoke the 1930s well and is an excellent portrait of Shanghai's varied international community and nightclub scene of the time. The Topaze Nightclub featured in the book is probably based on Dekobra's own experiences in Shanghai, and likely on Sir Victor Sassoon's Ciro's nightclub. It's a reasonably light novel that becomes progressively darker and ends with the Japanese invasion of the International Settlement. Claudette is born and raised in French Indochina, the beautiful daughter of a French mother and an American father. After the death of the latter, her mother takes her to Shanghai, hoping to find there a rich husband for

in Japan for unflattering depictions of the country's army general staff and prostitution in Tokyo. Sessue Hayakawa (and the Paris-based Japanese actress Michiko Tanaka) also starred in that movie.

293 *Lune de Miel à Shanghai,* (Paris: Baudinière, 1943); *Shanghai Honeymoon,* (London: T Werner & Laurie, 1946).

the girl. Her suitors include sybaritic Italians and supposedly aristocratic Russians before she spends some time in a Japanese jail.[294]

Returning to France in 1946, Dekobra largely ditched his trademark mix of cosmopolitanism, exotic charm, and travel journalism to write a series of whodunnits, which were very successful. His earlier works continued to sell well and fund his lifestyle. He was translated into 32 languages. Dekobra continued writing until the early 1960s and died in Paris in 1973 at 88 years of age.

294 Though not identical, readers of 1940s foreign literature set in Shanghai will notice the similarities between *Shanghai Honeymoon* and Emily Hahn's slightly later novel *Miss Jill,* (New York: Doubleday, 1947).

Stanley's War

The Wartime Adventures of Stanley Ho Hung-sun (1941-1945)

A young Stanley Ho

...Macao, the streets were crowded with pedestrians, a sea of humanity. Everyone walked. There was no longer any gasoline for buses. People cobbled together radio receiving equipment...
– Caroline Petit, *Deep Night: A Novel* (2008)

'Macao was paradise during the war.'
– Stanley Ho

Becoming the King of Macao

When Stanley Ho Hung-sun, the man who made Macao a global gambling mecca, died aged 98 years old in May 2020 he was reportedly worth US$14.9 billion.[295] Known as Macao's "King of Gambling", the biggest of Macao's *du wang*, or "gambling tycoons", Ho was the owner of 19 casinos, the founder and chairman of the ubiquitous conglomerate *Sociedade de Turismo e Diversões de Macau* (STDM, founded in 1962), and had held a government-granted monopoly on gambling in Macao for 40 years, having taken over the monopoly after the death of Macao's former major *du wang*, Foo Tak-yam. Through his publicly listed company Shun Tak Holdings, founded in 1972, Stanley Ho had interests in everything from the Hong Kong-Macao ferry service to local aviation, banks, and property investments. At one time he supposedly employed fully one-fourth of Macao's entire workforce. He had made overseas investments in mainland China and Hong Kong, as well as back in Portugal, and in the former Portuguese colonies of Mozambique and East Timor. Other investment locations Ho dabbled in included Vietnam, Indonesia, the Philippines, and North Korea where, in 1999, he opened a casino in Pyongyang.[296]

As well as his outsized influence over affairs in Macao, his business interests made Stanley Ho an important figure in Hong Kong and mainland China, and he was for a time a member of the Standing Committee of the Chinese People's Political Consultative Conference (CPPCC). He was arguably the most influential businessman in East Asia in the latter half of the twentieth century and the start of the twenty-first. He was rarely out of the newspapers.

But before Stanley Ho made Macao, he had to make himself.

*

295 'Obituary: Macau Casino Tycoon Stanley Ho Dies Aged 98', *Asia Times*, May 26, 2020.

296 Ho's Casino Pyongyang was opened in the basement of the Yanggakdo International Hotel on the Taedong River's Yanggak Island. It was a small venture by Macao standards: two blackjack tables, one for Baccarat, and a table for the Chinese game of luck Big/Small (akin to roulette). All the staff were foreign, either from the Chinese mainland or Macao. It has reputedly never turned a profit.

Born in Hong Kong in 1921, Stanley Ho was the ninth of 13 children. Eurasian, he had mixed Chinese, Dutch-Jewish, and English ancestry. His grandfather was Ho Fook (1863-1926), the Eurasian brother of the merchant and Jardine Matheson comprador (or local agent) Robert Ho Tung (1862-1956), known as "the grand old man of Hong Kong". However Stanley's branch of the extended family clan hit hard times when his father Ho Sai Kwong (1886-1974) fled Hong Kong to Saigon following the collapse of his business (referred to delicately as a 'misguided share speculation') in the late 1920s. This left the family penniless.[297]

Ho studied at Queen's College, the oldest Government secondary school in Hong Kong, but did not excel academically. Still, he got a scholarship to Hong Kong University to study humanities though showed little book-learning promise there either. Mid-way through the course his studies were curtailed due to the Japanese invasion of Hong Kong.

After the attack on Pearl Harbor on December 7, 1941, Britain and America instantly declared war on Japan. The Imperial Japanese Army invaded Hong Kong where, despite fierce resistance, the city fell on Christmas Day. Ho had worked as an air-raid warden but hearing of the surrender threw away his uniform in fear of being executed as an enemy combatant as Hong Kong succumbed to Japanese domination.[298]

And Stanley Ho had an out. His great uncle, Sir Robert Ho Tung, though almost 80 years old, was living in Macao running an import-export firm profiting from the triangular trade between Macao, Hong Kong, and southern China.[299] He invited young Stanley, then barely 20 years old, to join him in the Portuguese colony. Ho was far from the only new arrival from fallen Hong Kong and Japanese-occupied southern China. British subjects, Chinese nationals, and many Eurasians who claimed Portuguese nationality were arriving too.

297 Rahul Jacob & Tom Mitchell, 'Stanley Ho, Macao Gambling Tycoon, 1921-2020', *Financial Times*, May 26, 2020.

298 Quoted in Stanley Ho's contribution to, Ed. Jill McGivering, *Macao Remembers*, (Hong Kong: Oxford University Press, 1999), p.105.

299 Robert Ho Tung lived at #3 Largo de Santo Agostinho, originally built in the 1850s as a home for Carolina Antonia da Cunha, the widow of a former Portuguese governor Pedro Alexandrino da Cunha. Ho Tung purchased the property in 1918. On his death in 1956 he bequeathed the house to the Macao government. The Biblioteca (Library) Sir Robert Ho Tung was officially opened on the premises in 1958.

Meanwhile in Kowloon the acting Portuguese consul in Hong Kong, Francisco "Frank" Soares, had made a significant decision. Soares had been born in Hong Kong in 1868. He was a keen horticulturalist and had been key to the development of the Kowloon suburb of Ho Man Tin in the 1920s as a "garden city". Shortly after the fall of Hong Kong, Soares began registering British subjects of Portuguese descent and providing them with certificates as "neutrals" allowing them to seek refuge in Macao as Portuguese citizens.[300] The Azores-born historian Jorge Forjaz has estimated that approximately 85 per cent of Hong Kong's Portuguese population fled to Macao while Soares's hastily issued visas may have saved 600 people from internment.[301]

Some from Hong Kong thought to perhaps spend the war in Macao and wait it all out, or at least wait and see if another Nederland Line Royal Dutch Mail steamship passed through (the traditional route back to Portugal from Macao).[302] And, if you were rich enough, you could sit out the duration in a decent hotel. Chinese, Portuguese, European Jewish refugees, and others spent much of the war years in Macao in cheap and invariably overcrowded lodging houses, small pensions, and hotels.[303] But the grand hotels of Macao were also accepting guests, if they could pay.

Those British and allied nationals arriving in Macao wealthy enough to afford a long stay in some style were disappointed to find that the luxury Hotel Bela Vista, off the Avenida da República, was off-limits. The Bela Vista was colonised almost entirely by German Nazi officials and their supporters mingling with their Japanese allies. The Bela Vista, and several nearby streets of commandeered houses became known as "Axis Alley", effectively German-controlled territory.

Consequently the Riviera Hotel, on the Praia Grande at the junction with the Avenida de Almeida Ribeiro, became occupied by wealthy, and often horribly snobbish, decamped British residents of Hong Kong. They

300 Soares moved the Portuguese Consulate from the Bank of East Asia Building on Des Voeux Road to his home at #2 Liberty Avenue in Ho Man Tin after the Christmas Day fall of Hong Kong.

301 Jorge Forjaz, *Famílias Macaenses* (1996), 2nd ed., V-489.

302 Royal Dutch Mail liners specialised in the route between Europe and the Dutch East Indies (Indonesia) often included a stop at Macao.

303 For more on the Jewish refugees who arrived in Macao from Europe or via Hong Kong or Shanghai, see Paul French, *Strangers on the Praia: A Tale of Refugees and Resistance in Wartime Macao*, (Hong Kong: Blacksmith Books, 2020).

jealously guarded the establishment's well-stocked kitchens and brought their own supplies of everything from tinned milk to boxes of chocolates. The British, to the fury of some other nationalities, dominated the Riviera bar's traditional daily "whisky hour" and didn't much care for the billiards tables that attracted many Portuguese guests.[304]

Still, the Riviera was a good location. The Avenida de Almeida Ribeiro was the centre of Portuguese retail life in the colony – with shops like the Agência Mercantil Limitada that stocked all manner of Portuguese goods from tinned food to sports equipment and traditional musical instruments, the Oriente Commercial bookstore, and the famous As Delícias patisserie with its popular 5pm high teas. But the English, used to their rather stodgier tastes being accommodated in Hong Kong, apparently insisted on 'plain' food, avoiding the hotel's menu. The Peking-sojourning English aesthete Harold Acton had dined at the Riviera a few years before the war and bemoaned the 'Portuguese dishes, rich and oily'.[305]

But the life of the Bela Vista or the Riviera was only for the privileged elite. For most the war would be a time of shortages, hunger, and impoverishment, despite finding sanctuary in Macao. However, for others it would be an opportunity. A half century later, in the 1990s, Ho told the historian Philip Snow, then researching a book about the fall of Hong Kong and the subsequent Japanese occupation: 'I made a lot of money out of the war.'[306]

Here's how he did it.

Macao's *Mercado Negro*

By the early 1940s, with most of China under Japanese control and Hong Kong occupied, Macao found itself in a unique position in the Asian theatre of war. Portugal had determinedly remained neutral, and so its

304 The Riviera's equivalent to the cocktail hour, or "Sundowners", popular in Hong Kong and Shanghai. Men invariably drank whisky-soda and women vermouth.

305 Harold Acton, *Memoirs of an Aesthete*, p.297.

306 Joe Studwell has this quote via Philip Snow. It is taken from Snow's original notes of an interview with Ho in 1995 while Snow was preparing a book on Hong Kong. Snow then shared these notes with Studwell for *Asian Godfathers: Money and Power in South East Asia*, (London: Profile Books, 2007), p.20. Philip Snow, *The Fall of Hong Kong: Britain, China, and the Japanese Occupation*, (New Haven, Connecticut: Yale University Press, 2003).

colonies were also deemed neutral territory. Macao was administered by the Portuguese Governor and Commander-in-Chief Gabriel Maurício Teixeira along, with Major Carlos da Silva Carvalho as his chief of staff, and the enigmatic Timorese Dr Pedro José Lobo, known by everyone simply as Dr Lobo, in charge of the key Economic Services Bureau.

However, the seas and ports immediately around Macao were controlled by Japan – across in French Indochina, from Hong Kong and southern China right up the Chinese coast to Shanghai and Tientsin. That meant Macao was forced to accept some form of cooperation with the Japanese in order to ensure food, fuel, and other supplies could enter the colony. Macao, with no worthwhile natural resources, limited land for agriculture, and sparse reserves of drinking water, would not last long in any blockade. For Teixeira, a young and rather handsome governor (he was only in his early forties when appointed in 1940), and Lobo, the war years were to be a delicate balancing act between preserving the colony's neutral integrity and avoiding overtly collaborating with the Japanese.

And if they got that balance wrong then they knew that they could lose the colony. In February 1942, Japanese troops invaded both Portuguese and Dutch Timor to oust the small and under-equipped combined British, Australian, and Free Dutch Forces occupying the territories. This sparked fears that Japan would move to occupy Macao next. They also knew that if they overly favoured the Japanese and then Britain and America won the war, let alone if Nationalist China defeated the Japanese, their reckoning would be harsh.

Inevitably with the sea lanes and traditional trading routes disrupted, wartime conditions meant very tough times in Macao. Food supplies were short, choice limited. The usually crowded stalls inside the pre-war Almirante Lacerda Market, housed in the three-storey Red Market building at the junction of Avenida Almirante Lacerda and Avenida Horta e Costa, were noticeably bare.[307] The stores along Rua Central near the Praia Grande and the Avenida de Almeida Ribeiro that specialised

307 The Red Market Building that housed the Almirante Lacerda Market is worthy of note. A three-storey art-deco building with a clock tower it is officially the Edifício do Mercado Vermelho or Mercado Almirante Lacerda. It was designed by the Macanese architect Júlio Alberto Fernandes Basto (1888-1936). It opened in 1936 and is so-named due to its distinctive red brickwork. It was originally closer to the docks (pre-landfill) and also surrounded by flower sellers. Basto also designed Macao's most overtly art-deco residence, Casa Skyline in Penha.

The Red Market after its completion in June 1936

in foreign imported goods were seriously denuded, and even the old Rua da Praia do Manduco (also called Hawker Street) had little for anyone to haggle over. At the popular and long-established (so old Chinnery had painted it several times) São Domingos Mercado (Saint Domingos Market) on the Travessa do Soriano, primarily a fish and shellfish market but which also sold fuel, supplies were strictly limited.

Similarly so at the Mercado Municipal on the Rua Da Praia Do Manduco and the Largo do Pagode do Bazar on the Rua de Cinco de Outubro and Rua do Guimarces. The latter was a traditionally more itinerant and ad-hoc market, now equally low on stock and relegated to being effectively a flea market as desperate people and refugees sold their few possessions. People wandered from *mercado* to *mercado*, bags at the ready, desperately hoping for new supplies to arrive.

Fuel stocks (primarily kerosene) ran particularly low, inflation became rampant, and the colony had to deal with the rapidly growing number of Chinese and European refugees arriving. Macao's population swelled from approximately 158,000 people before the war to half a million within a few years. The cold winter of 1942-43 was particularly severe with a record death rate.[308] Indeed 1942-43 was Macao's coldest winter on record. A poor rice crop in Kwangtung, worsened by the Japanese army destroying much of it before it could be harvested, accentuated hunger and restricted supplies to Macao. A boat sent by the Governor to French-controlled Kwangchowan for rice, the tramp steamer *Wing Wah*, was accidentally sunk by an American submarine mistaking it for a

308 As well as the camps established by the authorities many refugees were housed in other communal lodgings such as the Albergue da Santa Casa da Misericórdia on Calçada da Igreja de São Lázaro, formerly known as the "Old Ladies House" when it was a home for elderly spinsters and widows, and later known during the war as "the shelter of the poor".

Japanese vessel, while the Japanese Navy chased Macao-registered fishing boats back into the harbour before they could get out to sea and catch anything.

To prevent a repeat of this tragedy, and to make up the short falls, smuggling, and the *mercado negro*, the black market, flourished. To circumvent the problem of black markets being technically illegal Dr Lobo effectively legitimised a secondary and parallel black market by creating the Companhia Cooperativa de Macau (the Macau Co-operative Company, CCM) tasked with going out and sourcing whatever the colony needed from wherever, and largely however, it could. Lobo, a small framed bespectacled man always well dressed in linen suits, white shorts and ties, his black hair pomaded back on his high forehead had darting eyes, a quick intelligence, and, most importantly, a superb grasp of Macao's wartime balancing act. He asked Sir Robert Ho Tung if there was someone he could trust to work as the company secretary. Sir Robert recommended his keen young great-nephew Stanley, newly arrived in the colony.

The CCM was arguably the most important institution in Macao during the war. It was the organization that kept the colony fed. Its main role was to keep Macao economically alive, able to feed itself, and function as a vehicle for balancing the delicate relationship with the Japanese without the political hierarchy, notably Lisbon's appointed Governor Gabriel Teixeira, becoming involved. It was decided from the start that Teixeira could have little formal contact with the Japanese authorities in order not to jeopardise Portuguese neutrality.[309] Consequently, the necessary structure of the CCM and the requirement not to antagonise the Japanese were to lead to a lifetime of accusations that Stanley Ho had collaborated with the Japanese in World War Two.

The problem was that while CCM was one-third owned by Dr Lobo himself, another third owned by several of Macao's wealthiest Portuguese families, the final third was owned by the Imperial Japanese Army who had things they wanted which were traded through Macao including wolfram, candlenut oil as a machine lubricant and fibrous matting for army and navy uniforms. The structure of CCM had been a non-negotiable and later the Japanese involvement did not go unnoticed. The

309 In case of an invasion by Japan Teixeira had only an estimated 400 army and navy men at his disposal to resist any incursion by the Japanese.

primary intelligence agency of the United States in Asia during World War Two, the Office of Strategic Services (OSS), noted in a report that Stanley Ho was, 'a member of a Japanese military advisory board' and 'attached to a Japanese naval department' while working for CCM.[310]

Stanley Ho maintained that he had known the setup when he joined, but that the Portuguese authorities in Macao (by which he most probably meant Dr Lobo rather than a direct order from anyone in Lisbon) told him to work with the Japanese at CCM, and that without the food CCM sourced Macao would have starved. In an interview with Simon Holberton of the *Financial Times* over half a century later, Ho said: 'I was in charge of a barter system, helping the Macao government to exchange machinery and equipment with the Japanese, in exchange for rice, sugar, beans. I was a semi-government official then. I was the middleman.'[311] A rather bland, but still technically accurate statement. As Secretary of the CCM, Ho was authorized by Lobo to keep Macao fed by bartering anything the island had to offer in return for essential supplies. This barter system apparently involved swapping cash, goods or spare parts for machinery, food, and oil.[312]

Shapeshifting in the South China Seas

This was no office job, no mundane bureaucratic form filling, or dreary paper pushing task. In his memoirs, Ho recalled that his first and most urgent task was linguistic, to learn both Portuguese and Japanese because his job was to barter between the two.[313] Secondly, he needed to be able to distinguish from a distance between pirate and Japanese ships as he was regularly travelling by boat in the treacherous waters around Macao. Japanese naval vessels and submarines as well as various pirates, including ones loyal to the Japanese, to Nationalist China, or to nobody but themselves (allegiances which regularly switched with circumstances and mood) all plied the surrounding waters.

310 João FO Botas, 'Macau 1937-1945: Living on the Edge: Economic Management Over Military Defences', in Ed. Geoffrey Gunn, *Wartime Macau: Under the Japanese Shadow*, (Hong Kong: Hong Kong University Press, 2017), p.59.

311 *Financial Times*, May 20/21, 1995.

312 Liu Yisong, *A Full Biography of Macau Casino King Stanley Ho,* (Beijing: Huazhong University of Science and Technology, 2013), p.33.

313 McGivering, *Macao Remembers*, p.105.

Ho was transporting payment in the form of cash, or machine parts, and receiving valuable goods he had then to get back to Macao intact. The job involved playing off all sides: the Portuguese authorities, the Japanese military, rogue triad and pirate gangs, and the various factions of China – Free China guerrillas as well as those sympathetic to Wang Jing-wei's puppet pro-Japanese (and mostly purely self-interested) regime. One, probably apocryphal, post-war rumour said that Ho always sailed with five flags – Portuguese, Japanese, Nationalist Chinese, French Indochinese....and a skull and crossbones![314]

This seaborne "shapeshifting", as it has been termed, was not uncommon in World War Two. Everyone did it when they could. The British, Vichy French, Free French, Germans, and Japanese all ran Blockade Runners during the war (merchant vessels under assumed flags and surreptitiously carrying contraband goods, war matériel, or personnel) in both European and Asian waters, often sailing as far as from Bordeaux in France to the Dutch East Indies or Japan. The British ran sophisticated shapeshifting smuggling fleets out of the Channel Islands, Gibraltar, Tangier and Malta (among other locations), moving contraband cigarettes, as well as radios, explosives, and spies, to key locations. They sailed under false flags, flags of neutral nations (mostly Spain) or, as Stanley Ho perhaps did in the waters around Macao, ran up whichever flag was most convenient and likely to allow them to avoid confrontation and gain safe passage.[315]

There is a significant element of derring-do to Stanley Ho's life in wartime Macao. Sailing rice, vegetables, beans, flour, sugar and other supplies between French Indochina and Macao, along the southern Chinese coast and around Japanese-occupied Hainan Island, meant avoiding pirate gangs who would take your gold on the outbound voyage and then your supplies on the inbound. Nationalist Chinese or pro-Communist guerrillas were equally keen to secure the goods or cash for themselves, and many saw the CCM's activities as collaboration with the

314 This is probably an apocryphal story – the skull and crossbones is more legend than South China Seas reality. The novelist Daniel Carney has his Macao-based smuggler Nicolai, a White Russian émigré known as the "Snake Boat Man", sail with multiple flags and when nearing the Inner Harbour hoist the Portuguese flag. Daniel Carney, *Macau* (London: Corgi, 1984), p.183.

315 There is a good discussion of "shapeshifter" blockade runners in the waters between Spain, Portugal, Gibraltar and Tangier in Damien Lewis, *Agent Josephine: American Beauty, French Hero, British Spy,* (London: PublicAffairs, 2022).

enemy and an instant death sentence. Japanese naval vessels were known to take pot shots at all manner of civilian craft while, later in the war, according to the historian of wartime Macao, Geoffrey Gunn, American and British submarines were liable to sink any vessels they thought were dealing with the Japanese while the United States Air Force took control of the skies above and could easily mistake Ho for any number of other things.[316]

Dr Lobo's legitimised smuggling was also operating in competition with local freelancers from both Macao and southern China. In 1943 in an attempt to tackle rampant inflation Governor Teixeira banned the use of Chinese money and insisted only specie issued by Portugal's overseas Banco Nacional Ultramarino (BNU) would be legal tender to crack down on smuggling and the spread of the black market.[317]

Ho does seem to have branched out beyond the not-so-strict confines of Dr Lobo's remit. According to the author Joe Studwell, who conducted a range of in-depth interviews with Ho family associates for his book *Asian Godfathers*, towards the end of the war, in 1944, Ho opened a kerosene factory that supplied the colony when fuel supplies were running perilously low. His kerosene refining business (smuggling if you like) took oil he obtained from supplies in French Indochina and the Japanese-controlled oil refineries in Sumatra in the Dutch East Indies and resold them back in Macao at a considerable mark-up. The business earned him the nickname "The Kerosene King".[318] Those kerosene shipments would bring in other supplies to the colony – luxuries such as British and American cigarettes along with all manner of booze, again all sold on at significant mark-ups.

The fuel situation went from bad to worse in January 1945 when the United States claimed that neutral Macao was drawing up plans to sell aviation fuel to Japan. Aircraft from the carrier *USS Enterprise* bombed and strafed the hangar of the Macao Naval Aviation Centre, targeting the fuel dump, which exploded, killing five civilians, and destroying the

316 Gunn, *Wartime Macao*, p.86.

317 BNU was established in Lisbon in 1864 with branches throughout Portugal's colonial possessions opening its first Macao branch in 1902 with an impressive building on the Avenida Almeida Ribeiro (where the building and the bank's headquarters remain today).

318 Joe Studwell, *Asian Godfathers*, p.19.

Macao Maritime Museum.[319] The attack, wiped out Macao's only other source of kerosene, inadvertently making Ho the sole supplier – essential to the continued functioning of Macao and now extremely rich.

Then in February 1945 and again in June that year further American Air Force raids hit strategic targets including the Porto Exterior and the Dona Maria II Fort causing still more fuel shortages.[320] But in August 1945 Japan surrendered unconditionally, Hong Kong was liberated, and Macao returned to unfettered Portuguese control.[321] Throughout this tense period Stanley Ho's kerosene had literally kept the lights on and the wheels turning in Macao.

'Macao was paradise during the War'

By the end of World War Two young Ho had made four vital gains. Firstly, he cemented a lifelong relationship with Dr Lobo, Macao's unofficial boss who would prove most useful to Stanley as he expanded his range of legitimate and other business interests post-war. Secondly, in 1942, he married Clementina Leitão, the daughter of a wealthy Portuguese family in Macao, which afforded him additional protections, privileges, and social position. She was said to have helped him with mastering the Portuguese language. The couple would have four children. Clementina was often referred to in the newspapers as the most beautiful woman in Macao and her father, Dr Leitão, a lawyer, and notary public was one of the richest and most influential men in the colony. Third, Ho

Clementina Leitão

319 The Naval Aviation Centre had been opened in 1927 with a small contingent of Portuguese air force planes participating in anti-piracy works in the South China Sea. The Centre officially closed in 1933 but was reopened for a time during the war. The original Macao Maritime Museum was established by Admiral Artur Leonel Barbosa Carmona and was located in the Capitania do Porto.

320 The Dona Maria II Fort was built in 1852 and lies between the Guia and Mong-Há Fortresses.

321 Following the Japanese surrender, the Portuguese government protested and, in 1950, the United States paid US$20,255,952 compensation to Lisbon for the wartime bomb damage.

amassed a sizeable fortune and was a millionaire by the end of the war and still only 24-years-old. And fourth, he had established ongoing and profitable businesses in rice trading, kerosene supply, and construction.

Ho now had cash, position, family, and good friends in useful positions. He commented in his memoirs, 'Macao was paradise during the war'.[322] And it was true that Ho had, as they used to say, a very good war. And he was far from ready to relax and enjoy the peace. Within weeks of the Japanese surrender Ho was back in Hong Kong making strategic investments, such as buying a boat to restart the first post-war ferry service between the two colonies. He was all set to remake Macao and invest massively in post-war Hong Kong too.

The post-war Stanley Ho

In the immediate aftermath of the war Stanley Ho faced criticism that he had collaborated with the Japanese, particularly from some in Hong Kong government and business circles. The truth was that Macao's wartime neutrality was always subject to Japanese influence – especially after the fall of Hong Kong. And in 1943, when Tokyo demanded the installation of Japanese advisers to oversee Macao, something akin to a virtual Japanese protectorate was created on the island. So contact was unavoidable. Ho didn't see any embarrassment in this, it was the *realpolitik*

322 McGivering, *Macao Remembers*, p.105

of the Portuguese colony during the war. He even admitted to having given English lessons to Colonel Eisaku Sawa, a short, stocky, and highly manipulative former sub-chief of Japanese intelligence in Manchuria transferred to act as Japanese vice-consul to Macao, commander of the Japanese garrison, and (by far his most important wartime role) head of the *Kempeitai* military secret police in the colony.[323]

And while Ho's wartime activities were officially sanctioned by Dr Lobo (and by extension Governor Teixeira) others involved in similar schemes at the same time were more obviously criminals and collaborators. Wong Kong-kit and his wife were referred to as the "Bonnie and Clyde" of wartime Macao by the Diocesan priest, historian and Kristang creole language expert, Father Manuel Teixeira (no relation to the Governor).[324] The pair travelled around in two cars with eight bodyguards on the running boards. They ran pro-Tokyo espionage and rice price manipulation rackets backed by the Japanese. According to Father Teixeira they regularly assassinated rivals, engaging in machine gun fights on the streets near their heavily fortified (including a machine gun nest on the roof), sandbagged, and Japanese gendarme-protected HQ on the busy thoroughfare of Avenida Horta e Costa.[325] Wong Kong-kit's gang did try to "tax" Ho's rice importation through the CCM along with that of other smugglers such as the three contraband-running brothers Wong Cheong, Wong Kan, and Wong Sam as well as the rice merchant Fernando de Senna Fernandes (who was assassinated and several assassination attempts made on his two daughters). Wong Kong-kit at various times threatened not just Stanley Ho and other smugglers but also Dr Lobo and Macao's police commander Captain Rodrigues Ribeiro de Cunha. It was a dangerous time; the stakes were high.

Eventually the formal accusations in Hong Kong receded, though many still muttered behind Ho's back. The truth was that an element of collaboration had been practised by many of the major British and Chinese *hongs* (business conglomerates) during the war. Singling out

323 The presence of Sawa's *Kempeitai* contravened the neutrality regulations, but realistically what could the Macao authorities do?

324 Manuel Teixeira (1912-2003) was Portuguese but lived most his life in Macao between 1924 and 2001. Kristang is a creole language of mixed Portuguese and Malay spoken largely in the Malacca region and Singapore. It is classified by UNESCO as a "severely endangered" language with perhaps only 1,000 speakers remaining.

325 Philippe Pons, *Macao*, (London: Reaktion Books, 2004), p.121.

anyone in particular was likely to raise questions about the conduct of all during the occupation. Best not poke that rattlesnake for a reaction.

But still China's Nationalist government had questions, and many considered Dr Lobo and Ho, and CCM's wartime business transactions, treacherous and supportive of Japan's war on China. Chinese officials attempted to arrest Ho for collaboration but, according to his own account of the attempt, the Portuguese colonial police protected him (unlike the avowed gangster Wong Kong-kit who was arrested in Hong Kong, extradited back to Macao, and assassinated by Chinese Nationalists en route). By late 1945, Stanley Ho was too entrenched, too wired into the Hong Kong-Macao-southern China post-war recovery nexus for the Portuguese administration to hand him over to China or for China vociferously to demand he be delivered to them. By 1949, as Nationalist China lost the civil war to the communists and decamped for Taiwan, Ho was living well in Macao and flying around the region in his own private plane.[326]

The Lisboa Hotel and Casino, 1970s

And so Stanley Ho moved on to become Macao's post-war gambling king. His empire came to include the iconic Lisboa Hotel and Casino, the Hong Kong-listed Shun Tak corporation and the TurboJET subsidiary

326 A visiting American to Macao, Margaret Bunyard Allen, recalled being offered the use of Ho's plane to fly from Macao to Saigon in the summer of 1949. *San Angelo Evening Standard* (Texas), August 8, 1949, p.4.

running hydrofoil ferries between Macao, Hong Kong and throughout the Pearl River Delta. It seemed nothing was beyond Stanley's reach – STDM came to control the Macau Jockey Club and the local lottery. And it all began – the success and the scandal – with Macao's unique position in World War Two.

A Russian Painter on the Praia Grande

George Smirnoff
(1944)

George Smirnoff and his wife Nina Pleshakoff in Shanghai, 1937

'Smirnoff's work has left us with a collective memory of each individual house and tree, every street and alley in Macao during the period of the Second World War.'
– Ung Vai Meng, Director of the Museu de Arte de Macau (1999-2008)

Leaving Russia

Yuri Vitalievich Smirnoff, aka George Smirnoff, was born in October 1903 in the Siberian port city of Vladivostok – the very eastern end of the Empire where Tsarist Russia met the Pacific Ocean. After 1917, as the Bolshevik Revolution rolled rapidly across the vast country from its beginnings in St Petersburg, George Smirnoff, barely in his teens and with only his mother for company, joined the massive "White Russian" émigré exodus.

The exact number of Russians who escaped the Bolsheviks for lives in exile is unknown. The best guess is somewhere between 800,000 and two million. Many went north and left Russia through the Baltic States and Finland, eventually destined for Western Europe and perhaps on to America. Others reached the Ukrainian port of Odessa and the Black Sea where they boarded ships to Turkey and Constantinople (today's Istanbul) where a vibrant Russian exile community settled. The Smirnoffs, no doubt fortunately, already lived in the major port of the third route of exodus: Vladivostok. From here an estimated 250,000 men, women and children embarked on mostly rusty and barely seaworthy old boats to flee Russia. It was a chaotic embarkation on often dangerously overburdened craft. Some were bound for destinations in Japan or perhaps Japanese-controlled Korea, but most, including the Smirnoffs', made land either at the port of Seishin (now Chongjin in North Korea) or rounded the Korean peninsula and reached the Chinese port of Dairen. They then headed by train for Harbin in Manchuria.

Harbin was a significantly Russian town even before the Bolshevik Revolution. It housed the many Russians who worked on the Tsarist-controlled China Eastern Railway that ran from the borderlands on the Amur River (the Heilongjiang to the Chinese) across to China's most northerly ice-free port, Dairen, then connected to China's burgeoning train services running south to Shanghai, Nanking, onwards to Canton and eventually Hong Kong. Harbin was technically a Chinese city, but by the turn of the twentieth century had a sizeable Russian community of 34,000. The city had Russian schools, Russian Orthodox churches, Russian-language newspapers, literary journals, a symphony orchestra of Russian musicians, Russian-style cabarets, restaurants, tea houses with samovars, Siberian furriers, tailors, dressmakers and cobblers, trades of every type. For sure though, Harbin could be a tough town. After the 1917 revolution so many refugees swelled the population that there was intense competition for work. Crime, vice, gangs, violence all spiralled in the 1920s as the town filled to bursting with refugees from the Bolsheviks.

It was George Smirnoff's natural talent at drawing that saved him from the street gangs or long hours of arduous labour in the city's great pig slaughterhouses, or railway engineering workshops. He was accepted into the Department of Architecture at Harbin Polytechnic Institute. By all accounts he excelled as a student, winning a gold medal for his designs and a bursary to study in the United States of America. However, he felt unable to leave his mother behind alone in Manchuria and so didn't take up the scholarship offer. Still, his life in Harbin seemed to have found an even keel. His hobbies included the theatre and he apparently painted sets for various productions, particularly liking light opera and ballet.[327]

Smirnoff graduated in 1927 and swiftly found work as an architect in Harbin. He courted a fellow Russian émigré Nina Pleshakoff and they soon married and set about making their own home in the city. But the Japanese annexation and occupation of Manchuria in 1931 forced Smirnoff to flee a second time. This time to Tsingtao, right across the vast plains of Manchuria into neighbouring Shantung Province.

Tsingtao was a pleasant enough city – built largely by the Germans back when it was their concession, with elements of their Teutonic style. It was expanded by the Japanese who took control in 1914 on the eve of World War One. Tsingtao was a manufacturing town – producing the beer that took the town's name, the nearby sorghum fields provided cereal to eat and straw for brooms as well as straw-braid, famously fashioned into Eton boaters. But it was also a seaside town, a coastal resort, a tourist destination for those escaping the heat of Shanghai and other cities for Tsingtao's beaches, regattas, and seafront restaurants and hotels. In the 1920s and 30s the tourist brochures proclaimed – "Tsingtao, the Riviera of the Far East".

In Shantung George again found architectural design work. He and Nina once more started to make a home for themselves. Their first daughter Irina (later Irene) was born in December 1934. George was

327 'Russian Artist from Harbin Here', *South China Morning Post,* June 14, 1939, p.5.

commissioned to work on a project for 200 planned new residences, villas, and bungalows, on the city's outskirts. On his weekends off he began to paint and sketch seaside scenes around the town. He worked in water colours and oils before teaching himself the palette knife technique that he was to often employ in his later work. The sojourn in Tsingtao was, by Smirnoff's own later recollection, a happy and contented time in the young family's life.

But then, still only in his thirties, he was forced to flee for the third time as Japan invaded northern China in 1937. His natural route might have been south to Shanghai, the International Settlement or French Concession where approximately 25,000 Russian émigrés lived and worked in relative safety. And it seems the Smirnoffs did move to Shanghai briefly, though perhaps only stopping a matter of weeks (perhaps even just days) before moving on. The Japanese invasion had affected Shanghai too, the bombings of "Black Saturday" (August 14, 1937) in what they believed was a safe and well-defended city-state had traumatised its residents. The foreign concessions were panicked. Many Shanghailanders were looking to evacuate ahead of an expected full Japanese invasion of the city. So George and Nina looked further south.

Hong Kong Refuge

The Smirnoffs made it to Hong Kong at the end of 1937, a city where there was also a noticeable White Russian émigré presence. After an initial period of discrimination when Russians first arrived in the British colony they had found ways to make themselves vital to Hong Kong. Since 1930, approximately 30 former Tsarist soldiers had served in the hundred-man strong Anti-Piracy Guard Contingent under the Hong Kong Police. Numbers are hard to ascertain as many remained in Hong Kong for only a short time or did little more than transit through while others remained for their entire lives. Among those who stayed a while, many worked in hotel orchestras, hotels, or in local retail businesses. A community formed around the Russian Orthodox Church that had opened in 1934 in Kowloon Tong. The Church's establishment meant that the Kowloon Tong area became a focus for Russian émigrés to settle or sojourn. The Smirnoffs found a house on Nathan Road in Tsim Sha Tsui, Kowloon.

Once again George was lucky and found work as an architect, and once again he attempted to rebuild his now thrice-thwarted domestic life with a family home in a Kowloon apartment block. He had hoped that this would be a starter home and that eventually the family could move to enjoy life on one of Hong Kong's outlying islands. But history caught up with him once more.

George Smirnoff as a Hong Kong Defence Volunteer, 1941

Smirnoff had joined up as a Hong Kong Defence Volunteer in 1941 as the Japanese closed in on the colony. In December 1941, on Christmas Day, Hong Kong fell to the Japanese. At the time of the surrender Smirnoff was working for the firm of Marsman and Co. who had the contract to construct the colony's bomb shelters under the government's Air Raid Precautions scheme.[328] It was fairly dull work in terms of

328 Founded by Dutch civil engineer Jan Hendrik "Hank" Marsman who worked in the Dutch East Indies and the Philippines around World War One. The company initially supplied machinery, tools, and services to mining operations in Baguio. With these profits they moved into engineering, insurance, air transportation, machinery, hardware, pharmaceuticals, and foodstuffs with their corporate headquarters in Manila. They also had a significant interest in the Needle Hill Tungsten Mine, the largest mining operation ever established in the colony. Marsman was to escape from Hong Kong in early 1942 to avoid being interned at Stanley.

architecture and Smirnoff spent much of his days in the Marsman offices sketching and doodling.[329] In his spare time he continued his painting using both brushes and palette knives. He painted the harbour, boats, and background scenery. War preparations were ever present – submarines jostling Chinese junks.

As stateless Russian émigrés George and Nina were not immediately liable to internment after the Japanese invasion. Unlike allied nationals, the relatively small number of stateless White Russians remained free, though were closely monitored to see if they either tried to help the British or engaged in espionage for the Soviet Union. It became increasingly difficult to move around, change lodgings, and food was short. George's long-term plan of moving the family to a home/studio on Cheung Chau island now proved impossible.[330]

His drawing skills noted, Smirnoff was ordered to produce murals for the Japanese Public Works Scheme, a project that aimed to put pro-Tokyo patriotic images around Hong Kong to win local support for the Japanese. Smirnoff refused. This refusal would seem to be the reason that he fell afoul of the much-feared Japanese military police, the *Kempeitai*. They charged him with suspected espionage (though had he been a spy he would surely have done what the Japanese asked and kept on spying without attracting attention to himself!). They ransacked the Smirnoff home on Nathan Road several times. It didn't help that it was virtually next door to the Japanese-occupied Police Training School. Eventually, while the *Kempeitai* found no evidence of espionage activities, they did find some illegal home brewed *samogon* vodka George had made for personal use. Illegal hooch was enough to get George sent to the Stanley Civilian Internment Camp. While he had not been a professional spy, Smirnoff did engage in acts of passive resistance to the Japanese, such as drawing cartoons of various Japanese officials which he left conspicuously in public places.

Smirnoff managed to get released from Stanley under an amnesty in late 1943. He had spent only a month in the internment camp. But his luck didn't hold. The United States Fourteenth Air Force intensified bombing raids on Hong Kong through the late summer, autumn, and winter of

329 *Hong Kong Sunday Herald*, October 28, 1945.

330 Smirnoff told a reporter this ambition in, 'Russian Artist from Harbin Here', *South China Morning Post*, June 14, 1939, p.5.

1943. Kowloon was a target.[331] After the family's house on Nathan Road was partially destroyed in an American bombing raid just after George's release from Stanley, the couple decided to leave Hong Kong for Macao. Smirnoff went ahead with his daughter Irina, by then nearly ten. Nina, their son Alexander and second daughter, also Nina, stayed behind in Hong Kong for a while as George looked for accommodation until the family could eventually reunite in Macao.

George and Nina with their children Irina, Nina and Alexander, Macao, 1945

George Smirnoff's Macao

The Smirnoffs stayed briefly at the Bela Vista Hotel before they managed to find lodgings on Pátio das Seis Casas (The Patio of Six Houses) between Travessa do Mata-Tigre and Pátio do Padre António in São Lourenço. It was a cramped two-room late-nineteenth-century second-floor apartment for the whole family, but at least Macao was safe. As a refugee in the Portuguese colony Smirnoff eked out a living giving painting classes and designing theatrical sets for productions (and even reputedly appearing as

331 'Hong Kong Harbor Like Quiet Lake, Thanks to American Bombing Raids', *The Austin American-Statesman,* December 16, 1943, p.14.

an actor in one production) at the Teatro Dom Pedro V that staged plays, concerts, and operas.[332]

Pátio das Seis Casas

Smirnoff was helped out by José Maria "Jack" Braga, whose family had left Portugal and settled in Macao in 1712 and then moved across to Hong Kong when the British colony was first established in 1842. José's father was José Pedro Braga, a businessman, journalist and the first Portuguese member of the Hong Kong Legislative Council (LegCo). José junior had worked briefly for the Hongkong and Shanghai Bank before moving back to Macao in 1922 to teach English language and literature at St Joseph's Seminary (Seminario de São Jose), and later at the Liceu (Lyceum) de Macau.[333] In the 1920s Braga helped found the *Diario de Macau*

332 The neo-classical Dom Pedro V Theatre is one of the first western-style theatres in Asia built in 1860 with a façade added in 1873. It could be converted into a ballroom, housed a reading room which stocked a decent library, and received newspapers from Portugal as well as hosting meetings of the Clube União (Union Club). During the latter stages of World War Two it was also a refugee shelter.

333 The Igreja e Seminário de São José, St Joseph's Seminary and church in São Lourenço established in 1758 by the Jesuits and later administered by the Lazarites. The church is still standing on Rua do Seminario. The Liceu de Macau was a Portuguese-curriculum public secondary school in Sé parish. The original building is gone and the Liceu has been amalgamated into the Macao Polytechnic University.

newspaper and, for much of the 1930s and during the war years, was also the Reuters representative in Macau. Additionally, Braga was an amateur historian as well as a philanthropic supporter of the arts in the colony. He knew of Smirnoff's painting, had acquired several for his own collection, and arranged for him to give painting classes at the St Luiz Gonzaga College.[334] He also found him work designing the logo of the Portuguese newspaper, *O Clarim* (owned by the Roman Catholic Diocese of Macao).[335]

José Maria "Jack" Braga

It seems George and Nina made friends in Macao, enjoyed the social life of the colony, felt safe and somewhat secure despite the deprivations of wartime. One friend, Vincente Yvanovich who had been born in Hong Kong in 1896, visited them regularly and Smirnoff gifted Yvanovich's daughter a painting of her choice from his work. Another of Yvanovich's daughters would visit Macao from Hong Kong for the *Enrontro* when Macanese from abroad were (and still are) invited back to Macao to make cultural connections. While there Smirnoff painted her, and her friends', portraits.[336]

And then in 1944 Smirnoff's luck really turned. The head of the Economic Services Bureau (and arguably the most politically powerful man in the colony), Dr Pedro José Lobo awarded him a commission on behalf of the Government of Macao to provide a series of watercolours depicting the colony. Quite why Lobo commissioned the paintings is unclear. He certainly did take an interest in the arts in Macao, particularly music, but perhaps it was his own version of a President Roosevelt-style

334 Works by Smirnoff and correspondence related to them are included in the Braga Collection, National Library of Australia, Canberra. They include a landscape of Praia Grande Bay, looking southwards (1944). After the Japanese occupation of Hong Kong, approximately 4,000 Portuguese families returned to Macau from the British colony. Macao's governor Gabriel Maurício Teixeira asked the Hong Kong Jesuits to set up a school for these returnees, St Luiz Gonzaga.

335 Now the oldest continuous Portuguese newspaper in Macao.

336 From a conversation over email with Teresa Borden Howell, granddaughter of Vincente Yvanovich. The portraits mentioned were later donated to the Museu de Arte de Macao (Macao Museum of Art).

New Deal programme to create work and employment for refugees in the colony? Whatever the reason, George Smirnoff had finally, perhaps only momentarily at least, secured a steady income and safe harbour. The Smirnoffs moved to larger and better lodgings at Rua da Prata, not far from Pátio das Seis Casas.

*

Despite the vicissitudes of war, this period of Smirnoff's life, spending his days painting Macao, were among his most settled and happy. Smirnoff's commission was for 63 watercolours that were all to be urban depictions of Macao's famous buildings, streets, churches, and notable sights. Later Smirnoff's daughter Irina recalled that he would spend days sketching and painting, simply staring at scenes he would later return to his studio to better depict on paper or board (wartime restrictions meant there was no canvas available). Smirnoff worked in watercolours from sketches and was also adept at the so-called "wash" technique whereby the artist uses a large amount of solvent with little paint applied to either paper or canvas. It's not clear when and where Smirnoff first used the wash technique. It may have been back at college in Harbin, or in Tsingtao, Shanghai, Hong Kong, or Macao, but it is a technique more closely associated with Chinese and East Asian traditional artistic style than European.

The Igreja de Sao Agostinho from Patio doc Cules

The Guia Lighthouse

Irina maintained that at times he would simply go fishing and thinking. His final paintings of Macao reflect a calmness and tranquillity he may have been feeling himself for the first time in a long time, if ever. He was apparently able to recreate a remarkable likeness of whatever he had observed and could sketch and colour everything from memory. Despite the war and the family's precarious refugee status, Irina believed that her father was at peace in Macao. As stateless Russians the Smirnoff's were classified as "Third Nationals" – neither Allies, Axis, or Neutrals. As ever the Russian émigrés found themselves in a legal no-man's land with nobody wanting to take responsibility for them, but nobody determined to persecute them either.

View of Penha Hill and the Statue of Governor Ferreira do Amaral

Smirnoff's pictures of Macao, mostly pencils and watercolours on paper, included churches, fortresses, seascapes, and street scenes. All of them exhibited a trademark aura of calm, peace, which perhaps contrasted with the wartime shortages, refugee crisis and general chaos.[337] Many of the paintings are depopulated, but others, for instance Smirnoff's painting of the main façade of Igreja de São Domingos (on Largo de São Domingos and built by Spanish Dominicans), show Macao as crowded, bustling with shoppers, children, and rickshaw pullers. They capture elements of everyday life in 1940s wartime Macao. For instance, Smirnoff's view of Igreja de São José (St Joseph's Church) showing the adjacent Seminário (Seminary) and Chinese dwellings has as its central focus a woman hanging out washing on a line. At times, as with Smirnoff's study of Rua da Prata or the old houses at Praça Lobo d'Ávila, Macao looks lost

337 Smirnoff completed between 63 and 74 paintings of Macao, according to differing sources.

in time, as if still in the early 1800s, scenes that could have been painted by Chinnery himself.

Main façade of the Igreja de Sao Domingos

Most of Smirnoff's Macao recreates tranquillity, a timelessness, a city devoid of motorcars and technology, new buildings, signage, any modern encumbrances. However, the Central Hotel can be glimpsed in Smirnoff's painting of the *Leal Senado* as seen from Travessa do Roquete. All in all the collection Smirnoff delivered to Dr Lobo form an incredible snapshot of Macao scenes and life during the 1940s.

View of the Igreja e Seminário de São José and adjacent Chinese dwellings

As part of the commission Smirnoff had a number of assistants and apprentices assigned to him to help complete the work. Luís Demeé was little more than 16 years old when he began working with Smirnoff, having studied under him at the St Luiz Gonzaga College.[338] Eventually the paintings were collected together and exhibited for the first time in December 1945, just a few months after the end of the war. They were shown in the Colégio Sao Luís (St Louis College), on the Praia Grande, in a joint show together with Smirnoff's apprentices, including Luís Demeé who went on to win a place at Portugal's Fine Art School in Lisbon, the Faculdade de Belas-Artes da Universidade de Lisboa.

*

338 Demeé went on to study at the Lisbon School of Fine Arts, the Oporto (Porto) School of Fine Arts, and then in Paris after the war before eventually becoming a professor at the Oporto School of Fine Arts.

In October 1945, after his exhibition, George and his family left Macao and moved back across to Hong Kong, finding lodgings in Tsim Sha Tsui once again. This time, a third-floor apartment at #15 Cameron Road. Smirnoff had obtained a position with the Architectural Office of the Public Works Department designing and building public urinals. Not glamorous, but a wage. At first he seemed happy enough, painting in his spare time, becoming active in the local Artists' Guild.

Macao Harbour

Despite the satisfaction his painting had briefly brought him in Macao, Smirnoff's entire life had been one of forced rootlessness and disruption. Clearly there were happy times, as the picture with Nina shows. Despite Irina's assertion that he had been content working on the Macao commission, a life of being rendered stateless and chased from Russia to Harbin, Tsingtao to Hong Kong, Hong Kong to Macao and back again took its toll. It was reported that his health had deteriorated and that he had to take time off work due to a 'disease of the nerves'. According to a police report, George Smirnoff either jumped or fell from the bathroom of his apartment at 10.30pm in February 1947. He was just 44.[339]

In a letter sent to Jack Braga in Macao just after the war and his move back to Hong Kong, Smirnoff wrote:

> 'I feel myself perfectly insignificant, shrinking to zero and am developing … an inferiority complex.'[340]

A requiem mass was held at the Russian Orthodox Church of Saints Peter and Paul in Kowloon Tong.[341] George Vitalievich Smirnoff was buried in the Colonial Cemetery at Happy Valley.

Smirnoff is far from forgotten in his adopted temporary home of Macao. Many of his paintings remain in the collection of the Macao Museum of Art and Museu Luís de Camões (Luís de Camões Museum) which has held retrospectives of his work.

View of the Igreja de Santa Clara and the Jardim de São Francisco

339 'Found dead in Yard – Russian Civil Engineer and Architect', *South China Morning Post*, February 8, 1947, p.6.

340 This final letter to Braga noted in Patricia Lim, *Forgotten Souls: A Social History of the Hong Kong Cemetery*, (Hong Kong: Hong Kong University Press, 2011), pp.529-530.

341 #12 Essex Crescent, Kowloon Tong (closed 1972).

A Macanese Writer in the Greater Chinese World

Deolinda da Conceição
(1913-1957)

Deolinda da Conceição

'She had been regaled with beautiful things, perfumes and jewellery, sumptuous gowns. She had been infatuated by luxurious and elegant surroundings, she had sat at abundant dinner tables, and tasted the most precious wines, in short, she had lived, lived life to the full…'

Deolinda da Conceição, *Cheongsam* (1957)

China's Wartime Women Writers

Deolinda da Conceição (fully Deolinda do Carmo Salvado da Conceição) only became a household name in Macao in the years after World War Two.[342] Her fame came primarily from journalism, regularly writing book and art gallery reviews, as well as essays, for the *Noticias de Macau (Macau News)* and other *feuilleton*-style supplements in a golden age of post-war Macao newspaper publishing.[343] She also pioneered the *Noticias's* women's page. These articles and commentaries on the Macao of the day, the colony's history, literary salons, and arts scene, were widely noted for their stylish flourishes. She was urged to try fiction and, feeling encouraged, began to write short stories. In 1957 some of her fiction was gathered together in the first published collection of her work: *Cheong-Sam: a Cabaia*. *Cheong-Sam* was a compendium of 27 short stories, all set in Macao, often harking back to the wartime period, and mostly dealing with the situation of Portuguese, Chinese, and Macanese women in the colony.[344]

Though of Portuguese heritage, da Conceição was born and raised in Macao. She spent some years in Shanghai in the 1930s just before the Second Sino-Japanese War broke out, and did not visit Europe until the 1950s towards the end of her life. These days – whether in the original Portuguese or in English translation – Deolinda da Conceição is largely overlooked and unfortunately almost totally forgotten outside Macao. And, when and if she is discussed, it is invariably without reference to any of the other twentieth-century female writers who lived or sojourned in Greater China and with whom she shares so many traits and common concerns. She is typically discussed as a "one-off", a somehow unique writer seemingly operating in a vacuum.

But da Conceição did share attributes with other writers – Chinese and foreign – of the inter-war and wartime period in what we can term Greater China, that is to say the mainland (in both its Nationalist and

342 Conceição is pronounced kõ.sɐjˈsɐ̃w̃.

343 The *Noticias* was founded in August 1947.

344 Deolinda da Conceição, *Cheong-Sam: a Cabaia*, (Lisbon: Livraria Francisco Franco, 1957). To slightly confuse matters most English translations of the main story, *Cheongsam*, use a one-word spelling where the title of the Portuguese publications either hyphenates or leaves a space – i.e. Cheong-sam/Cheong Sam.

Communist formations), as well as Taiwan, Hong Kong, and Macao. While admittedly she does not fit neatly in any of the various loose groupings of women writers of the time, either in terms of race, heritage, or nationality, she does have feet in various camps. It is worth considering her literary output as part of these loose writerly affiliations.

*

Da Conceição can be considered among the many interesting, and often highly perceptive, European and American expatriate women writers who spent time in interwar Greater China and wrote novels and short stories set in the societies they encountered. They include the English writers Ann Bridge, a diplomat's wife in Peking; Stella Benson, who lived in Hong Kong and various small treaty ports in China with her Chinese Maritime Customs Service (CMCS) husband; the American poet Margaret Mackprang Mackay, who married a hotelier in northern China of Scottish ancestry and lived and wrote largely in Peking and Tientsin; Nora Waln, a writer and journalist whose Pennsylvania family had long standing trading links to Hopei province; and the American *New Yorker* correspondent Emily "Mickey" Hahn who lived in both Shanghai and Hong Kong and was in relationships with, first, the poet Sinmay Zau (Shao Xunmei) in Shanghai and then the British intelligence officer and leading English Portuguese studies scholar Charles Boxer in Hong Kong.

Cheong-Sam a Cabaia, first edition, 1956

However, unlike da Conceição, all these women were sojourners: all were born outside the region, and all (except Benson who succumbed to pneumonia in French Indochina) eventually left the region to return home or moved on to new adopted countries.[345] Their work regularly touches on women's issues in China, albeit usually focussed on expatriate women: Bridge's often frivolous comments on the affairs and dalliances of the Peking Legation Quarter clique; Stella Benson's descriptive blends of fiction and reality set in volatile, occasionally quite remote, colonial settings; Mackprang Mackay's novel of an American woman's attempt to live independently in inter-war Peking in *Lady With Jade;* Waln on the changing position of women after the collapse of the Qing; and Hahn, in her 1947 novel *Miss Jill,* on the role of western women as "coasters" or courtesans in Shanghai.[346]

*

Also, in many respects da Conceição might be read alongside her Chinese female contemporaries who dealt with feminist subjects in various ways. Reading da Conceição's post-war short stories, such as *Cheongsam*, *O Calvário de Lin Fong* (*The Suffering of Lin Fong*) and *O Anel de Jade* (*The*

345 Ann Bridge (Lady O'Malley, 1889-1974) went to China with her husband, British diplomat Owen O'Malley. Her novels of the north China "Foreign Colony" include *Peking Picnic* (1932), *The Ginger Griffin* (1934), and *Four-Part Setting* (1938). Stella Benson (1892-1933), more overtly feminist than Bridge, went to China in the 1920s to work in a mission school and hospital where she met her husband, James (Shaemas) O'Gorman Anderson, an official in the Chinese Maritime Customs Service. They lived in various southern China treaty ports including Nanning and Pakhoi, as well as in Hong Kong. Her best-known novels include *The Far-Away Bride (1930)* and *Tobit Transplanted* (1931). Margaret Mackprang Mackay (1907-1968) wrote a number of novels and poems concerning China including *Lady With Jade* (1939) which concerns a single American woman making her way in interwar Peking. Nora Waln (1895-1964) was a best-selling American writer and journalist in the 1930s–1950s. Her interest in China stemmed from her family's connections to Hopei province where she lived for a time and which became the subject of her best-known novel set in China, *The House of Exile* (1933). Emily Hahn (1905-1997) is of course still well known for her many books, *New Yorker* columns, and marriage to Charles Boxer. Less well known is her novel of an American mother and daughter struggling to survive in interwar Shanghai, *Miss Jill* (1947).

346 The most famous "China coaster" of course being Shanghai Lil, played by Marlene Dietrich in *Shanghai Express* (1932) – 'a woman who lives by her wits on the China Coast.' Hahn's *Miss Jill* was based on a real woman, an Australian in 1930s Shanghai, Lorraine Murray – see Nick Hordern, *Shanghai Demimondaine*, (Shanghai: Earnshaw Books, 2023).

Jade Ring), we can identify the themes and preoccupations of many mainland Chinese writers like Eileen Chang (Zhang Ailing) in her shorter works – such as *Love in a Fallen City* (1943), and *The Golden Cangue* (also 1943) which feature issues of arranged marriage, or the much later published, though 1940s-set, *Lust, Caution* (1979).

Similarly so with the Hunanese writer Ding Ling's first novel *Meng Ke* (1927) and her short story *Miss Sophia's Diary* (also 1927), to take just two of her works. As well as Eileen Chang and Ding Ling, we could also add Lu Yin, a prominent figure of the May Fourth (1919), intellectual movement whose many short stories and several novels, perhaps notably *The Heart of Women* (1933), explore overtly feminist themes. Among Lu's work was *The Ivory Ring* (1934), a novel based on the life of her good friend, and another Chinese feminist writer of the period who could easily be included in this informal grouping, Shi Pingmei, who died tragically young.

Other writers that could be included were Xiao Hong, who died in the chaos of wartime Hong Kong, and Lu Jingqing, who spent time in London during the 1930s. Indeed Lu Yin, Shi Pingmei, and Lu Jingqing were all friends though they, and the others mentioned, never formed a "movement" as such and had many political and social differences of opinion. The oldest among them was born in 1898, the rest between 1902 and 1907, and the youngest, da Conceição, in 1914.

The important common thread between these women writers in Greater China was a similar form of feminist understanding. A notion of the plight of women in general, and the specificity of their situation and in the extremes of wartime, runs through all their work. Though of European heritage and writing in Portuguese, da Conceição shares many attributes with her Chinese contemporaries – her upbringing in Asia; an early and dedicated commitment to feminism; her adoption of the short story format; the primacy of (European, Eurasian, and Chinese) female characters in her work; and a life of movement between various Greater Chinese cities – Macao, Shanghai, and Hong Kong in her case. Reading da Conceição alongside Eileen Chang, Ding Ling, Lu Yin, Lu Jingqing, Shi Pingmei, and others – perhaps right through to later writers such as the Taiwanese Chen Mao-ping (aka "Echo" Chen Ping or "Sanmao") who wrote of her travels to the Western Sahara in the 1970s – we can see similar sympathies, styles, and approaches to da Conceição's work.[347]

*

For Deolinda da Conceição, as it was for Eileen Chang and Ding Ling, the interwar period, and the long-drawn-out years of the Second Sino-Japanese War, were a time of prolonged trauma, sometimes featuring extreme hardship, impoverishment, and hunger. Lu Jingqing returned from London with her husband, the poet "Shelley" Wang Lixi, to support the fight against Japan. Sadly Wang died of sepsis while at the front with the Chinese Writers' Association's War Area Interview Group. Widowed, Lu retreated to Shanghai but continued to participate in resistance activities and to write. Ding Ling was persecuted by the Communist Party for supposed pro-Nationalist activities that led to long-term trauma.

Admittedly they all, in different ways, had certain privileges compared to many women. For instance, da Conceição was able to move about relatively freely as a "neutral" Portuguese citizen; Chang was from a relatively well-off family and, during the war, connected to the collaborationist government in Shanghai; while Ding Ling, though later suffering persecution, was initially in the relative safety of the communist base at Yan'an far behind the front lines of battle. But they saw others suffer hunger, hardship, tortures, internment, and death…. and they all wrote about it.

All of these women writers were involved in journalism in various forms, and at various points. Eileen Chang started out writing for her school magazine in Shanghai, and then during the war for *XXth Century* magazine, funded by German Foreign Ministry money and in favour of

347 If wishing to extend the remit we could also mention several Japanese female writers who spent time in Shanghai. Notably Toshiko Tamura (born 1884), an early feminist author from Tokyo who controversially left her husband to follow her journalist lover to Canada in the inter-war years. In 1942 she moved to occupied Shanghai to edit a Chinese literary magazine, *Nu-sheng* (*Women's Voice*). She died of a brain haemorrhage in Shanghai in 1945. Though in a city occupied by the Japanese army it has been said that Tamura mostly recruited Communist party staff and writers to *Nu-sheng* and that she was seen as generally sympathetic to the left and against Japanese militarism. For more see Wu Peichen, 'Sato (Tamura) Toshiko's Shanghai Period (1942-1945) and the Chinese Women's Periodical "*Nu-Sheng*."' *US-Japan Women's Journal*, No.28, December 2005, pp.109–124.

Wang Jing-wei's government. She reviewed movies as well as covering wartime fashions. Ding Ling also worked in journalism during the war, though from a very different angle, editing a pro-communist newspaper's literary supplement in Yan'an. Lu Jingqing contributed to both Shanghai and British newspapers, while Lu Yin wrote for the *Shishi Xinbao* (*New Current Affairs Times*), one of the four main Chinese commercial daily newspapers in Shanghai and sympathetic to the May Fourth Movement. As mentioned, when she returned to Macao from Shanghai, via Hong Kong, and with the war over da Conceição would have a long post-war career translating for and contributing to *Notícias de Macau*, and occasionally *A Voz de Macau (The Voice of Macau)*.[348]

A Macao Merchant's Daughter

Before considering her published fiction perhaps we should look at da Conceição's biography. She was born in July 1914 in Macao's São Lourenço parish, the fourth daughter of a Portuguese merchant, António Manuel Salvado, and his wife Áurea Angelina da Cunha Salvado, a Macanese woman.[349] Her mother died in 1919, when Deolinda was just six. She was educated at the Portuguese-speaking Liceu de Macau.[350] In November 1931, at 17 or 18 (depending on her correct birth date), Deolinda married Luís Gaspar Alves, a Portuguese man just a few years older than her. The newly-wed couple decided to move to Shanghai. Presumably Luis was seeking greater business or career opportunities than were available in rather sleepy early 1930s Macao. In Shanghai

Young Deolinda

348 Founded in 1887 and also publishing an English-language edition, from 1939 *A Voz de Macau* was pro-British in its stance (according to Helen Lopes, *Neutrality and Collaboration in South China*, (Cambridge: Cambridge University Press, 2023). The paper was not published between February 1945 and September 1945 due to the paper's premises being bombed.

349 Some sources list her birthdate as July 1913.

350 During Deolinda's time at the Liceu it was largely based at the Asilo das Inválidas building on Avenida Conselheiro Ferreira de Almeida.

the couple had two children: José Maria Salvado Alves (born in August 1932), and Rui Cândido Augusto Alves (born November 1936).

The marriage didn't last, and the couple split up in 1937. The Chinese portions of Shanghai came under attack from the Japanese in the summer of that year and Deolinda decided it was too dangerous a place for her children. After "Black Saturday" – August 14, 1937 – when bombs fell on both the International Settlement and the French Concession sparking mass panic and killing thousands of innocent civilians in what was a terrible accident by the Chinese air force, evacuations southwards were common. Deolinda opted to leave. Many foreigners living in Shanghai who could evacuate chose to. Rui was still a babe in arms, José Maria just barely five-years-old. They left by coastal steamer for Hong Kong.

Of course the war followed her. Several years later Deolinda, who had found work as the director of a Portuguese school in Hong Kong, was trapped in the British colony after the Japanese occupation in 1941. As a neutral Portuguese she managed to remain out of internment, kept her job at the school, and supplemented her income translating articles from English to Portuguese for the newspaper *A Voz de Macau*.

Deolinda with António Maria da Conceição on their wedding day, May 1948

At the end of the war Deolinda and her children finally returned to Macao where she found a steady job with the newly founded *Noticias*. Again she supplemented her income working as a teacher of stenography at the Pedro Nolasco Commercial School.[351] In 1948 she married her second husband António Maria da Conceição, a teacher and sometime colleague at the *Noticias*, and in 1951 they had a son, António Maria Júnior.[352]

351 The school, at the time one of two trade schools in Macao, opened in 1878. It was folded into the Portuguese School of Macao after the 1999 handover.

352 António Maria da Conceição (1910-1985) studied at the University of Coimbra in Portugal. He was a teacher at the Liceu Camões and later director of Pedro Nolasco

Cheong-Sam

Deolinda da Conceição's literary work is linked to the aspirations and struggles of women in Macao. These are often reasonably well-educated women, feeling restricted within the confines of traditional marriages or relationships, such as concubinage. As noted these are also themes we see in the work of Chang, Ding Ling, and other Chinese contemporaries.

Da Conceição's best-known story is *Cheong-Sam*.[353] We meet Chan Nui, a smart young Chinese woman from a relatively prosperous merchant family in northern China, with some western-style education, entering into an arranged marriage. *Cheong-Sam* starts with A-Chung, Chan Nui's husband, in a prison cell having being sentenced to life imprisonment. He is ranting, incoherent. He is 32. He claims he will take 'that cheongsam, tear it up, throw it in the fire. It's got a curse, it's laughing at me, it's alive, it's got her life in it....the one I killed...'

The guards seek to calm the man having no idea what he is shouting about, telling him there's no cheongsam in his cell. Da Conceição writes, 'What a cursed war! A cursed war, that had taken everything away from him and turned him into a criminal, a murderer, a heartless father, a man incapable of rational thought.' The story then flashes back to their marriage being brokered by Chan Nui's father with another merchant clan with whom he wishes to consolidate business relations. A-Chung is obviously intellectually inferior to Chan Nui though she accepts the union out of tradition and respect for her father. The couple have a child. However, war threatens to ruin the family financially. The couple leave

---

Commercial School. He also wrote regularly for both *O Desporto* and *Notícias de Macau*. He was also a keen sportsman. In the 1950s António was President of the Board of Directors of the football club, Sporting Clube de Macau (founded in 1926). Later the club was to become rather moribund until, in 2008, his son, António Conceição Júnior, revived it. It is also claimed (perhaps apocryphally) that António introduced the rickshaw to Macao having imported one from Swatow (Jorge P Forjaz, *Macanese Families, Vol. 1* (Macao: Fundação Oriente, Instituto Cultural de Macau & Instituto Português do Oriente, 1996), p.776.

353 This and all other quotes from *Cheong-Sam* from Deolinda da Conceição, 'Cheongsam' in *Visions of China Stories from Macau*, translation by David Brookshaw, (a joint publication of Gávea-Brown (Providence, RI) and Hong Kong University Press (Hong Kong), 2002).

Japanese-occupied northern China and Chan Nui loses any hope of possible independence. They move south to Shanghai, but the war follows them. After Bloody Saturday they move again, further south, apparently to Kwangtung, and then finally to Macao. In Macao A-Chung can find no work and Chan Nui must work as a taxi-dancer in a nightclub. The only dress she has good enough is her wedding dress – a 'sumptuous dress *(cheongsam)* of scarlet satin embroidered in gold. A-Chung, forced to stay home and look after their child is consumed by jealousy seeing his wife leave for work each night in her scarlet cheongsam.

The climax of *Cheong-Sam* is extremely tragic and surprisingly unexpected. The reader is left to ponder whose fault the tragic and violent final turn of events is – Chan Nui's actions, her husband A-Chung's jealousy, the family insisting on traditions that ultimately end in violence, the war itself, or some combination of all these things? In keeping with many stories from other Chinese writers, da Conceição shows in *Cheong-Sam* that within the overall horror of war there are very personal tragedies.

*

Other short stories in the collection (only a few of which have been translated into English) deal with the Portuguese community in the 1930s and during the war, describing both the privations suffered during the period of neutrality and the colonial regime's discrimination against the Chinese population of Macao. The stories also chart the rise of the independent, modern Chinese and Macanese women – those that had received some education and were, in terms of fashion and often their social politics, distinctly westernised and contemporary. Within these fictions is contained a version of da Conceição herself and her life in Shanghai, Hong Kong, and Macao. As the inter-war years in China came to be associated increasingly with the growing encroachment of Japan on the country the triangle of these three locations was crucial to the region's Portuguese and Macanese communities.

In the short story *An Act of Charity* da Conceição deals with the Eurasian dilemma of feeling out of place in both communities. A young mixed-heritage man in Macao feels deeply humiliated at what he perceives as the injustice of his life, his illegitimacy, his low-born Chinese mother:

'His father, he knew, had come from far, from the ancient continent of Europe, disillusioned by life, embittered and in despair, to hide his pain and maybe his humiliation in that distant part of China. His mother was a poor ignorant Chinese woman, who went around barefoot, had no education whatsoever, and had been brought home one day by his father.'[354]

The young man focuses on what he sees as his mother's common traits – eating with chopsticks rather than a knife and fork, her reliance on Chinese medicine. He desires affection, but his mother is too beaten down and his father too all-consumed in his own humiliation and grievances to give it to him. Eventually he decides to flee Macao. His last act is to treat his mother as a beggar, denying he even recognises her – 'he felt in his waistcoat pocket, and pulling out a coin, dropped it in her hands, which were outstretched before his eyes as if in prayer. Then, trembling nervously, he moved quickly away, and strode feverishly up the gangplank and onto the ship. His mother, distraught and sobbing, beseeches him from the quay below the ship, 'He gave me his charity, he gave me a dime, in return for the life I gave him!'

In *A Conflict of Feelings* the need to depart the claustrophobic society of Macao is again emphasised. A Chinese woman with her young son waits at the quay for a boat to the 'New World'. Encouraged by her teachers and friends she is leaving her husband (who has other wives) to start anew in the United States. It transpires she had been raised in America before finding herself in Macao in a polygamous marriage to a feckless, womanising man who 'frequents clubs and theatres and gambles heavily.'[355] She considers staying but concludes, 'He would never change. He had squandered his fortune but what he had left was used up on his expensive conquests.' She leaves her husband and Macao behind.

To emphasise the commonality of themes between da Conceição and other women writers in Greater China in the 1930s, 1940s and 1950s it is worth mentioning her short story, *The Suffering of Lin Fong*.[356] Illiterate Lin works in a Macao firecrackers factory for extremely low wages in

354 All quotes from da Conceição, *Cheongsam* in *Visions of China Stories from Macau*, pp.37-41.

355 Both quotes from da Conceição, *Cheongsam* in *Visions of China Stories from Macau*, pp.42-46.

356 From da Conceição, *Cheongsam* in *Visions of China Stories from Macau*, pp.47-50.

poor conditions. She falls pregnant to a 'foreign soldier' she had met before and fallen in love with. The soldier tells her he is returning to 'his distant country' but promises to return for her. At the end of the story we see Lin Fong, now with a child, returning to the factory and waiting for the soldier to return to her. She has hope, though we know he will never come back for her.

Reclaiming Deolinda da Conceição

In interviews later in her life Eileen Chang always maintained that she wrote about the 'small things', by which she meant personal stories rather than the tales of war and revolution. But, of course, in reality Chang did write about big things – loyalty, love, resistance, patriotism, and betrayal, among them. Deolinda da Conceição's stories can also appear to be insular tales of the 'small things', though are in actuality about big themes too. In *Cheong-Sam* male-female relations are turned on their head, traditional notions of face overridden, male superiority undermined. In other stories the guilt and shame of family secrets, of abandoning parents, of fleeing bad marriages recur. In *Cheong-Sam* da Conceição notes that in occupied Shanghai 'only those prepared to sell themselves to the cruel enemy got any work.'

If da Conceição is justified in being included among the crop of better-known Chinese women writers of the same period, then she is also a writer who has been influential on a number of Macao writers who emerged slightly later.

Henrique de Senna Fernandes was born in Macao in 1923, a decade after da Conceição. His family had been established in Macao for several centuries and he had grown up in wartime Macao before studying at university in Portugal and returning to Asia in the 1950s. Like da Conceição he worked for *A Voz de Macau* and *Notícias* (as well as other Macao publications such as *Gazeta Macaense*, *Mosaico*, and *Revista de Cultura*). In many ways his work follows and extends many of the themes pioneered by Deolinda da Conceição.

His 1993 novel *A Trança Feiticeira* (*The Bewitching Braid)* is a searing indictment of established Portuguese families in Macao, their arrogance and dismissiveness of the poor working class Chinese elements of society. Fernandes is exploring the foundations of Macanese society, evoking the sense of a common Macanese identity while looking at the racial and colonial inequalities and considering the beginnings of the dismantlement of the Portuguese empire in Asia. As with da Conceição, Fernandes's short stories and two novels are set within an entirely Macanese world of local Chinese, Portuguese colonial officials, and self-important business dynasties.[357]

In *The Bewitching Braid* Fernandes continues the theme da Conceição explored through her own experiences in Shanghai. His character, the ghoulish over-reaching, gold-digging widow Lucretia has sojourned in Shanghai. Now back in Macao she is desperate to remarry – not just to money, but to ensure that she never has to return to her provincial home village in northern Portugal. A new marriage, any marriage is preferable to returning to what she sees as backwater Europe.[358]

*

Today Deolinda da Conceição remains little known or remembered outside of literary circles in Macao. This is a great shame. She deserves to be more widely read, and read alongside her contemporaries in the region.

While visiting Portugal in 1956 Deolinda was diagnosed with an incurable disease. She died at just 43 in St Paul's Hospital in Hong Kong in May 1957. Not long afterwards *Cheong-Sam: a Cabaia* was first published, posthumously.

357 Fernandes (who died in 2010) also wrote the novel *Amor e Dedinhos de Pé* (*Love and Tiny Toes*) published in 1986 and adapted as a film by Luís Filipe Rocha in 1992. It also is a portrait of the Portuguese colonial society of Macao.

358 Henrique de Senna Fernandes, *A Trança Feiticeira*, translated by David Brookshaw and published as *The Bewitching Braid*, (Hong Kong: Hong Kong University Press & Instituto Cultural do Governo da RAE de Macau, 2004).

Mayhem in Macao: Josef von Sternberg's Fantastical Macao of the Mind

Josef von Sternberg (1952)

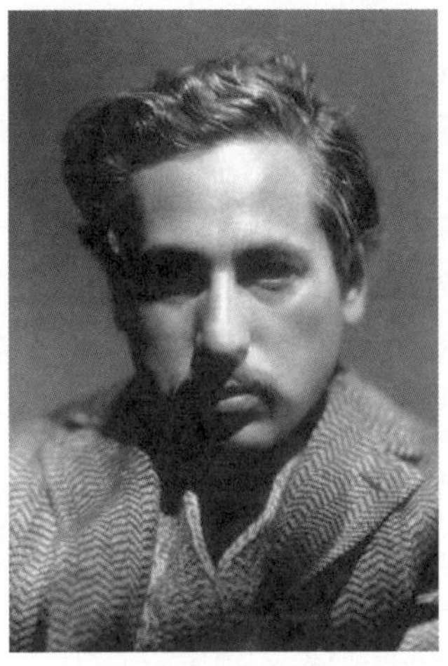

Josef von Sternberg

'Macao has two faces: one calm and open; the other veiled and secret'.

– From the opening voice-over of *Macao* (1952)

The Dream of Macao

To repeat a theme from the introduction to this collection, Macao is so often an abstraction, something imagined rather than actually known. Often it stands as a symbol; invariably, rightly or wrongly, as one for lassitude and vice. Macao is portrayed as an outpost, a backwater, a place largely forgotten, and so therefore a site where anything, often things usually deemed prohibited, immoral, or transgressive, can take place. A covert location where troublesome human desires and tastes can become overt. Where people can hide, seek refuge, start over. Macao as a dream, a humid fever dream. And so this collection includes references to a number of films and novels that have been set in Macao (it still surprises me that more have not used the location). Hollywood's best-known and biggest budget Macao-set movie to date is titled simply (no more was needed to draw the crowds, it seems) *Macao*.

*

Few dreamt of Macao more than Jonas Sternberg – he changed Jonas to Josef and added the "von" later – a Viennese Jewish kid born in 1894 to an Orthodox family. His father was a military man in the army of the Austro-Hungarian Empire, his mother a former child circus performer. The family emigrated to America when he was seven. They bounced around, came back to Vienna for a while, and then finally settled permanently in New York around 1908. Throughout his career von Sternberg was to embrace extraterritoriality, be drawn to cosmopolitan places – colonies, treaty ports, international settlements, liminal zones, and disputed territories. His work is set in criminal underworlds, docks, ports, and cities in collapse (French Morocco, post-Great War Vienna, Tsarist Russia…) and, of course, Shanghai (twice). Naturally a place such as Macao would interest von Sternberg and he spent many hours there in his mind, even though he never actually visited.

In his introduction to the published screenplay of *Macao* the film and theatre critic Andrew Velez calls von Sternberg a 'masterful cinematic magician.'[359] *Macao* was going to be the culmination of his long-held

359 Velez, introduction to *RKO Classic Screenplays: Macao*, (New York: Frederick Ungar Publishing, 1980 – copyright RKO: 1952). The screenplay is credited to Bernard

dream – the last in a trio of films about the Far East. After his triumphs with *Shanghai Express* (1932) and *The Shanghai Gesture* (1941), *Macao* would be von Sternberg's crowning glory. He had a script, money, a big studio behind him, and a plethora of top stars at his disposal: Jane Russell as a Dietrich-like cabaret singer and the handsome *noir* actor Robert Mitchum. Von Sternberg was almost unique as a film director, having had a 30-year-long stellar career with hardly any duds along the way. He'd made a lot of money for Hollywood.

Jane Russell and Robert Mitchum

His early years had seen him directing silent movies in Berlin; Germany's first "talkie" in 1929 *Der Blaue Engel* (*The Blue Angel)* was a box office hit that made a star of his muse and later regular collaborator Marlene Dietrich. The movie caught Hollywood's attention. There followed a slew of successes – *Morocco* (1930), *Dishonored* (1931), *Blonde Venus* (1932), *The Scarlet Empress* (1934), and *The Devil is a Woman* (1935) among them. In 1950 when filming on *Macao* began von Sternberg was only 57 years old, still youthful for a movie director. He had just signed a lucrative exclusive two-picture deal with the fabulously wealthy Howard Hughes and his RKO Studio. Budgets, he had been assured, would be enormous. *Macao* was the second movie of their agreement after the not-

C Schoenfeld and Stanley Rubin from a story by Robert ("Bob") Creighton Williams.

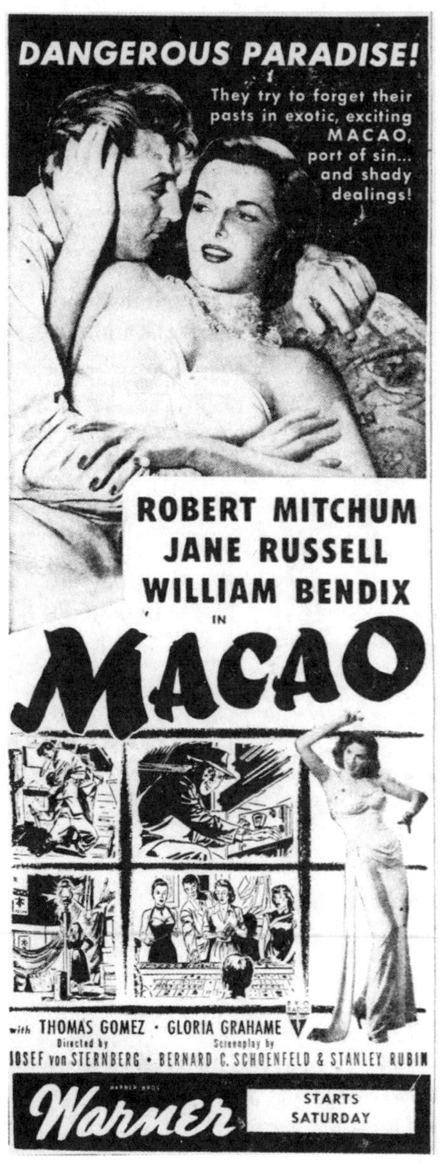

A movie poster for Macao, 1952

so-well-remembered *Jet Pilot*, a Cold War romance penned by Jules Furthman (who had scripted *Shanghai Express* and *The Shanghai Gesture)* starring John Wayne and Janet Leigh. (*Jet Pilot* wasn't actually released until 1957, after *Macao,* despite having been made first).

Robert Mitchum and Jane Russell had enthusiastically (at least initially) signed on as the leads with reliable supporting actors William Bendix and Gloria Grahame in secondary roles. The basic story was pretty good, even if von Sternberg found the early versions of the script problematic. For instance, much to her annoyance, Grahame's character changed from Eurasian to White Russian, and then to an American called "Marge" within the space of a 15-minute script discussion![360]

All Aboard the Hong Kong-Macao Ferry

Nick Cochran (played by Mitchum) is an American World War Two veteran who has bounced around from Iraq to Cairo to Singapore and is now in self-imposed exile in the

360 Bernard Eisenschitz, *Nicholas Ray: An American Journey*, (London: Faber and Faber, 1993), p.170.

Far East after getting in 'a jam' back in the States. He is given a chance to restore his good name by helping to capture an international crime boss. We first meet Nick aboard the Hong Kong-Macao Ferry steaming towards the Portuguese colony. He's stand-offish and tough in true *noir* style, but, as we soon see, willing to jump into the sea to save a drowning Chinese man who's a complete stranger to him.

Soaking wet but back onboard (his passport and wallet conveniently lost) he meets and is instantly attracted to Julie Benton, a beautiful, but hard-boiled, caustic and chippy, nightclub singer (Russell) heading to Macao after sojourning in Saigon and Hong Kong for reasons she is not keen to discuss. The scriptwriters were in no doubt Julie Benton was to be a classic film *noir* femme fatale:

> 'She is dressed in tropical clothes and a large hat. Her valise and an old traveling phonograph are on the deck. She constantly fans herself because of the intense heat and humidity. Life has obviously given Julie a severe beating, but she has retained a kind of defiance and self-respect. Many women like her might have become tramps – but part of Julie's strength lies in the fact that she has not.' [361]

Also aboard is Lawrence C Trumble, played by Bendix, apparently a friendly Brooklyn salesman of silk stockings though, as it turns out, really an undercover New York cop. His target is fugitive American racketeer, murderer, and owner of Macao's The Quick Reward casino, Vincent Halloran (played by B-movie tough guy specialist Brad Dexter).

> Driver: Mr Vincent Halloran. Very important man. Big boss.
> Nick: What's he boss of?
> Driver: Most of Macao…[362]

Halloran runs the biggest casino in town, pays off the Portuguese police to let him know if any undercover cops arrive at the ferry terminal, and has a vicious henchman, Itzumi ('a cold hoodlum of the Orient'), played by Philip Ahn.[363] Ahn was a Korean-American born in Los Angeles and

361 *RKO Classic Screenplays: Macao*, p.2.

362 *RKO Classic Screenplays: Macao,* p.17.

363 *RKO Classic Screenplays: Macao*, p.18.

the first Korean-American to receive a star on the Hollywood Walk of Fame. He had worked with Douglas Fairbanks on *The Thief of Baghdad* as a schoolboy in 1924. He played mostly Chinese in the movies – von Sternberg spotted him opposite Anna May Wong in the B-movie *Daughter of Shanghai* (1937) and was impressed by his performance.

When Halloran hears from the corrupt Portuguese Commissioner of Police, Lieutenant Felizardo José Espirito Sebastian (played by the Spanish-French American Thomas Gomez), that an undercover New York detective is in Macao to get him he suspects everyone. He is fooled by the genial Trumble and convinced that Nick is the cop sent to investigate and arrest him for a murder back in the States.

Robert Mitchum and Gloria Grahame

Halloran hires Julie as a lounge singer, thus rousing the ire of his moll and chief croupier Margie (Gloria Grahame) – 'a most attractive wench in her middle twenties', say the script notes, and jealous of Russell's sultry *chanteuse* act.[364]

> Halloran: Diamonds would only cheapen you.
> Margie: Sure – but what a way to be cheapened.[365]

364 Ibid.

365 *RKO Classic Screenplays: Macao*, p.18.

Nick and Julie take a smoochy midnight sampan ride around the Porto Interior. The next day Cochran turns up at The Quick Reward exacerbating Halloran's concerns about him. He tries to persuade Nick to leave town, return to Hong Kong, forget about Julie, and Macao. Nick is recruited by Trumble and agrees to try and sell a US$100,000 diamond to Halloran. He'll be paid for US$4,000 for his trouble. Halloran, as Trumble knows he will, recognises it as one of a cache he sent to Hong Kong to be sold and which disappeared (unbeknown to him seized by the police). The twist is Halloran must leave the Portuguese colony and come to the British colony to do the deal where he can be apprehended in international waters (for the sake of the plot beyond a supposed "Three-Mile-Limit" of Portuguese waters within which the "international police" have no jurisdiction).

Nick and Halloran meet at Largo do Pagode da Barra (Barra Square) where Halloran keeps his speedboat. Halloran coshes Nick and lets him know he believes he's an NYPD detective and that he's not falling for the three-mile-limit trap – 'You're in Macao – this is my precinct.'[366] Halloran and his henchman Itzumi stash him at Margie's apartment.

Brad Dexter, Philip Ahn and Gloria Grahame

Julie, concerned about Nick's disappearance, is helped by a recurring character, Kwan Sum Tang, a blind Chinese beggar played by the

366 *RKO Classic Screenplays: Macao*, p.56.

Moscow Arts Theatre-trained Russian émigré actor Vladimir Sokoloff in yellowface. He takes her to Margie's apartment. Nick acts as if he's been with Margie all night in the hope Julie will leave, annoyed, and not be caught by Itzumi who is there hiding and eavesdropping. Julie, unaware of Itzumi, is hurt at this apparent desertion by Nick and leaves in a huff. Eventually Nick escapes from Margie's apartment but is hunted by Itzumi and his troupe of knife-wielding thugs. Nick meets up with Trumble who is fatally knifed in the back by Itzumi. In his dying breath he tells Nick the three-mile-limit plan and that a Royal Navy vessel is waiting to apprehend Halloran in international waters.

Thinking Cochran is safely stashed at Margie's apartment, Halloran decides to head to Hong Kong. He takes Julie with him on his speedboat. Once aboard and heading out to sea Halloran realises the boat's skipper is actually Nick. They fight, long enough to reach the three-mile-limit and the waiting police who arrest Halloran. Nick and Julie then reunite, kiss and…

FADE OUT
THE END

Though there is some rough stuff and gun play in the background, the movie is essentially a dance between Mitchum and Russell (reminiscent of the sexual byplay between Dietrich and Cooper in *Morocco* or Dietrich and Clive Brook on the *Shanghai Express*), attracted at first sight but both too worldly wise and toughened by experience to fall head-over-heels so fast. Presumably, along with the liminal Macao location, it was this element that initially attracted von Sternberg to the project.

Filming was to be in California, but there was a second unit trip to Macao for authenticity with some locally shot footage. Most of the Hollywood trade press predicted movie gold – the sort of gold von Sternberg, Mitchum, and Russell had delivered repeatedly. How could Russell's dark beauty and Mitchum's almost decade-long string of *noir* hits (*Undercurrent, The Locket, Pursued, Crossfire…*) not suit the legendary depravity and outré sexiness of Macao! Von Sternberg envisioned Russell as another in his string of ice-cool beauties – a brunette Dietrich. He wanted Mitchum to recreate the Gary Cooper of *Morocco* 20 years before, emphasising the languid, the cool, the flip off. Everyone was excited.

But it was all to be an unmitigated disaster on set. Russell was Russell, an actress with a drollness and wry approach that transcended the simplistic sex-symbol box the studios tried to force her into. She was not the continental ice queen Dietrich. Mitchum was his own man with his own particular brand of post-war cool; more anti-hero than all-American hero. Soon after shooting began, cast and director fell out, leading to brutal firings, bitter fights, lifelong hatreds, a significant loss of money, although ultimately not such a terrible movie if we just appreciate it aesthetically and forget the script.

So, how did *Macao* fall apart?

"A Fabulous Speck off the China Coast"[367]

Josef von Sternberg loved Asia, China particularly. He had spent a prolonged sojourn there, a trip he recalls in his autobiography *Fun in a Chinese Laundry*.[368] His two previous cinematic ventures to China had been box office successes. *Shanghai Express* was a sexy pre-code movie, originally from a 33-page treatment written by the gay Savannah-based writer and Asia hand Harry Hervey. The established screenwriter and frequent von Sternberg collaborator Jules Furthman wrote the script. Dietrich signed on (for the fourth of the seven films she and von Sternberg would make together) along with the English actor Clive Brook and Anna May Wong. The Swedish-American actor Warner Oland, who had just appeared in the first of the long-lived and extremely popular Charlie Chan movies, appeared in yellowface.

Dietrich smouldered as Madeline, aka Shanghai Lily, a notorious "White Flower of the China Coast" living off her wits. Anna May Wong was equally captivating as the courtesan Hu Fei – von Sternberg lit both of them remarkably. Furthman's script has some great lines – 'It took more than one man to change my name to Shanghai Lily' being the most famous. *Shanghai Express* won an Oscar for cinematography and was nominated for best picture and best director.[369] It was to be one of

367 As the movie's opening voiceover describes Macao.

368 Josef von Sternberg, *Fun in a Chinese Laundry*, (London: Secker & Warburg, 1966).

369 For more on *Shanghai Express* see the chapter *Harry Hervey's Peking of the Imagination* in Paul French, *Destination Peking* (Hong Kong: Blacksmith Books, 2021).

the greatest cinema hits of the Depression, grossing US$3.7 million in 1932 money on its initial run, the highest grossing movie of that year by some considerable margin.

The Shanghai Gesture (1941) is equally good. Based on John Colton's stage play that scandalised audiences, critics, and the Broadway censors in 1925 with its opium addiction, lost white girls in the Far East, and casual racial mingling. The movie somehow manages to retain much of that original 1920s edginess despite the imposition of the Hays Code that most definitely did not like drugs or miscegenation, two major themes of *The Shanghai Gesture*.

Gene Tierney, as "Poppy", appears effectively drugged throughout (nominative determinism!). Her flawless beauty, heavy lidded eyes and (to Hollywood's way of thinking at least) European mannerisms, repeatedly led Tierney to be cast in ethnically ambiguous roles. The swarthy Victor Mature in his fez and *djellaba* is suitably indefinable as Dr Omar ('the matter-of-fact Arab despoiler', as he is described in the script). There is Mother Gin Sling – Madame Goddam in Colton's original play – played by Ona Munson in yellowface as the sexually ambiguous (as indeed Munson was in real life) queen of Shanghai's gaming tables. Perhaps the best performance in the movie is given by Phyllis Brooks as the China Coasting show girl Dixie Pomeroy, stranded in Shanghai and with a ladder in her nylons to symbolise her descent into the netherworld.

Again the movie got great reviews. Von Sternberg repeated his stylistic black-and-white chiaroscuro cinematography of *Shanghai Express*, the butterfly lighting (placing the light above and directly centred on the actresses' faces) that he instituted as the effective in-house lighting style of Paramount Studios, the trademark obscuring effects of gauze curtains, were all employed again. The Chinese-American actor and artist Keye Luke (who appeared in over 60 movies but is best remembered as Charlie Chan's eldest son in the long running Fox Studios franchise) provided vivid background art for Madame Gin Sling's apartment. Her Shanghai casino resembles Dante's *Inferno* (The Quick Reward in *Macao* would be a smaller, more modern version a decade later) with Dr Omar orchestrating the frenzied revelry of the gambling. Perhaps von Sternberg had seen Jean Delannoy's *Macao, L'enfer du jeu*? Madame Gin Sling's joint is not

---

Hervey's own visit to Macao is described in his travelogue, *Where Strange Gods Call: Pages Out of the East*, (London: Thornton Butterworth, 1925).

dissimilar to Delannoy's Eldorado casino. The film is decadent in the extreme and, frankly, rather druggy. It is also, being released in 1941, a film that symbolises the end of an era for Shanghai – mired in Japanese occupation and with only civil war and revolution to look forward to.

An artist's representation of von Sternberg's Macao

So when von Sternberg turned his attention to the Far East once again (which in 1950 now meant Hong Kong or Macao given the inconvenience of China having just turned Red) audiences could be forgiven for anticipating another dark and *noir*-y ride. They had enjoyed von Sternberg's previous Oriental dreamscapes and so anticipated the early images released by RKO's press department of the Macao waterfront – the latticework fishing nets, stray black cats, blind beggars, crowded gaming houses, cheongsams, a myriad of bobbing sampans in the harbour… Surely the master had done it again? His Macao of the mind would be as glorious as his Shanghai had been.

Action!

Filming got underway in California in August 1950, though it was immediately obvious that von Sternberg's directorial style was not to everyone's taste. Some saw the script as a melange of other "exotic" thrillers of the 30s, 40s and 50s. They saw elements of 1938's Charles Boyer and Heddy Lamarr's *Algiers* (itself a remake of Julien Duvivier's 1937 French movie *Pépé le Moko)*, the phenomenally successful *Casablanca* (1942), and the 1947 Alan Ladd and Veronica Lake vehicle *Saigon*. Some concluded therefore that *Macao* was too derivative of a genre overly familiar to cinema audiences. Despite over half a dozen full-time RKO scriptwriters getting involved the plot line had major holes in it. A classic case of too many cooks spoiling the broth.

Talking of which, von Sternberg banned the crew from eating while on set, working them long hours without breaks. They were soon starving and tired. Mitchum, keen to ingratiate himself with the lighting and cameramen, as well as perhaps to annoy von Sternberg, brought in baskets of fruit and muffins every day for the crew. Von Sternberg threatened to fire him. The main talent bonded in adversity with Russell defending her friend and co-star. Von Sternberg called her a 'beautiful but stupid girl'. He tried to drive a wedge between the actors, telling Mitchum, 'She has as much talent as this cigarette case'. Relations between the director and his two stars, as well as Gloria Grahame, went downhill from there. What stars of an earlier generation might be willing to have put up with from von Sternberg was past (Dietrich described him as 'the man I most wanted to please'). He was now seen as extremely arrogant and not someone to whom his two current stars were willing to kow-tow.

Mitchum and Russell had become good buddies a year before while making *His Kind of Woman* for Howard Hughes and RKO. That movie is not actually very different in many ways from *Macao* – gambling is central, a down-on-his-luck American, Russell in a relationship with a bad guy etc.... except that it takes place in Mexico rather than Asia. What *His Kind of Woman* (released in 1951) did prove conclusively was that the pair had undeniably great screen presence together – chemistry. Hughes loved their joint screen test so much he told them they were immediately teaming up again for *Macao* even as they made *His Kind of Woman*. As actors still in the rigid studio system and signed exclusively to RKO they didn't actually have much choice.

Hughes was a massive Russell fan, though slightly creepy in his adoration. He took great delight in commenting on her dresses in the movie, obsessing about her figure (in the 1943 film, *The Outlaw*, Hughes effectively invented the underwire bra as a means to enhance her chest). He wrote long detailed notes to von Sternberg after viewing the rushes:

> 'The fit of the dress around her breasts is not good and gives the impression, God forbid, that her breasts are padded or artificial.'

Von Sternberg thought Hughes interfering. Hughes felt the director didn't understand the concept of being an employee. They were both right about each other. For her part, Russell thought Hughes a pest who repeatedly tried to sleep with her.[370]

Gloria Grahame didn't want to be in the movie at all. She knew that the part of Margie, Vince Halloran's girl, had been earmarked for Jane Greer who, like Grahame, made her name in *noir* movies and was yet another of the many sexual obsessions of Hughes. However, his fixation with Greer was love/hate and around the time of casting *Macao* he was in the latter mode. Grahame, like everyone, hated the script, and thought all she had been given to do was to go and pout in the corner, look sexy, and blow on some dice for luck. She had just had a big hit and garnered serious critical acclaim for her role opposite Humphrey Bogart as Laurel Gray in *In a Lonely Place* (1950). That movie was based on the *noir* novella by Dorothy B Hughes and dealt with the dark subject of men returning from World War Two and being so damaged as to turn into killers, unable to readjust to civilian life.[371] The movie adaptation is watered down considerably from the novel, but Grahame excels as the woman drawn to a damaged man despite the threat to herself.

Grahame was a talented actress. François Truffaut remarked that 'It is always sad to see her die.' Signed to Hughes and RKO since 1947 Grahame wanted to be loaned out to Paramount to do *A Place in the Sun*, based on the Theodore Dreiser novel about a complicated love triangle *An American Tragedy*. It would have been a great follow-up movie for her, with some literary heft. Hughes, who admitted he hadn't seen *In a Lonely Place*, refused point blank, and told Grahame she was making *Macao,* whether she liked it or not. Elizabeth Taylor got the lead in *A Place in the Sun* (1951) playing opposite Montgomery Clift. Shelley Winters got the part Grahame wanted, and an Oscar nomination.

Eventually Grahame's career would take off as better parts came along – 1952's *The Bad and the Beautiful* (for which she did get the Best Supporting Actress Oscar), *The Big Heat* (1953), and *Oklahoma* (1955) among them. But not being allowed to work on *A Place in the Sun* long rankled. So, Grahame hated everything about *Macao* even before filming

370 Karina Longworth, *Seduction: Sex, Lies, and Stardom in Howard Hughes's Hollywood*, (New York: Harper Collins/Custom House, 2018) and Christina Rice, *Mean…Moody…Magnificent! Jane Russell and the Marketing of a Hollywood Legend*, (Lexington, KY, University Press of Kentucky, 2001).

371 Dorothy B Hughes, *In a Lonely Place,* (New York: Duell, Sloan & Pearce, 1947).

began. She was in the process of divorcing her husband, the film director Nicholas Ray (who had directed *In a Lonely Place*). The two had married in 1948 and had had a son, but it had been a rocky and tempestuous relationship from the get-go. Grahame and Ray's philandering, her insecurity about her looks and repeated plastic surgeries, and finally Grahame's sexual relationship with her stepson Anthony "Tony" Ray destroyed the marriage.[372] By coincidence Grahame's older sister, an actress called Joy Hallward, had married Robert Mitchum's younger brother John. Her niece by her sister's marriage, Vicky Mitchum, said, 'Over the years, she [Grahame] carved herself up, trying to make herself into an image of beauty she felt should exist but didn't. Others saw her as a beautiful person, but she never did, and crazy things spread from that.'[373]

In the midst of her divorce Gloria Grahame told Ray she would waive any claim for alimony if he got her out of the movie. He couldn't, but they finalised their divorce anyway – and Ray himself was about to become embroiled in *Macao* mayhem.

Discord and Rewrites

Mitchum and Russell's working relationship with von Sternberg was in tatters. Much as the director came to dislike Mitchum he couldn't fire him – Mitchum's star was just too high. And it was Mitchum's role in the film as the war vet washing up in Macao that gave the film its *noir* credentials. Martin Scorsese has said that 'Mitchum *was* film noir,' though he was continuing the tradition pioneered by Humphrey Bogart and Alan Ladd.[374] Mitchum was tall and could be physically intimidating on screen. His film personas – honed in early *noir* movies like *Out of the Past* (1947) were a little more morally ambiguous than even Bogart's self-interested Sam Spade in *The Maltese Falcon* (1941). Mitchum rarely

372 Grahame and Anthony Ray reconnected in 1958 and married in May 1960. The couple went on to have two children: Anthony, Jr. (born 1963) and James (born 1965). The couple divorced in 1974 after 14 years of marriage.

373 Ray Hagen & Laura Wagner, *Killer Tomatoes: Fifteen Tough Film Dames*, (New York: McFarland, 2015), p.73.

374 Joel Dinerstein, *The Origins of Cool in Postwar America,* (Chicago: University of Chicago Press, 2017), p.109.

resists a chance to make some easy money or get some sex, where Bogart has more of a moral code.

For contemporary audiences of *Macao* the tension was heightened by the fact that several of Mitchum's previous movies had seen him perhaps uncharacteristically outsmarted and outclassed by his *femme fatale* opposite players, despite torrid affairs. This meant that the outcome of a Robert Mitchum movie was always in doubt therefore heightening audience expectations. In *Macao* Mitchum is as cool, distanced, nonchalant and sexy as ever. However, his trademark trench coat and rain are absent making Macao perhaps the original "Tropical Noir".[375]

A *noir* hero needs a *femme fatale* and Russell had already proven that she simmered in that role. But she too was rowing constantly with von Sternberg. Brad Dexter was a friend of Russell's, having worked with her the year before on RKO's *The Las Vegas Story,* (also released in 1952) and so took her side in the arguments. Along with Grahame's dislike of being forced to work on the film it does seem that everyone's performances are rather strained at times, though it is hard not to read that into their faces when you know how acrimonious things were on the set. It was agreed by everyone, including the director, that the shooting script made little sense in terms of plot, and nobody understood how one scene connected to another.

*

After roughly a third of the movie had been shot Howard Hughes stepped in, probably on the insistence of Mitchum and Russell, and fired von Sternberg. He brought in Nicholas Ray, Gloria Grahame's husband (mid-divorce proceedings), to direct the rest of the film including the brutal fist fight between Mitchum and Dexter that is a high point of the movie. Action and fight scenes were never von Sternberg's strength; he knew this and rarely included them in his films. Mitchum, who had come to know the sub-standard script inside out, started rewriting it himself to try and join up all the loose plot ends. He was never officially credited but did

375 There are of course other movies that could claim the title. Among them is the 1934 pre-code movie *Mandalay*, directed by Michael Curtiz and featuring Kay Francis as a stateless Russian émigré cabaret singer nicknamed Spot White and stranded in Mandalay (Burma) in a bordello-cum-nightclub run by foreign gangsters.

apparently write some real hard-boiled zingers. The movie's final scene is pure Mitchum:

> Russell (mildly resisting a clinch): 'You're all wet.'
> Mitchum (pulling her closer): 'You'd better get used to me fresh out of the shower.'

Film critics will argue forever about whether or not the film is really von Sternberg's or Ray's. Certainly, many characteristic elements of von Sternberg's style remain – the chiaroscuro cinematography, the expressionistic butterfly lighting, wonderfully over-dressed sets, and the plethora of his trademark motifs such as fishing nets (a style the director had first used back in 1928 on his movie *The Docks of New York*). The film's climax of a pursuit through the harbour amidst hanging nets, and with bobbing sampans in the distance is also classic von Sternberg. When Mitchum encounters Russell on the humid Hong Kong-Macao ferry she rebuffs his initial advances with her electric fan. Mitchum mock defends himself with a pillow and the room is filled with a storm of feathers – another classic von Sternberg moment.[376]

Nicholas Ray biographer Bernard Eisenschitz admits that von Sternberg introduced many of the subsidiary characters that give the movie a foreign feel and show Macao as cosmopolitan – 'a rickshaw man, a Russian émigré doorman, bus driver, barman, Sikh policeman, Portuguese pilot, old fisherman, coolie, captain, Dutch tourist, female barber, Arab. He had the night-club pianist play *Pavane for a Dead Infanta* and an unpublished piece by Granados.'[377] It's also the case that von Sternberg added in the insert of a lizard on a wall that gives a tropical feel and for Vladimir Sokoloff to speak several lines of Chinese. However, Ray spent an estimated US$100,000 on reshoots (estimated at a third of the movie von Sternberg left) and hired two new scriptwriters. Gloria Grahame, who had divorced Ray mid-picture, repeated a version of her previous offer – if he'd cut her scenes out of the movie she'd waive any alimony claims. She stayed in the picture.[378]

376 As noted by Velez, introduction to *RKO Classic Screenplays: Macao.*

377 Bernard Eisenschitz, *Nicholas Ray: An American Journey*, (London: Faber & Faber, 1993), p.171. Some of these cameos and inserts were cut eventually.

378 Eisenschitz, *Nicholas Ray*, p.172.

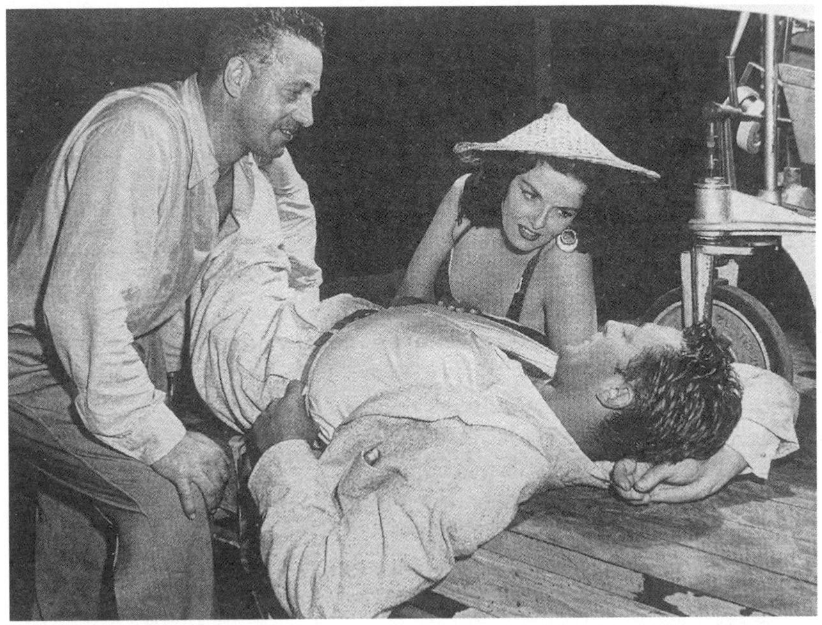

Nicholas Ray with Jane Russell and Robert Mitchum on the set of Macao

In his memoirs, *Fun in a Chinese Laundry*, published in 1965, von Sternberg notes only that after filming the mediocre RKO Cold War thriller *Jet Pilot* (1951), he made, '…one more film in accordance with the contract I had foolishly accepted. This was made under the supervision of six different men in charge. It was called *Macao*, and instead of fingers in that pie, half a dozen clowns immersed various parts of their anatomy in it. Their names do not appear in the list of credits.'[379] In an interview with Kevin Brownlow von Sternberg was more direct: 'Nicholas Ray is an idiot. He did terrible things to *Macao*, he cut it and ruined it. His name did not appear but mine did. It was a great injustice.'[380]

*

Individually the characters and actors in *Macao* are great – Mitchum is trademark cynical and handsome, pioneering the eternal outsider type that would become much more common in a later generation of

379 Von Sternberg, *Fun in a Chinese Laundry*, p.283.

380 Eisenschitz, *Nicholas Ray*, p.173. Kevin Brownlow is a British film historian, television documentary-maker, filmmaker, author, and film editor.

American movies. Russell is an equally cynical and sultry nightclub singer – performing the hit song of the movie *You Kill Me* and then *One For My Baby* in "torch" style on The Quick Reward's stage – and all with a chip on her shoulder the size of the Great Wall.[381] But somehow the characters never quite come together in anything resembling an ensemble. Script-wise it's a wildly stir-fried *noir* that never sticks together. The initially mooted plans to film in Hong Kong and Macao were scrapped and only some stock footage of the two locations (shot earlier by second-unit cameraman Dick Davol) was used.

When the movie was released in 1952 Nicholas Ray's role was not mentioned and von Sternberg was credited as sole director, though he completely disowned the movie. His name is still on the cinema print titles, the DVD, the published screenplay – Ray is never mentioned. Ray may have been mildly and momentarily annoyed by this, but it didn't hurt his career. *Johnny Guitar* (1954), *Rebel Without a Cause* (1955), *The True Story of Jesse James* (1957), and other hit movies were to follow including a return to China (on sets anyway) with the big-budget Boxer Uprising movie starring Charlton Heston, David Niven, Ava Gardner, and Flora Robson in yellowface as Empress Dowager Cixi*: 55 Days in Peking* (1963).

Most reviewers praised the various set pieces within the movie while remaining confused by the plot. The serious critics noted that von Sternberg's trademark unity of form and function was not as strong as in previous movies. However, the movie is (and Ray was in the von Sternberg mould as a director in this sense) often atmospheric and steamy. It is also, as all good *noir* should be, in black and white.

Russell perhaps lacks the exoticism and world-weariness Dietrich might have brought to the role, but still gives a great performance. Grahame, resisting the film to the last both under the directorship of von Sternberg and Ray, clearly couldn't care less, which perhaps ultimately just adds to her couldn't-care-less character. Michael Woulfe's gowns and jewellery for the leading ladies stand out – Russell's *lamé* dress for her nightclub scenes was rumoured to weigh 26lbs!

381 Incidentally, the 2012 film *The Last Time I Saw Macao* (*A Última Vez Que Vi Macau*) directed by João Pedro Rodrigues and João Rui Guerra da Mata, which merges memoir of the Portuguese colony with elements of neo-noir, is bookended by Jane Russell singing *You Kill Me* (music by Jule Styne/lyrics by Leo Robin) from *Macao*.

*

Macao premiered at the New York Paramount Theater in late April 1952. Von Sternberg ignored the premiere. He went on to only direct one more film – in 1953 he made *The Saga of Anatahan*, a dramatization of the true incident about Japanese Marines who refused to believe that they had lost the war.

Howard Hughes wasn't happy – *Macao* lost US$700,000 on release (though now, after numerous TV repeats and video/DVD/streaming sales it has finally made a profit of reportedly US$1.1 million). The much-vaunted long relationship intended for Hughes and von Sternberg at RKO came to a crashing halt.

And one last disaster. Second Unit Cameraman Dick Davol, sent to shoot footage in Hong Kong and Macao, eventually got around to sending Hughes an itemised list of all the bribes he'd had to pay in order to be allowed to film:

Macao Chief of Police
Macao Propaganda Minister
Macao Immigration Officers
Macao Customs Officers
Macao Harbour Police
Hong Kong Immigration Officers
Hong Kong Policemen
PRC Communist Custom Patrol Boats
Macao Sampan Owners
Macao, Hong Kong and PRC Junk Owners and Crews
Pro-Communist Business Owners

If they'd been better-connected they would have known. The CIA had issued a Confidential Information Report in May 1950 on Waterfront Lawlessness in Macao – the waterfront luggage porters were a racket; refusal to pay their inflated fees could lead to a beating or stolen baggage. Additionally the CIA noted racketeers hanging around ticket-selling offices and travel agencies demanding commissions on customers they brought. It was alleged the threats and extortion of the ferry companies was so severe that they were afraid to complain to the Macao Harbour Police (which would probably have been useless – see above list!)[382]

The list of pro-communist front organisations likely to seek bribes was noted in another Confidential CIA Information Report, also from 1950, that listed several dozen "Red" organisations under communist influence including the Vice-Commissioner of Customs, department store workers, the plumbers' and carpenters' unions, down to the peddlers', tailors', and barbers' unions, all hotel workers, and not forgetting the all-important Salted Roast Pork Workers' Union. The hidden costs of the second film unit were always going to be enormous.[383]

Indeed, the second film unit might have agreed with Julie Benton, standing on the deck of the Hong Kong-Macao Ferry watching the Praia Grande come into view:

> Trumble: First trip to Macao?
> Julie: Yes – and from what I hear, once is too much.[384]

In Macao everything is a gamble – Good Luck[385]

However von Sternberg inspired a mini fashion for Macao movies. Though made slightly later, Russian-born B-movie director Edward Ludwig rushed his *Smuggler's Island* (1951), set in Macao (courtesy of some stock footage and filmed on a set in Los Angeles) about some sunken gold off the coast, into cinemas. It didn't get very good reviews (it didn't really deserve any) and largely went straight into second-run and drive-in cinemas. It was run-of-the-mill fare despite the exotic location and, though it was pretty low budget, still didn't manage to turn a decent profit for Universal Studios. Slightly later 1953's *Forbidden* retrod ground familiar to audiences from von Sternberg's *Macao*. Again from Universal

382 CIA Information Report – *Waterfront Lawlessness in Macao* – RDP82-00457R004900590009-9, May 31, 1950.

383 CIA Information Report – *List of Communist Organisations in Macao 1950* – RDP82-00457R004300490005-0, February 23, 1950. RKO made a little money back by selling Davol's footage of Macao to Universal who used it in the opening credits of their 1953 Tony Curtis/Joanne Dru Macao-set noir, *Forbidden*.

384 *RKO Classic Screenplays: Macao*, p.8.

385 *RKO Classic Screenplays: Macao*, p.13. As spoken by a Portuguese Customs Officer to Trumble who has expressed his hope that 'the dice will get as hot as the weather.'

Studios the not-quite-yet movie star Tony Curtis and Joanne Dru star as gangster Eddie Darrow and a mobster's widow Christine Lawrence falling in love in Macao and incurring the wrath of the gangster owner (played by Lyle Bettger) of the Lisbon Club casino. Despite some location shots it was entirely filmed on the San Diego waterfront.

Piraten von Macao: the German poster for Smugglers Island, 1951

Those location shots would get one more outing when Clark Gable visited Macao filming *Soldier of Fortune* (released 1955). Many might have expected Gable's movie to give von Sternberg's *Macao* a run for its money – it was directed by Edward Dmytryk, often touted as a von Sternberg rival in the *noir* filmmaking stakes. But *Soldier of Fortune* is really a Hong Kong movie – at least for Gable; his co-star and love interest in the movie Susan Haywood never left America and shot all her Hong Kong and Macao scenes on a Hollywood studio set alongside Gable and Mel Welles, who plays Fernand Rocha, a Portuguese gambler and cheat based in Macao.

And finally audiences had Jennifer Jones as the Chinese-born bi-racial "Eurasian" physician and author Han Suyin visiting 1949 Macao briefly from Hong Kong in the Hollywood adaptation of Han's autobiographical novel *Love is a Many Splendored Thing* (1955). The movie features location footage of Hong Kong shot by second-unit director Otto Lang, but with sets standing in for Macao. But once again, fleeting though Macao's role is in the film, it is important, and Macao plays to type. This is essentially a 'dirty weekend' – Han Suyin is taken to Macao by her married lover Mark Elliot (William Holden), supposedly on assignment in the colony.[386]

386 Holden plays Elliot as an American though in reality Han Suyin's lover was Ian Morrison, the Peking-born journalist and son of George Morrison 'Morrison of China', the long-time London *Times* journalist in Peking. As with Holden's character Morrison did die in Korea killed by a landmine. The film is of course an adaptation of Han Suyin's *A Many Splendoured Thing*, (London: Jonathan Cape, 1952).

She makes the journey from Hong Kong on the ferry.[387] Arriving, she checks into the hotel, meets with Elliot, has dinner, some dancing, and then on the way back to their room (presumably to consummate the relationship) Elliot is called away to the Korean War. This particular message of the movie is clear: Macao is where you go to sin, to indulge baser passions, to avoid the censorious stares of the nearby British colony.

In the subsequent 70 years since its release, *Macao* has sunk into obscurity, certainly not one of von Sternberg's better remembered movies. It's a shame. Ultimately it is, as von Sternberg originally envisioned, a vivid *noir*, a Macao of the mind, a *Casablanca* of the South China Seas.

387 Stock footage of the *SS Fatshan* is used in the movie. The *Fatshan* famously started out in the 1930s as a Hong Kong-Canton ferry, was seized by the Japanese during World War Two, spent some time as the Hong Kong-Macao ferry, and eventually, in 1971 tragically sank off Lantau Island during Typhoon Rose with a terrible loss of life.

Harbin Boxer, Shanghai Gangster, Manila Smuggler, Macao Refugee

Paul Lojnikoff
(1956)

Paul Lojnikoff

'I beg you, let me stay'
– Paul Lojnikoff (1956)

'I beg to stay!'

Admittedly the story of Paul Lojnikoff's life involves only a very brief time in Macao. Throughout the twentieth century he spent much more time in many other places – Harbin, Shanghai, Manila, Rio de Janeiro among them. But Macao was to be a highly significant turning point that ended one phase of Lojnikoff's quite extraordinary journey and began another that was to be equally remarkable. And, in that sense, Lojnikoff's brief unintended sojourn in the colony is an instructive story about Macao in the 1950s. It shows Macao as a post-war, post-1949 Chinese revolution place of refuge; Macao as a place to escape past indiscretions; Macao as a potential launchpad to another life. Paul Lojnikoff's story is also perhaps an insight into how the newly communist People's Republic of China treated Macao as a place in which to rid itself of foreign undesirables, a dumping ground for unwanted *laowai* troublemakers.

When Paul Lojnikoff arrived in Macao in the summer of 1956 he had already lived a tumultuous and morally questionable life. Only in his mid-to-late-30s, he had already endured terrible poverty and hardship in Manchuria, survived the hard-scrabble underbelly world of pre-war Shanghai, spent time in occupied Manila, and then some years in a Chinese prison. Macao was his next staging post, and his arrival was to be perhaps one of the most dramatic the Portuguese colony had ever seen.

*

On an August afternoon in 1956 a motorised junk called the *Sanfatlee* motored into Macao's harbour and attempted to dock at Wharf No.10. On board was a crew that included two Communist Chinese guards and a single rather skinny and shaggy-bearded European man. The *Sanfatlee* had sailed from Canton and then crossed to Macao from the small outlying island of Lapa. Before World War Two Lapa had been under largely (though contested) Portuguese control. The Japanese then occupied it in 1938 as they overran southern China. At the end of the war, Nationalist China reclaimed the island and so it eventually came under, as the American media had started to say in the 1950s, "Red Chinese" control. Alerted to the *Sanfatlee's* presence nearby, the Macao authorities expressly forbade the junk to land.

The Portuguese maintained a constant guard at Wharf No.10. It had already been used several times by Chinese soldiers defecting from the nascent People's Republic to Macao – a major headache for everyone involved. A couple of years previously a disaffected Chinese soldier posted at a People's Liberation Army (PLA) sentry post on Lapa had stolen a sampan and made for Wharf No.10 accompanied by a Thompson submachine gun, one hundred rounds of ammunition, and four live hand grenades. He had eventually been disarmed and taken ashore. However, there had been a subsequent diplomatic row, angry accusations of kidnapping from Peking, and so now the Portuguese were not keen on encouraging any more defections across the narrow strait between the PRC and the *Província da Macao*.[388] The *Sanfatlee* however confused the Macao authorities as it appeared that the Chinese wished simply to disembark their European passenger and then return to their guardhouse on Lapa.

When the Chinese guards aboard the *Sanfatlee* attempted to hand the European man over to the Macao authorities, they initially refused to accept him. The Portuguese immigration officials claimed that he did not have the correct papers. It was true, he had no passport nor any form of formal identification. Indeed, it was unclear if the man had any way at all to corroborate himself. The Chinese guards on the *Sanfatlee* did not wish to return to Lapa with the European, having been ordered by officials in Shanghai and Canton to deliver him to Macao. The man himself was, for reasons that would soon become clear, not eager to make the return voyage. When it became obvious that the *Sanfatlee* would not be allowed to land, and that the Portuguese were not going to accept the man in transit onto their territory, there was a stand-off.

A Maritime Police cutter blocked access to Wharf No.10 while the *Sanfatlee* idled just offshore refusing to return to Lapa. This situation lasted for several hours – enough time for some local newspaper stringers to show up and ensure that the situation made the newspapers around the world, at least in a couple of paragraphs, the next day. Seeing a crowd of curious folk gathering on the shore, and hoping they might be

388 *Chinese Press Review*, American Consulate General Hong Kong, July 1953 summarising a report that appeared in the pro-Nationalist *Chung Nan Jih Pao*, September 4, 1953.

sympathetic to his plight, the man decided to end the stalemate himself by jumping overboard and attempting to swim ashore.

At this point nobody was quite sure what to do. The Chinese onboard the *Sanfatlee* wanted to turn around and motor away, leaving the problem to the Portuguese. The Portuguese Maritime Police did not wish to drag the man ashore without knowing who he was. Both sides hesitated, fearing possible repercussions from the man drowning. Neither side wanted the attendant bad publicity of, for the Chinese, not having discharged their orders and, for the Portuguese, letting a man, possibly a refugee from "Red Communism", drown on their territory. The man himself, treading water, pleaded to be allowed to remain in Macao – 'I beg you, let me stay' the newspapers reported him crying out and then repeatedly 'I beg to stay'.[389] Eventually the Portuguese relented, the man was pulled from the water onto the wharf; the *Sanfatlee,* satisfied they had got rid of their problem, swiftly turned round and headed back to Lapa Island presumably breathing a large sigh of relief. The man was given a towel and taken to the nearest police station for questioning. The inquisitive press followed behind.

*

Quite what the man told the *Polícia de Segurança Pública* is not clear. The American newspapers claimed he told them that he had spent the last five years in a 'Red China concentration camp'.[390] What is certain is that he did not tell them the full story of his life and career in China. Still, he apparently did tell them enough to get 'special permission' to remain in Macao for the time being as a refugee.[391]

Direct from Shanghai People's Prison

The man identified himself as Pavel, or Paul, Ivanovich Lojnikoff, a "White", or stateless, Russian émigré.[392] He claimed to have spent the last five years in a Chinese prison, specifically the Ward Road Gaol in

389 'Russian Permitted to Land in Macao', *Honolulu Star-Bulletin*, August 1956, p.2.

390 Ibid.

391 Ibid.

392 Lojnikoff is sometimes, in various newspaper accounts, official documents and memoirs, spelled as Lojnikof. He is variously referred to as Paul Ivanovich, Paul I., and sometimes as Paul J.

Shanghai. This was enough to gain Lojnikoff temporary leave to remain in Macao and he was, according to newspaper reports, extremely grateful. He reportedly began crying in relief when told he had been granted temporary asylum.

In the summer of 1956 the Macao Police would not be surprised to hear that a foreigner was being released after spending time in a Shanghai prison. After 1949, Shanghai's Ward Road Gaol, aka the "Shanghai Bastille", originally administered by the Shanghai International Settlement, its Municipal Council, and the Shanghai Municipal Police, was brought under the control of the communist government's Municipal Military Control Commission and renamed the Shanghai People's Prison.[393]

Within the massive facility, the largest prison in Asia at the time, were a number of foreigners convicted of various crimes. These included some who had been incarcerated by the Nationalist Chinese District Court in Shanghai and remained in the prison during the transfer from the Nationalists to the Communists half a dozen years previously. Those accused of minor crimes or with short sentences were released and deported quickly. But others, most of whom were convicted of serious crimes including murder, and often had life sentences, remained on the cell block becoming prisoners of the new PRC. These hard-core criminals were joined by a number of foreigners who committed crimes in the early years of the PRC along with a number of American missionaries in Shanghai accused of espionage. Regardless, one by one most of the foreigners left the Shanghai People's Prison having finished their sentences, died inside, or been released for one reason or another.

But a few remained. And they eventually needed to be dealt with. Habitual criminals, murderers, accused missionary-spies, and those who had openly collaborated with the Japanese during the war. The new communist government certainly didn't care to continue providing free lodging and food to these people. And so, prisoner releases of the final incarcerated foreigners, often people largely forgotten by anyone in the outside world, began to happen in the summer of 1956.

For instance, in July 1956 long-time Shanghailander and British subject Charles Archer, who had been convicted of the murder of a Chinese gold dealer in Shanghai in 1947, was taken in the sealed compartment of a train from Shanghai to Canton. From there he was taken by PLA guards

393 Later known as Tilanqiao Prison and eventually closed in 2013.

to the border with Hong Kong at the Lo Wu checkpoint. He was handed over to waiting Red Cross officials, who signed for him and then took him for a medical check-up in a Hong Kong hospital. To be fair nobody back in Britain appears to have paid much attention, though *The Straits Times* in Singapore ran the headline – "KILLER FREED".[394] Archer was repatriated to England as soon as his health allowed. It was a country he didn't know, and had never visited previously, having spent his entire life in Hong Kong and Shanghai.[395]

Lojnikoff, it appears, fell into a similar category. But his case was slightly more confusing in that he had been imprisoned as a stateless citizen with no nation to claim him or ever enquire about him. Whether they remembered him or not, and whether he'd ever set foot on English soil, Charles Archer was provably, and with a paper trail to show, undeniably a British subject. Lojnikoff's entire background was unclear, and nobody was claiming him. Indeed, given the many upheavals in his life – both the vicissitudes of history as well as his own purposeful obfuscation – he had not a sheet of paperwork to show the Macao authorities. It seems likely that given this situation the Chinese weighing up what to do with Lojnikoff, realised that the route they usually used for British and American freed prisoners – across the Lo Wu border – wouldn't work. The British would simply refuse to accept him. And so they thought that maybe Macao, and the Portuguese, would be an easier option.

For his part, Paul Lojnikoff was telling anyone who'd listen that he was grateful to the Macao authorities and Portugal for being able to stay, at least temporarily, in the colony. But there is a lot more to the Paul Lojnikoff story. It begins in an Eastern Europe in turmoil, then the Manchurian city of Harbin, a career as a professional boxer, two decades in one of the most notorious gangs of the inter-war Shanghai underworld milieu, a questionable relationship with the Japanese occupiers of Shanghai and Manila as a collaborator throughout the war, and then a renewed criminal career in the chiaroscuro of post-war Shanghai while on the run from American Military Intelligence.

When W Somerset Maugham described the French Riviera as, 'a sunny place for shady people' he could also have been describing post-

394 'Killer Freed', *The Straits Times* (Singapore) via United Press, July 27, 1956, p.1.

395 I have told the more complete story of Charles P Archer, his life and trial, in my Audible Original, *Murders of Old China*, (London: Audible Originals, 2019).

war Macao.[396] Paul Lojnikoff wasn't the only shady type to turn up on its sunny shores in the 1950s, but he is one of the most fascinating characters through which to tell an alternative history of his era.

Harbintsy

In the story of Paul Lojnikoff there's what he'd like us to know, what he'd not be so keen on us knowing, what he purposefully obscured, and what we simply don't, and will probably never, discover. All four stories are equally interesting. He'd like us to know he was Russian-Polish, that he was a rated and successful boxer in Shanghai, that he enjoyed a wartime romance with one of the most beautiful and notorious women in Japanese-occupied Manila, that he later enjoyed a successful and legitimate career as a gem dealer. He's less keen on us knowing that he spent much of the war shuttling between Shanghai and Manila on dubious business for the Japanese army, or that he was part of a notorious gang of Russian and Russian-Polish criminals in the Shanghai International Settlement. He purposefully obscured his role as a collaborator with the Japanese in Shanghai during the war, perhaps from as early as the summer of 1937 until the war's end. And then there's the short interregnum period after the Japanese surrender until his arrest by American Military Intelligence in Shanghai and his imprisonment in Ward Road Gaol.

So, here's what we know…

Lojnikoff was born some time between 1913 and 1922 in Harbin, Manchuria, of Catholic Russian-Polish parents – that is to say his family was ethnically and culturally Polish and Catholic, but from when it was a part of the Russian Empire.[397] His origins in China are somewhat obscure. His parents may have come to work on the Russian-run Chinese Eastern Railway or may have been part of the massive emigration of Russians and Russian-Poles eastwards to escape the Bolshevik Revolution, the so called "White Russians". As with so many other Russian émigrés they ended up in Harbin, by far China's most Russified city.

396 W Somerset Maugham, *Strictly Personal*, (Doubleday, Doran & co., inc., 1941), p. 156.

397 Lojnikoff's birth date is extremely unclear. The American newspapers in 1945 reported him as 32 – i.e. approximately 1913. However, one man who claimed to be his good friend later in life claimed he was born in 1922 while others throw in dates in between.

In the 1920s Harbin was one of the world's most cosmopolitan places. Though nominally under Chinese rule, Harbin had quickly become a distinctly Russian city – with 120,000 White Russian émigrés, street names and neon signs in Cyrillic, and nine daily Russian language newspapers and magazines sold from street corner kiosks. There was also an English language newspaper, six in Chinese, two in Japanese, another in Ukrainian, and one in Yiddish. Onion-domed churches including the looming cathedral of Saint Sophia and the ornate wooden cathedral of St Nicholas served the Orthodox community, alongside the Church of the Holy Annunciation. Two large and imposing synagogues – one on Artilleriskaya Street and a second on Diagonalnaya Street served the Russian Jewish community and included a soup kitchen, free clinic, and a home for the aged and destitute.

Russian style paddle steamers lined the Sungari River (the Songhua to the Chinese), tramcars and horse-led droshkies screeched and clattered along the cobbled streets. There were monasteries for the devout, Russian schools and technical colleges for the aspirant; theatre, opera, and an all-Russian orchestra for the culturally inclined, and department stores along Kitayskaya Street ("Chinese Street", and the location of the landmark Hotel Moderne) in the city's downtown Pristan district. You could eat at Russian delis, buy black bread at Russian bakeries, street kiosks sold a local version of kvass made with sorghum. Hotels, like the Moderne, the Orient, and the Grand, housed Russian commercial travellers while Russian-run flophouses were billets to the indigent and poverty stricken. Russian-staffed brothels catered to the émigré's baser needs with card games and other illicit attractions also provided. Suicides were common as refugees decided to end it all stripped of their former wealth and position and with no chance to return to their homeland.

Most Poles fitted easily into Russian society although Polish children could attend the Henryk Sienkiewicz Polish Middle School. The Lojnikoffs attended the Polish-administered neo-Gothic Cathedral of the Sacred Heart of Jesus. There were numerous Polish businesses including the city's major brewery and a daily Polish language newspaper.

However, it would seem that things were not that great at the Lojnikoff house. At a young age Pavel, or Paul, and his younger brother Pyotr (or Peter) ran away from home for unspecified reasons. They appear to have fended for themselves on the streets of Harbin, where temperatures

Shanghai in the 1930s

could fall as low as 25 or even 30 degrees below zero in winter. According to different sources the brothers were informally adopted by a local gym, the *Russky Sokol*. There both became talented and fairly successful lightweight class boxers.

Quite when the Lojnikoff brothers moved to Shanghai is unclear, probably sometime in the mid-1930s as the Japanese began to consolidate their occupation of Manchuria and the situation got tougher for the White Russians in Harbin. Certainly it seems that by 1937 the brothers had established themselves as keen amateur boxers in the city, which had an interwar population of approximately 25,000 Russian émigrés.

Paul's boxing career lasted into the war and the Japanese occupation of the International Settlement. It was reported that Paul Lojnikoff won the 1942 China Lightweight Boxing Championship beating a Japanese challenger, "Knocker Nokano", knocking him out in the third round. He was taller than the average lightweight but rangy with a long reach for the weight class. Overall he fought 13 professional fights, winning seven, losing four and drawing two. Though Lojnikoff had very little formal education he was said to be talented in languages, speaking Chinese (which dialect is not stated), some Japanese, English, Russian, and Polish (and later after his stay in Macao, Portuguese).

Shanghai Vice

In the late 1930s Shanghai Lojnikoff became a face about town. The historian of the inter-war Shanghai underworld Bernard Wasserstein claims he was known as a "pretty boy".[398] Part of his charm came from being a champ in the ring. He had also apparently served with the Russian Regiment in the Shanghai Volunteer Corps. He fought at the Burlington Hotel on Bubbling Well Road (Nanjing West Road) and at the Canidrome in the French Concession. He was one of several Polish boxers well known in Shanghai at the time that included his brother Peter and a former merchant seaman turned welterweight boxer, Edward Kowaliski, known as "Big Teddy". A number of Lojnikoff's fights were referred to the Shanghai Boxing Commission – in short he was widely believed to be involved in fight-fixing.

Lojnikoff was also working for the Japanese, employed by a front company buying up scrap metal and industrial diamonds for the Japanese military in China. He was arrested by the Frenchtown *Sûreté* several times, once for apparently defrauding his brother Peter's mother-in-law. Paul was courting too and in the war, doing well from his collaborationist activities, married an eccentric and rich American socialite in Shanghai, the Baroness Ksenia Girard de Soucanton, who had actually been born in Gatchina, near St Petersburg in 1917, and who lived permanently in a suite at the Cathay Hotel on the Bund. His socialite friends and collaborationist activities soon brought him into the sphere of Eugene

398 Bernard Wasserstein, *Secret War in Shanghai: Treachery, Subversion and Collaboration in the Second World War,* (London: Profile Books, 1998), p.235.

Pick, an actor, opera singer, impresario, criminal, and spy who ran the so-called Hovans Gang in wartime Shanghai in league with Japanese Naval Intelligence.

This collaboration with the Japanese took Lojnikoff to occupied Manila in the early 1940s. There the Hovans Gang traded commodities between Shanghai and Manila, did a little gem and silver dealing and apparently informed widely on members of the Filipino resistance and their contacts in Shanghai. The Baroness Ksenia Girard de Soucanton seems to have disappeared. Lojnikoff reportedly took up in Manila with a nightclub singer, Españita de Vidal, who, as well as being beautiful, talented, and a minor star in early Philippines cinema, was from a well-connected family close to the wartime collaborationist leader of the Philippines, Jose P Laurel. Lojnikoff gained protection and valuable intel for his Japanese masters. Bernard Wasserstein claims Lojnikoff provided protection to de Vidal from patriotic Filipinos who saw her as a traitor.[399]

Manila's Escolta Street, 1930s

Through this alliance in Manila Lojnikoff usurped Eugene Pick as head of the Gang and expanded their activities into blackmailing resistance fighters, stealing industrial grade diamonds and gun running.

Shanghai Bastille Regular

When the war ended, the position of the foreign collaborators was precarious with both the Chinese authorities and American military intelligence in Shanghai hunting for them. Quite how Lojnikoff survived

399 Wasserstein, *Secret War in Shanghai*, p.253.

in Shanghai post-war is not entirely clear. There are rumours of large-scale black marketeering, which make sense given the scale of the black market in Shanghai at the time and Lojnikoff's partially still-at-large connections from his wartime dealings. It seems at some point, and with the relationship with the Manila showgirl not surviving the end of the war, he became involved with a Czechoslovak woman in Shanghai. Again it is uncertain if they formally married or not, but it does appear they had a son. Lojnikoff's freedom didn't last long – really only a matter of months after the city's liberation. In November 1945 he was arrested on espionage charges and sent to Ward Road Gaol.[400]

IN TROUBLE

SHANGHAI, Nov. 15. (Delayed) (AP)—An army announcement said today that American intelligence officers have arrested a man they identified as Paul Lojnikoff, 32, onetime lightweight boxing champion of China, for investigation of alleged war criminal activities.

The Reno Gazette Journal, November 16, 1945

The record then gets a little hazy – Lojnikoff wasn't overly forthcoming in Macao later, the records from that time in Shanghai as the Nationalist government collapsed and the Communists took control are unclear, buried deep, or lost. After his first arrest he seems to have spent at least the next six years in the Shanghai Bastille. No easy incarceration – the prison was overcrowded, disease outbreaks were common, and treatment basic. Ward Road was still damaged from bombing in the war, infested with bugs and rats, the food terrible. Casual punishment for minor infractions was meted out frequently by the guards, beatings with bamboo lathis

400 'Boxer Rebellion is Over in China', *Spokane Chronicle* (Washington), November 16, 1945, p.6. An admittedly pretty good pun from the subs desk at the *Spokane Chronicle*.

were regular. There was little news of the outside world while executions by hanging regularly occurred. It seems Lojnikoff was released around 1951, though he seems to have ended up swiftly back in Ward Road (though on what charge is not stated). Overall, it seems he survived the best part of a decade in Ward Road.

And then one day in 1956 he was taken from his cell, accompanied by guards to the railway station, taken to Canton and put on a boat with other guards heading towards Macao. There was then the stand-off alongside Wharf No.10 before Lojnikoff decided to leap overboard and swim towards the Portuguese colony crying out 'I beg you, let me stay'. And the authorities at Macao did, at least for a while.

*

Post-1949 relations between Portugal and the People's Republic of China were tense. Portugal was withholding its recognition of the PRC; official contact was non-existent despite 400 years of relations and a shared border. In January 1950 Portugal saw its old ally Britain recognise Beijing, but America, which Lisbon could not now ignore, was more hesitant.[401] Macao remained in an indecisive and potentially difficult place not unlike the neutrality balancing act the colony had had to undertake during World War Two.

1956 was a particularly tense year in Macao and Hong Kong – both seeing a swelling number of arrivals of Chinese refugees across the border. In January that year the US Army added Macao to a list that included the Soviet Union and Eastern Europe, Cambodia, and Vietnam as a place that 'officers and personnel with special intelligence information' should not visit due to fears of kidnapping.[402] Tension between the PRC and the Republic of China on Taiwan had been high, political clamp downs in China intensifying and the first effects of famine were being felt in parts of the country that would be exacerbated in the following few years. Visiting Macao in February 1956, Dr Carl J Giers, a Baptist pastor from

401 For a more in-depth look at post-1949 Portugal-Macao-PRC relations see Pedro Aires Oliveria, 'Portuguese Consuls and Diplomats and the Coming of the People's Republic of China', c.1945-1950, pp. 186-211, within Sue Onslow and Lori Maguire (Eds), *Consuls in the Cold War,* (Leiden and London: Brill, 2023).

402 'Experts "May be Kidnapped"', *The Daily Telegraph* (London), January 7, 1956, p.7.

the United States, noticed Chinese refugees 'spreading their wares on the pavement, one next to the other, for blocks.'[403]

The "Bamboo Curtain" was not totally enforced though. When the PRC government opened the borders in February 1956 an estimated 50,000 Chinese from Hong Kong and Macao visited mainland relatives and attended Canton trade fairs around Chinese New Year. The borders were closed again on March 10.[404]

The refugee problem was an issue for the Macao authorities…and not just the Chinese fleeing "Red China". A reported 450 Portuguese who had originally settled in Macao and then moved to locations in China – Foochow, Shanghai, Amoy, Tientsin, Peking and elsewhere – sometimes remaining for several generations now had to leave the PRC and arrived back in Macao (or in Hong Kong) as refugees. They were mostly broke, living in camps maintained by the Portuguese authorities and the US-based National Catholic Relief Service (NCRS). Officials of the NCRS managed to gain permission for about 200 of these refugees to move to California. The remaining 250 or so were relocated by the Portuguese to Brazil.[405]

*

Lojnikoff it seems was offered passage to Brazil. He took it and settled in Rio de Janeiro. He adopted the name Paolo and became a jeweller and gem dealer – skills he had partly learnt in the war trading between Shanghai and Manila for the Japanese. His store supplied crystals, tourmalines, and other gemstones to many North American jewellers from San Francisco to Idaho.

But it seems he probably never left his old black marketeering and smuggling ways completely. Trouble was never far away from Paul, or Paolo, Lojnikoff. In 1974 it was reported that a 74-year-old man called Humphrey Wallace Toomey from Coral Gables, Florida, and a former vice president of Pan American Airlines Brazilian operation, was shot to death through the heart while in his pyjamas at his daughter Gail's

403 'Dr Giers Visits Port of Macao, Under Portuguese for 300 Years', *Chattanooga Daily Times*, March 9, 1956, p.8.

404 '50,000 Chinese Cross Red Border to Visit Families', *The News* (Paterson, New Jersey), March 13, 1956, p.25.

405 'Catholic Missionary Priest Asks Aid, Housing for Portuguese Refugees', *Stockton Evening & Sunday Record* (California), March 29, 1956, p.37.

home in the wealthy Copacabana district of Rio. Nothing was reported stolen. Police investigator Ayrton Luzada de Abreu Lima interviewed the daughter, a night guard, the maid, Toomey's friends in the city, and several never formally named women, as well as his former son-in-law and still current business partner in a Brazil-USA gem trading venture, Paolo Lojnikoff.[406]

After months of getting nowhere 'arresting all the prostitutes in Copacabana', the *Los Angeles Times* described the investigation as a 'comedy of errors'. Enticingly the *LA Times* also noted that a lead suspect had undergone a blood test which proved nothing except, to their apparent surprise, that they were positive for syphilis. Unfortunately the paper does not tell us if this suspect was Paul Lojnikoff or not.[407] Eventually in March 1975 a local woman accused her former lover, a small-time bank robber and burglar, of murdering Toomey. However, few bought the theory – nothing of value was stolen, Toomey's daughter's missing Yorkshire Terrier dog was never seen again after that night, and there was no sign of forced entry at the apartment. The trail ran cold.

*

Paul Lojnikoff's life never got any less exciting. His own Rio home was robbed in 1984. He was reported as 65 years of age in the Brazilian papers and still looking like a fit lightweight. The raiders smashed up his house and tried to bust into his safe. Police shot several of the robbers trying to escape, leaving them dead on his lawn.[408] Lojnikoff bought a condo in Barra de Tijuca. He was rumoured to keep a pistol on the nightstand by his bed. His status as a legendary ladies' man was maintained and he may have married as many as seven times – certainly to Gail Toomey in Rio, but whether any of these seven weddings included the Baroness Ksenia Girard de Soucanton, Españita de Vidal in Manila, or the Czechoslovakian woman in post-war Shanghai is hard to ascertain definitively.

There is little evidence that Lojnikoff was particularly interested in religion as a young man in China. However, perhaps later in life he

406 'Rio Police Probe Death', *Akron Beacon Journal* (Ohio), December 12, 1974, p.63.

407 'Air Pioneer's Death Makes Headlines But No Progress', *The Los Angeles Times*, January 14, 1975, p.2.

408 'Bandidos Mortos Após Bebedeira No Assalto', *Última Hora* (Rio de Janeiro), September 27, 1984, p.7.

rediscovered his Catholicism. He wrote a short religious-themed book *Sete Anos Conversando Com Espíritos* (*Seven Years Conversing with Spirits*), told anyone who would listen that he considered himself a reincarnation of St Paul, and apparently did a lot of charitable work. Into his later years he remained rangy, thin and in apparently good shape. That's not to say he lived a particularly healthy life. He kept to many of his former sins – one person who remembered him recalled that he smoked two packs of cigarettes and drank a quart of whisky a day throughout his life.

Paul Lojnikoff and his safe, Rio de Janeiro, 1984

Pavel/Paul/Paolo Lojnikov (he had taken to spelling his name with a 'v' rather than 2 'f's in Brazil) died in Rio de Janeiro in 2002. He is buried in the Cemitério de São João Batista (St John the Baptist's Cemetery) in the Rio beachfront neighbourhood of Botafogo.

It's true he didn't stay in Macao long.... But it was a crazy moment in a crazy life.

The Beautiful Graveyard

Ian Fleming
(1959)

Ian Fleming

'All my life I have been interested in adventure, and abroad. I have enjoyed the frisson of leaving the wide, well-lit streets and venturing up back alleys in search of the hidden authentic pulse of towns.'
– Ian Fleming, *Thrilling Cities* (1963)

A Brief Sojourn

In 1959 the London *Sunday Times* approached Ian Fleming to write a series of articles on the world's most exciting places. Fleming, a dedicated *bon vivant* and serious gourmet, obviously couldn't resist an all-expenses-paid trip around the world. He was by now internationally famous for his James Bond books and making good money from his creation. He'd published seven novels featuring the British spy with an eighth, *For Your Eyes Only* just underway, though the movies that would catapult 007 to international superstardom were still some years away.[409]

Yet when Ian Fleming arrived in Macao in November 1959 the colony was somewhat down on its uppers, woefully under-subsidised by Portugal, whose intransigent ageing dictatorship was dealing with violent resistance in its African colonies while negotiating relations with the new Communist government bordering its primary remaining Asian possession. But Fleming came rapidly to like the place. What had been the Macao of his mind was in fact matched by the reality he encountered when he arrived. He sojourned for only a limited time, enjoyed a few good dinners, some gambling, sipped *vinho e licores* while watching visiting Hong Kong bachelors dance with Eurasian hostesses to a Filipino band at the Central Hotel. And then he wrote it all up.

*

Macao had experienced a steady period of decline throughout the 1950s, even as movies that played into the pre-war image of the colony, like Josef von Sternberg's *Macao*, and B-movies such as *Smuggler's Island* and *Forbidden* in 1951 and 1953 respectively, were still being made. Visitors such as Alonzo L Baker had come expecting to encounter the 'world's wickedest city' in the 1950s. Baker, a professor at a Methodist-affiliated college in California was evidently flummoxed by the Macao he

409 The half dozen being *Casino Royale* (1953); *Live and Let Die* (1954); *Moonraker* (1955); *Diamonds are Forever* (1956); *From Russia with Love* (1957); *Dr No* (1958); and *Goldfinger* (1959). For details on Fleming's *Sunday Times* commission and relationship with Leonard Russell see Fergus Fleming, ed., *The Man with the Golden Typewriter: Ian Fleming's James Bond Letters*, (London: Bloomsbury, 2015), pp.236-237. The first Bond movie was *Dr No*, released in 1962.

encountered.[410] On one level, as a religious man, he was glad to observe an apparent decline in gambling and prostitution (though he appears to be basing his assessment of the decline on somewhat hyped-up pre-war articles in the American press rather than any first-hand knowledge). Baker viewed the colony as 'harmless', a little low stakes gambling, bored croupiers, the once infamous red-light street of the Rua de Felicidade now home only to a few rather bored and intermittently employed prostitutes. The Rua de Felicidade was perhaps the most famous street in Macao, described in just about every sensationalist newspaper report and pulp novel, it features in Hendrik de Leeuw's *Cities of Sin*, and in von Sternberg's *Macao* – 'Mucho-fun – win plenty money – fan-tan – dice – big gambling…'[411] By the end of the 1950s it was more nostalgic tourist attraction than hardcore sin street.

Baker was concerned that Macao's economy – the fishing trade, the traditional fireworks and incense stick industry, as well as the casinos and 'pleasure streets' – were being strangled by a blockade launched by "Red" China. Untrammelled sin was bad, but (to Baker) communist influence was far worse. Macao was in fact suffering under a double blockade. There was firstly the drawing down of the "Bamboo Curtain" and the cessation of much cross-border business and travel between Macao and southern China. And secondly the blockade of "Red China" by the western nations stifling potential currency earning exports from Macao to the mainland. Beijing was also punishing Portugal for being a charter member of the United Nations (an organisation the People's Republic of China was displeased with over boycotts linked to China's support of the fledgling Democratic People's Republic of Korea, North Korea, during the Korean War). So Macao was adversely affected by sanctions from both East and West. Hong Kong, although better supported from London, was for many of the same reasons as Macao also in economic recession, adding to Macao's woes. The decline in visitors from Hong Kong meant that the flow of tourists to gamble, carouse (those expats sipping *vinho e licores*

410 Baker was a Professor of Political Science and International Relations at the Methodist-affiliated College of the Pacific, a private liberal arts school founded in 1851 with its campus in Stockton, California. He was a late life academic having spent most of his working life in the printing and publishing business. Alonzo L Baker, 'Macao Today: Two Blockades Squelch World's Wickedest City', *Oakland Tribune* (California), August 9, 1955, p.11.

411 *RKO Classic Screenplays: Macao,* p.16.

and waltzing with the taxi-dancers to the Manilaman band observed by Fleming at the Central Hotel) and do business in Macao, was significantly down.

Thrilling Fleming

Fleming, born in 1908, was 50 years old when he arrived in Macao. He had been born to a wealthy and titled family, though he was the second son – his older brother Peter who travelled and wrote extensively about China inherited the Oxfordshire estate, most of the money, and the title of the Squire of Nettlebed.[412] The Fleming children were all interesting – Peter as a bestselling travel writer and husband of the British film star Celia Johnson, while their younger half-sister (the illegitimate daughter of an affair between the painter Augustus John and Ian's mother Eve) became a notable cello player. Fleming attended Eton and then the military academy at Sandhurst (leaving after a year having contracted a scandalous dose of gonorrhoea). He dabbled in banking (boring), diplomacy (performing poorly in the Foreign Office entrance exams), and finally journalism (which he discovered he had a talent for to the relief of his family). This latter career choice led to a visit to the Soviet Union and interest in international affairs. He had what was considered a "good war" in Britain's Naval Intelligence Division, as did his brother Peter. Espionage and deception seem to have come naturally to him. Dashing and handsome, Fleming engaged in a long affair with Ann Charteris, the wife of Viscount Rothermere, the right-wing press baron. Somewhat scandalously for the times Rothermere divorced Charteris in 1951 because of her relationship with Fleming. The couple finally married in 1952 at Goldeneye, Fleming's home in Jamaica. In the early 1950s he began writing his Bond novels and the first, *Casino Royale*, was

412 Peter Fleming (1907-1971) wrote two travelogues involving China – *One's Company* (London: Jonathan Cape, 1934) and *News from Tartary* (London: Jonathan Cape, 1936). Additionally he translated the French doctor and travel writer André Migot's *Caravane vers Bouddha* (1954) as *Tibetan Marches* (London: Rupert Hart-Davis, 1955). He also wrote two history books concerning the region – the first covering the Boxer Uprising and the Siege of the Legations, *The Siege at Peking* (London: Rupert Hart-Davis, 1959) and *Bayonets to Lhasa: The First Full Account of the British Invasion of Tibet in 1904* (London: Rupert Hart-Davis, 1961).

published in 1953 – the rest is literary, cinematic, and popular cultural history.

In 1959 Leonard Russell, then the literary editor of *The Sunday Times,* and also Fleming's friend and golfing partner, couldn't think of anyone more suited to write a series of articles on the world's most exciting and sinful cities than the creator of James Bond. He approached Fleming (as ever in these sorts of British circles over lunch at their London club) with the idea for a series of articles covering six European and six international cities that were places Fleming had found interesting. Russell wanted *Thrilling Cities* to focus on the 'bizarre and perhaps the shadier side of life' rather than simply reviews of hotels, restaurants, and tourist sites.[413] Fleming was to travel to these cities in 1959 and 1960, capturing a snapshot of each during roughly the same period. In Europe he chose Hamburg, Berlin, Vienna, Geneva, Naples, and Monte Carlo. Further afield he opted for Honolulu, Los Angeles/Las Vegas, Chicago, New York, Tokyo, Hong Kong… and Macao. The commission, Fleming hoped, would also provide good source material for future Bond novels.

Thrilling Cities, 1964

To Macao with Dick

Thrilling Cities begins with Fleming flying with the old BOAC – British Overseas Airways Corporation, a forerunner to British Airways – to Hong Kong for a three-day look-see followed by his trip to Macao. He embarked on the *SS Takshing* ferry for the three-hour voyage from Hong

413 Fleming, *Thrilling Cities*, (London: Jonathan Cape, 1963), p.7. When the articles appeared details of hotels, restaurants, local cuisine, and night life spots were included. Further editions have been published by Vintage in 2013 and Ian Fleming Publications in 2023.

Kong to Macao (with third-class passengers still below the waterline while upstairs eager gamblers could play onboard slot machines or visit a mahjong room) with a very interesting companion, the Australian veteran Far East journalist and correspondent for *The Sunday Times*, Richard "Dick" Hughes.

In 1959 there was perhaps no better guide to Macao – its secrets and scandals – than Dick Hughes, whom Fleming referred to as his "comprador".[414] Originally from Melbourne, the son of a music-hall ventriloquist, Hughes had become a war correspondent, spent time in Shanghai, found himself in Tokyo on the eve of Pearl Harbor, covered the Casablanca landings in 1942, and then, after the defeat of Japan, settled in Hong Kong from where he covered regional politics and the war in Korea while running up a sizeable bar tab. Whether it was true or not most people considered him to be a British spy, and a few thought him probably a double agent. He did little to dissuade people and generally worked hard on his gregarious persona. He famously dominated the bar at the Hong Kong Foreign Correspondents' Club in its heyday.[415]

Richard Hughes

Fleming had first come to know Hughes during his time working as foreign manager for the Kemsley newspaper group (which then owned *The Sunday Times*). But Hughes was a man Fleming would have sought out one way or another. Fleming was obsessed with espionage and spooks, had indeed been a very effective one in Naval Intelligence, and knew two thing about Hughes that fascinated him. The first was that Hughes had met the pre-war Soviet master spy in Japan, Richard Sorge of the infamous "Sorge Spy Ring", in Shanghai and Tokyo, and the second

414 John Pearson, *The Life of Ian Fleming*, (London: Jonathan Cape, 1966), p.339.

415 When Fleming first met Hughes for a drink to talk Macao, the Foreign Correspondents' Club was located at 41A Conduit Road. It has since moved to Lower Albert Road.

was that in 1951 Hughes had gone to Moscow and got the scoop on the two British Intelligence officer/KGB defectors Guy Burgess and Donald Maclean.[416]

Hughes was larger-than-life – physically and socially – with a massive head and a nose that looked like it had been pummelled at some point. A big drinker, trencherman, and teller of tales often true, but also often very tall. He was though generally considered immensely knowledgeable on the Far East and a serious journalist. His book about his time in Asia, *Foreign Devil: Thirty Years of Reporting in the Far East*, is easily one of the best foreign correspondent memoirs of the period.[417] According to one early Fleming biographer, Hughes was a 'repository of the inside stories of all the biggest rackets and finest restaurants in the East.'[418] Back in his youth in Australia he'd been a keen amateur boxer, though somehow this got inflated into stories of him having been a heavyweight champion.

Hughes was certainly a man around whom legends grew up. Fleming described him as 'a giant Australian with a European mind and a quixotic view of the world.'[419] He was to become immortalised twice. Firstly as the inspiration for Fleming's Australian intelligence officer Dikko Henderson in *You Only Live Twice* (1964). Then by John le Carré who knew him a decade or so later in Hong Kong. Le Carré modelled his character "Old Craw" on Hughes in his magnum opus of Hong Kong espionage, *The Honourable Schoolboy* (1973) – 'he saw the gross figure of Old Craw in his kimono planted at the top of the staircase, hugely pleased, calling him "Monsignor" and "you thieving pommy dog," and exhorting him to haul his upper-class backside up here.' [420]

416 Nicholas Shakespeare, *Ian Fleming: The Complete Man,* (London: Harvill Secker, 2023), pp.400-407.

417 Richard Hughes, *Foreign Devil: Thirty Years of Reporting in the Far East,* (London: Andre Deutsch, 1972). Hughes also mentions Macao in his book *Hong Kong: Borrowed Place – Borrowed Time*, (London: Andre Deutsch, 1968).

418 Pearson, *The Life of Ian Fleming,* pp.338-339.

419 Fleming, *Thrilling Cities*, p.20.

420 Ian Fleming, *You Only Live Twice*, (London: Jonathan Cape, 1964). Fleming dedicated *You Only Live Twice* to Hughes. Fleming, who also visited Japan which would become a location for Bond, was essentially researching and sketching out ideas for the novel as he went. John le Carré, *The Honourable Schoolboy*, (London: Hodder & Stoughton, 1973), p.168.

Gold!

Especially after the commercial buzz of Hong Kong, Macao initially appeared outwardly quiet to Fleming. The cobbled alleyways, the thoroughfares traffic-less. But he felt adventure must lurk just beyond reach. Fleming wrote that Macao was, 'as picturesque as, and deader than, a beautiful graveyard.'[421] But there was one subject that really piqued Fleming's interest… gold.

From the inception of the *Thrilling Cities* project, Fleming had intended to visit Macao. The idea of the Portuguese colony had long interested him, reminding him of his wartime espionage exploits in neutral Lisbon, and the time he spent in the nearby casinos of Estoril and Cascais. As the *SS Takshing* neared the Macao terminal Fleming grew excited, noting a single 'Kiplingesque' Portuguese gunboat in the harbour and the Praia Grande 'of once grandiose private houses ornamented with the most exquisite, though dilapidated, baroque plaster and stonework.' The waterfront of 'rotting godowns announcing in sun-faded letters that they were, for instance,

> FABRICA DE AGUAS GASOSAS

or the

> KWONG HUNG TAI FIRECRACKER MANUFACTURING COMPANY…' [422]

From the outset Fleming knew that his piece on Macao would focus on the colony's gold smuggling reputation. Gold trafficking and Macao were a much-linked and much-repeated trope in the 1950s. Gold was a motif of numerous pulp fiction novels and sensationalist newspaper articles as well as the 1951 Hollywood B-movie *Smuggler's Island* that opened with the on-screen caption:

> Macao: isle of intrigue, of secrecy

421 Fleming, *Thrilling Cities*, p.31.
422 Fleming, *Thrilling Cities*, p.31.

The constant whisper is heard in a dozen languages:
Gold...
Gold: the lifeblood of Macao[423]

Or consider the previously discussed Josef von Sternberg/Nicholas Ray 1952 movie *Macao* where, on the ferry from Hong Kong to Macao, vagabonding ex-soldier Nick (Robert Mitchum) meets lounge singer Julie (Jane Russell) for the first time:

Nick: Smuggling anything in?
Julie: The way I hear it, you smuggle things out of here – not in.[424]

The colony's Economic Services Bureau director and *eminence grise* Dr Pedro José Lobo saw gold as being the solution to the double blockades and economic downturn. In a letter to Michael Howard, his editor at Jonathan Cape in London, Fleming noted early on in the planning for *Thrilling Cities* that it was gold smuggling that had caught his interest in Macao.[425] Gold... and Dr Lobo, 'the Gold King of the Orient'.[426] It's hard not to see the writer of James Bond in these twin fascinations – caches of gold moving through an exotic locale, smack bang up against the largest communist country in the world, and the whole place reputedly a nest of spies and adventurers. Add to this the mysterious and mercurial Dr Lobo

A smiling Dr Lobo

423 Opening voice-over of Smuggler's Island (Universal Pictures, 1951), based on a story and adaptation by Herbert Magolis and Louis Morheim, script by Leonard Lee. For more on this movie see Paul French, 'Smuggler's Island – *Em busca da força vital de Macau*', *Paragrafo* magazine (*Ponto Final*, Macao), #85, November 2023.

424 *RKO Classic Screenplays: Macao*, (New York: Frederick Ungar Publishing, 1980 – copyright RKO: 1952), p.11. See Chapter 13, *Mayhem in Macao*, on Josef von Sternberg/Nicholas Ray's movie.

425 Letter from Ian Fleming to Michael Howard at Jonathan Cape, November 26, 1957, contained in *The Man with the Golden Typewriter*, pp.183-184.

426 Fleming, *Thrilling Cities*, p.29.

who might easily, just by his name alone, potentially stand tall in the long line of Fleming's great villains – Octopussy, Auric Goldfinger, Le Chiffre, Francisco Scaramanga, Dr No, Dr Lobo!

What particularly intrigued Fleming was that Macao under Dr Lobo's influence had i) no income tax, ii) complete freedom of import and export of foreign currencies, and iii) was an active free gold bullion market. The notion of anyone arriving with cash, departing with gold and with no questions asked or taxes levied piqued Fleming's thriller writer antenna. While much of this may have been a legitimate, or at least semi-legitimate trade in the precious metal, Fleming was aware that profits derived from the burgeoning Far East heroin trade were being laundered through Macao's casinos and converted into gold to be retained away from the reach of the Hong Kong authorities or smuggled out of the country.

From the 1920s through to the mid-1960s Pedro José Lobo was to be at the centre of events in Macao. From the louche pre-war years, through the delicate balancing act of Portuguese neutrality in World War Two, to the colony's new relationship with communist China, Dr Lobo (he claimed a doctorate from a correspondence course at Chicago University), as he was known to everyone, was central to the twist and turns of events in Macao.

Lobo was born in 1892 in Manatuto, on the northern coast of Timor, 30 miles or so from the capital Dili. Lobo's heritage was mixed: Malay, Macanese-Chinese, Dutch, and Portuguese were all in the swirl of his genes. He gained a place to study at the prestigious Igreja e Seminário de São José (St. Joseph's Seminary and Church) on the Rua do Seminario in Macao. After he moved to Macao Lobo never looked back and made his life and career in the colony. In 1920 he moved up the Macao social scale when he married Branca Helena Hyndman, who came from a long-established Eurasian trading family. They had six children and established a home at the prestigious address of #6 Avenida da Praia Grande with a "holiday home" at the Villa Verde.

During World War Two Dr Lobo became a name everyone in Macao knew, respected and, in a few cases, feared. As director of the Central Bureau of Economic Services he had close contact with the Japanese and organised supplies of food, fuel, and medicines for the colony to keep things going.[427] On January 16, 1945, American planes bombed and machine-gunned the Porto Exterior. Lobo was inspecting his warehouses there as the gas tanks exploded, killing five and injuring several more. Lobo's official car was strafed but he survived by throwing himself out of the vehicle onto the ground. Then, with civil war raging on mainland China and the likelihood of the country turning communist, Lobo knew Macao needed new sources of capital to keep the colony afloat. The major source was to be gold trading.

Fleming requested a meeting with Dr Lobo, sat back and waited for a reply.

*

After a few waterfront G&Ts under a banyan tree at the Macao Inn on Travesso do Padre Narcisco, Fleming checked into a suite at the old Bela Vista Hotel with a balcony overlooking the bay – enjoying those *Sunday Times* expenses. The Bela Vista was perhaps somewhat past its 1930s heyday but still the best establishment in town. However, in *Thrilling Cities*, Fleming writes more about, and was clearly fascinated by, the Central Hotel on the Avenida de Almeida Ribeiro (colloquially referred as San Ma Lo) near the Largo do Senado. For many years the restaurant that occupied the ground and mezzanine floors of the hotel had been called simply "United States of America". The apocryphal line attributed to Fleming while sitting on the balcony at the Central Hotel, G&T in hand, gazing down on the crowds queuing for the nearby Victória Cinema, listening to Dick Hughes's tales of old times at the pre-war Hotel Presidente and high adventure in the Far East was, 'I suppose a man could be happier here than anywhere else in the world…For about a fortnight.'[428]

The Central Hotel had been built in 1928 and the casinos inside run by the local gambling and "entertainment" tycoon Foo (aka Fu) Tak-yam.[429] It was then the tallest building in Macao, and the first equipped

427 See Chapter 10, *Stanley's War – The Wartime Adventures of Stanley Ho Hung-sun (1941-1945).*

428 Pearson, *The Life of Ian Fleming*, p.339. The Central Hotel had been known as the Hotel Presidente before the war.

429 Foo Tak-yam (1894-1960) famously got into the casino business in the 1930s with the short-lived Shum Chun (Shenzhen) casinos that, for a while, threatened Macao's gambling business. After they were closed he moved into gambling in Macao

with elevators. Casinos were to be found on the fifth and sixth floors offering mostly fan-tan and three-dice games of chance, their entrances guarded by tall security guards recruited from Mozambique and usually ex-Portuguese Army in Macao. While recommending the establishment in *Thrilling Cities*, Fleming did admit that the Central Hotel, a 'House of Pleasures' for sure, was also 'the least recommendable place on earth', at least in polite company. As he noted, 'the higher up the building you go, the more beautiful and expensive are the girls, the higher the stakes at the gambling tables, and the better the music.'[430]

Senado Square with the Central Hotel in the background

Fleming enjoyed gambling but could make little sense of the games at the Central – pure chance games such as fan-tan and hi-lo, which Fleming thought childlike pastimes that led to inevitable losses and far inferior to his preferred roulette.[431] Fleming soon burnt through $100. Fleming and

and held the monopoly until he died, and Stanley Ho took it over in 1962. Obviously the casino business was always a little rough and ready – Foo was kidnapped in 1945 and lost part of his right ear during the prolonged negotiations for his release. In 1937 Foo bought the Presidente Hotel, renamed it the Central Hotel, and put casinos on the fifth and sixth floors.

430 Fleming, *Thrilling Cities*, p.33.

431 Though of course roulette is also a game of pure chance despite Fleming's advocacy of the so-called James Bond betting system, which involves spreading 20

Hughes then went up to the next floor to see the dancefloor. Here they found jazz, a taxi dancer named "Garbo", and a steady flow of G&Ts that prompted some rather stereotyped opinions on Asian women.

From the windows Fleming could see billboards and neon signs for Coca-Cola, Chesterfield cigarettes, and all manner of Chinese characters he couldn't make head nor tail of. Avenida de Almeida Ribeiro was a busy street of cars, single decker buses, bicycles, and a uniformed policeman directing traffic.[432] If you stood on the steps of São Paulo Cathedral facing away from the ruined frontage and out across Macao, the Central Hotel loomed up a half dozen or more storeys higher than any other building in the colony in 1959.

*

Fleming thought Macao's gold obsession ultimately down to a distrust of paper money in Asia. It's not an unreasonable theory when you consider how bad Chinese hyperinflation rates got: prices rose by more than a thousandfold in the 1940s, paper money was essentially useless, banks closed, defaulted, collapsed, investors queued for days, businesses failed, families were impoverished. It all arguably ended in a revolution as the Chinese population gave up on the Nationalist government's corruption and economic mismanagement.

But Macao's role in the gold trade was also a strategy of Dr Lobo's. In a territory with precious little manufacturing industry, a depressed post-war services economy, no raw materials, gold could be a way to invigorate the Macanese economy. Lobo wanted to encourage the trade while simultaneously not wanting to talk about it much – a tricky proposition. And it was hard to say no to a noted author like Fleming and the London *Sunday Times.* It's also worth considering who Lobo thought he'd be talking to? A *Sunday Times* journalist? The author of James Bond? Or a former (and perhaps still active) British Intelligence Officer?[433] Lobo could not have been unaware that in the late 1940s and 1950s rumours

---

units of stake unevenly across the board. Great thriller writing and movie action, but unfortunately it doesn't work.

432 Fleming didn't comment, but Simon Kent in his contemporaneous novel *Ferry to Hong Kong*, (London: Hutchinson, 1957) describes Macao's policemen as 'operetta-uniformed' (p.9).

433 Brigitta Olubas, *Shirley Hazzard: A Writing Life*, (London: Virago, 2022), p.71.

of gold smuggling in Hong Kong's neighbour Macao were rife in British Intelligence.

Fleming did get to interview Dr Lobo at his home, the swimming pool-equipped Villa Verde on central Macao's outskirts. Lobo greeted him 'in his trim blue suit, stiff white collar and rimless glasses, looking like a bank manager or a dentist.'[434] By the late 1950s Lobo was in his late sixties, yet he was trim, fit, chatty, and drinking Johnnie Walker whisky with his guests. Fleming flattered him, claiming that he had heard Lobo was a noted composer.[435] They dined on macaroni and vegetable soup. But Fleming got very little out of Lobo beyond tourist recommendations, some polite inanities (he railed against opium smuggling and the pernicious influence of the triads on the business) and a complimentary signed copy of his gramophone record *Gems of the Orient*. Lobo could afford to be reticent on the gold trade in 1959. He had effectively already decided that, with Hong Kong now recovered economically from the war and occupation, casinos, tourism, hotels, and leisure would be the driver of the colony's economy in the future. It was also the case that the days when a boat, or a Catalina, could slip unnoticed from Macao to Hong Kong were over. Those, from Shanghai or elsewhere in mainland China, who had gold to get out had either managed it or lost it by the end of the 1950s. And so the notorious gold trade had fizzled out by the mid-1960s as casinos were prioritised.

Macao in the 1950s

434 Fleming, *Thrilling Cities*, p.38.

435 Lobo was a composer and conductor. He had released several records including *Gems of the Orient* and composed an operetta about Macao's wartime experiences, *Cruel Separation*. He also founded Rádio Villaverde which broadcast music and live horse racing.

'What had I learned of Dr Lobo, the gold king whose name is whispered with awe throughout the East? Absolutely nothing at all.'[436]

Ultimately Fleming found the sin of Macao all perhaps a little packaged? Dick Larsh, the *Variety* correspondent who visited in the mid-1950s, noted that R&R-ing American GIs could pay enterprising local tourist agents US$20 (approximately US$225 in 2024) for an overnight hotel room, return ferry fare to Hong Kong, three meals, a sightseeing trip with professional guide, and a pipe of opium.[437]

Fleming drank, danced, gambled, talked gold and opium smuggling, and pondered the role of triads. Later, back in Hong Kong, antiquing on Cat Street ('the Portobello Road of Hong Kong'), sitting in the Jardines box at Happy Valley, playing a round at the Fanling Golf Course in the New Territories up near the border with mainland China, he decided that Macao was certainly less respectable than the British colony where his background opened plenty of doors, but that he rather missed Macao.

And then he moved on, Dick Hughes still in tow, flying out of Kai Tak, over Formosa in a Comet aircraft towards Okinawa, his next thrilling city.

Ian Fleming Recommends…

By the way, you may like to know Fleming's 1959 recommendations, what he called 'Incidental Intelligence', when visiting Macao? He recommended visitors stay at the Bela Vista Hotel up on tree-lined Penha Hill. The double bedrooms were the best and a room with a balcony a must. They should make time to dine (and drink the excellent G&Ts) at the two-storey Macao Inn, opposite the Governor's Residence at the junction of the Avenida da Republica, which was lined with smart residencies (including Central Hotel proprietor Foo Tak-yam's house at #23-34) and along the Travessa do Padre Narcisco, close to the British Consulate on the Praia Grande.

Fleming also recommended trying the local dishes of African chicken baked in coconut, *bacalao* (dried codfish), all manner of *peixe salgado* (salted fish of various types), and roasted Macao pigeon as well as

436 Fleming, *Thrilling Cities*, p.42.

437 'Adventure Still Rules Macao; Gals Serve Your Opium at Hotel Bedside', *Variety*, August 11, 1954.

sampling the excellent list of Portuguese wines. He advised gambling at the Central Hotel, that cricket fighting was an autumn activity, and the Grand Prix was in November. He also noted Fat Siu Lau restaurant (a specialist in roasted pigeon) on the Rua de Felicidade and the Long Kei fish restaurant.[438]

*

By the 1960s the chain-smoking and heavy drinking was catching up with Fleming and he had a series of heart attacks, though was still working hard. His *Sunday Times* travel articles were published as the collection, *Thrilling Cities*, in late 1963. The book was generally well-received and reviewed. Fleming was a 'tourist extraordinary' said the *Daily Express. The Times* liked, 'Fleming's smooth, sophisticated, personally conducted tours', while *The Listener* paid the perhaps backhanded compliment of, 'a fascinating informative mock-up, disarmingly snob-ridden'. Conversely *The Guardian* thought he, 'writes without any pretension at all'.[439] The American reviews were slightly less flattering, but generally acceptable. Fleming kept on with Bond and also moved into children's literature, his children's novel *Chitty Chitty Bang Bang: The Magical Car* (1964) was a hit movie in 1968.

Ian Fleming died in 1964 at just 56 years of age. He has achieved a sort of immortality thanks to Bond, the novels, and subsequent movies not to mention the luxury lifestyle of his Goldeneye estate in Jamaica, the legendary gold typewriter, his rumoured sexual appetites and infidelities, his serious chain smoking. He remains the subject of new biographies, and probably will do as long as Bond remains in the public consciousness around the world. [440]

438 The Fat Siu Lau remains, now run by the third and fourth generations of the same family, at #64 Rua da Felicidade. The Long Kei (formerly at Largo do Senado/Avenida de Almeida Ribeiro) is, I believe, no longer in business while the Macao Inn (formerly the Hotel Carmen) was demolished in the 1970s.

439 'The Oriental Lady and the Spy', *Daily Express*, December 12, 1963, p.6; *'City Couriers', The Times*, November 14, 1963, p.17; *'Book Reviews',* The Listener, November 14, 1963, pp.799–800; 'Two Flying Visitors', *The Manchester Guardian*, November 22, 1963, p.6A.

440 Bond only actually ventured to Macao on screen in *The Man with the Golden Gun* in 1974 when Roger Moore visits the Macau Palace floating casino in the Porto Exterior (opened in 1962, closed in 2007), and *Skyfall* (a story not taken directly from a Fleming

Despite being a couple of years older than Fleming and of similar appetites Dick Hughes lived longer. He remained the "doyen of the Far East foreign press corps" and a stalwart of the Hong Kong Foreign Correspondents' Club. Hughes died in Hong Kong in 1984.

---

novel) in 2012 when Daniel Craig visits the 'Golden Dragon Casino' (actually a set at Pinewood Studios near London).

Appendix: The Geography of Macao

The Macao discussed in this book consists of peninsular Macao, Taipa (sometimes referred to as Tamtsai Island or Typa in early English-language texts), and Coloane (sometimes referred to as Colowan in older English works). Today Macao can add to this trio its "New Urban Zone" of reclaimed land and Cotai, the reclaimed land now joining the islands of Taipa and Coloane. This may soon be added to with the inclusion of the former Hengqin Islands, but this had not been formally ratified at time of publication. Before land reclamation steam launches made the journey back and forth twice a day from the Porto Interior to the sparsely populated Taipa and Coloane.

During the Portuguese colonial period Macao was administratively divided into two municipalities (*concelhos*) and seven civil parishes (*freguesias*). The parishes were administrative subdivisions of the municipalities. The *concelhos* were Macao (the peninsula) and Ilhas (literally "Municipality of the Islands"), consisting of Taipa and Coloane, as well as the (Hengqin) islands of Dom João, Isla Montanha, and Lapa/Lappa (with some changes of ownership over the centuries, as outlined in the chapter dealing specifically with the islands).

The parishes:

Santo António – named after the St Anthony's Church – the area around the ruins of the Church of São Paulo (St Paul's) and the Leal Senado;

Sé – (a cathedral, or from the Holy See) – named after the Sé Catedral da Natividade de Nossa Senhora and Igreja da Sé (The Cathedral of the Nativity of Our Lady) – the area to the south-east of peninsula Macao including the Praia Grande;

Nossa Senhora de Fátima – Our Lady of Fátima – the area situated in the north of peninsula Macao and the largest of the civil *freguesia* (parishes);

São Lázaro – named after the St Lazarus Church, which used to house a leper community – the parish that occupies the central-east region of peninsular Macao and the smallest *freguesia*, though covers the area including the Guia Hill;

São Lourenço – Saint Lawrence – the southwestern portion of peninsular Macao;

São Francisco Xavier – after the Jesuit missionary Francis Xavier – covering Coloane;

Freguesia de Nossa Senhora do Carmo – named after Our Lady of Mount Carmel – the area covering Taipa.

Road Types in Macao

Portuguese	**English**
Alameda	Boulevard or Promenade
Avenida (Av.)	Avenue
Azinhaga	Alleyway
Beco	Lane (sometimes Crescent)
Calçada	Sidewalk
Caminho	Avenue/Road
Estrada (Estr.)	Road
Largo	Square
Rua	Street
Pátio	Yard
Pista	Private Road
Praia (Praya)	Waterfront
Ramal	an extension to an existing road or short side road
Travessa (Tv.)	Cross Street

Chinese Towns & Cities

Old	**New**
Amoy	Xiamen
Canton	Guangzhou
Chefoo	Yantai
Chengtu	Chengdu

Chuhai	Zhuhai
Chungking	Chongqing
Chungshan	Zhongshan
Chusan	Zhoushan
Dairen (or Dalny)	Dalian
Foochow	Fuzhou
Fort Bayard	Zhanjiang
Hankow	Hankou
Hsinking[441]	Changchun
Kiating	Leshan (Sichuan)
Kiautschou	Jiaozhou
Kwangchowan	Guangzhouwan
Kweilin	Guilin
Mukden	Shenyang
Nanking	Nanjing
Ningpo	Ningbo
Pakhoi	Beihai
Peking	Beijing
Shumchun (Shum Chun)	Shenzhen
Swatow	Shantou
Tientsin	Tianjin
Tsingtao	Qingdao
Weihaiwei	Weihai
Yunnan-fu	Kunming

Chinese Provinces

Old	**New**
Fukien	Fujian
Hopei	Hebei
Kansu	Gansu
Kwangsi	Guangxi
Kwangtung	Guangdong
Shantung	Shandong
Turkestan	Xinjiang

441 While under Japanese occupation from 1932-1945.

Acknowledgements

My thanks to the following: Gary Brown of Vibe Books at Mui Wo on Lantau Island, Samantha Culp, my former editors for many years at Hong Kong University Press Colin Day and Michael Duckworth, Mike Goodridge at Good Chaos, Jo Lusby of Pixie B, Shonee Mirchandani of Bookazine Hong Kong, Lawrence Osborne, Luis Corte Real and Margarida Damião of the publishers Saída de Emergência in Lisbon, Megan Stevenson of Group 8 Media, Jonathan Wattis of Wattis Fine Art in Hong Kong, Phil Whelan and Annemarie Evans of RTHK3.

In Macao my thanks to Gonçalo Lobo Pinheiro, Ricardo Pinto of the Livraria Portuguesa bookshop, *Ponto Final* newspaper (and *Paragrafo – Ponto Final's* bimonthly literary supplement), Agnes Lam of the University of Macao, and Sara Santos Silva at *Macao News*.

Libraries and museums are of course essential and my thanks to the London Library, The Special Collections Library of the University of Hong Kong, the Australian National University, the Museu do Oriente (Lisbon), The Macau Public Library, and the Arquivo de Macau (The Archives of Macao administered by the Cultural Affairs Bureau).

A special thanks to Dave Besseling, Long Reads Editor of the *South China Morning Post* weekend magazine in Hong Kong. Dave originally commissioned an article on Tokyo's attempt to buy Macao from Lisbon, My thanks also to John D Wong of Hong Kong University for his thoughts on the colony's early aviation developments and the Pan Am China Clippers. Additionally, the Pan Am Museum Foundation and (for the "China Scissors" translation footnote) the anonymous Tweeter "Telegram Sam". Dave also originally commissioned a version of the article on the history of the Hengqin Islands.

An earlier version of *Mayhem in Macao* first appeared in *Cha: An Asian Literary Journal*, Issue 33, September 2016. My thanks to the founding co-editor Tammy Ho Lai-Ming. Ricardo Pinto allowed me to write about the movie *Smuggler's Island* for *Paragrafo* magazine.

I was originally asked by the Shanghai publisher Graham Earnshaw to write an introduction to his reprint of Aleko Lilius's *I Sailed with Chinese*

Pirates. I also spoke about Lilius with Annemarie Evans on her RTHK3 show *Hong Kong Heritage*. My thanks also to Jan Kronholm who provided additional information to fill in aspects of Lilius's often rather dubious biography.

Jenni Marsh, my then editor at CNNi, commissioned and edited an earlier version of *Stanley Ho's War*, which was published shortly after Ho died in 2020. Once again Ricardo Pinto helped me locate various texts dealing with the history and biography of Dr Lobo. Laura Hemming of the University of Wisconsin-Madison Libraries and Georgia Brown of the American Geographical Society Library at the University of Wisconsin-Milwaukee kindly helped me locate Harrison Forman's photographs, diaries, and articles from his 1950 Macao visit.

I first became acquainted with the work of George Smirnoff during a tropical downpour in Macao around the early 2000s. I was visiting for a couple of days and wandering the old town somewhere up near the Camões Gardens when a rainstorm started. I dived into a tiny art studio-cum-tourist shop where an elderly Chinese gentleman was sketching away while his son attempted to sell the sketches to visitors. They were mostly, so they told me, sketches of Smirnoff's originals that tourists liked. I bought a few, though somehow over the years and over many moves have annoyingly lost them. Despite searching on repeated trips back to Macao I've never found the studio again. As that day recedes into the distance I wonder if I didn't perhaps dream it all – part of the Macao of my own imagination! I am indebted to the Gwulo.com website maintained by David Bellis for information on Smirnoff's time in Hong Kong, as well as to the research of Katya Knyazeva, and the writings of Jason Wordie for additional information.

The chapter on Deolinda da Conceição would have been impossible without the translation work of David Brookshaw.

Though the Macao shelf still remains significantly smaller than the bookshelves for Shanghai, Peking, or Hong Kong there are some extremely useful texts I should note that are not included in the footnotes throughout the text. These include:

Charles R Boxer, *The Great Ship of the Amacon: Annals of Macao and the Old Japan Trade, 1555-1640* (Lisbon: Centro De Estudos Historicos Ultramarinos, 1963).

JM Braga, *The Western Pioneers and Their Discovery of Macao* (Macao: Instituto Portugués de Hong Kong, Imprensa Nacional, 1949).

António Correia and Ernesto Matos, *Macau 22-113* (Lisbon: Mythos de Er, 2022).

Docomomo Macau, *Macau Modern Architecture* (Macao: The Urbanism and Architecture Research Center in Macao (Docomomo), 2022).

Duarte Drummond Braga, *As Índias Espirituais Fernando Pessoa e o Orientalismo Português* (Lisbon: Tinta da China, 2019).

Duarte Drummond Braga, *Cina e Macao: Camilo Pessanha* (Lisbon: Livros de Bordo, 2023).

Morris Collis, *The Grand Peregrination* (London: Faber & Faber, 1949).

Regis Gervaix (aka Eudore de Colomban), *Resumo da História de Macau* (Macao: Tip. do Orfanato da I. C., 1927).

Robin Hutcheon, *Chinnery, the Man and the Legend* (Hong Kong: South China Morning Post Publishing, 1975).

Gonçalo Lobo Pinheiro, *O Que Foi Nao Volta Ser...* (or *What Was Doesn't Come Back to Be*), (Macao: Ipsis Verbis, 2022).

Jonathan Porter, *Macau: The Imaginary City* (Boulder, Colorado: Westview, 1996)

Lindsay Ride, May Ride, and Bernard Mellor, *An East India Company Cemetery: Protestant Burials in Macao* (Hong Kong: Hong Kong University Press, 1995).

Tim Simpson, *Betting on Macau, Casino Capitalism and China's Consumer Revolution* (Minneapolis: University of Wisconsin Press, 2023).

Manuel Teixeira, *A Gruta de Camões em Macao* (Macao: Imprensa Nacional, 1977).

CX George Wei, *Macao: The Formation of a Global City* (London: Routledge, 2016).

Katrine K Wong and CX George Wei, *Macao: Cultural Interaction and Literary Representations* (London: Routledge, 2013).

Henrique Travassos Valdez (National Senator for Macau), *Por Macau!... Artigos e Discursos* (Macao: Tip. do Orfanato da I. C., 1922).

Clive Willis, *China and Macau* (Burlington, VT: Ashgate, 2002).

Jason Wordie, *Macao: People and Places Past and Present* (Hong Kong: Ansanga, 2013).

Anne Witchard kindly edited and commented on the evolving manuscript over several incarnations. And finally thanks to Cara Wilson for the cover design, Paul Christensen for editing, and Pete Spurrier of Blacksmith Books for publishing another *Destination...*

Image credits

Front cover – the ruins of St Paul's (São Paulo) Cathedral, Santo António, Macao. Built in the early 1600s, largely of wood, it was destroyed by fire in 1835. The stone façade that survives today was added in the 1630s. Philadelphia: C.H. Graves, publisher, circa 1902.

The blue edging is based on the design of Macao's street signage inspired by traditional Portuguese *azulejo* white tiles with blue surrounds.

Macao map – courtesy of Jonathan Wattis Fine Art – 12-13
Public domain – pp: 21, 22, 23, 26, 28 (Carl Van Vechten), 33, 43, 42, 46, 52, 61, 75, 80, 82, 95, 97, 111, 129, 132, 139, 142, 165, 170, 178, 179, 190, 191, 192, 194, 196, 199, 205, 210, 211, 213, 215, 219, 221, 223, 235, 236, 243 (self-portrait), 245, 246, 248, 249, 259, 263, 275, 281, 289, 294
Charles Toogood Downing, The Fan-Qui in China,1836 – 43
Author's collection – 44, 93, 115, 119, 128, 158, 177, 186, 222, 265, 292
Special Collections, University of Bristol Library – 49, 86 (Lai Fong Afong Studio)
Instituto de Ciências Sociais Universidade de Lisboa – 59
J Paul Getty Museum, Los Angeles – 72
Royal Asiatic Society of Great Britain and Ireland – 76
Jonathan Wattis Fine Art – 81
Yale Center for British Art, Paul Mellon Fund – 103
Museu de Macau – 114
Macao Archives' Exhibition on the History of Piracy in Macau (August 2020) – 125, 126
D. Appleton and Company – 130

Wisconsin News Record – 135
Património de Influência Portuguesa – 136
Instituto Cultural de Macau – 141
Arquivo Histórico Parlamentar, Lisbon – 146
Brooklyn Eagle – 149
John Wiley Books – 152
United Nations Office at Geneva Library – 153
Kansas City Star – 157
Berkshire Eagle – 166
The Morning News (Delaware) – 169
The Macon (Georgia) Telegraph – 171
United States Post Office – 180
Bibliothèque Nationale de France – 183
Studio Harcourt – 193
Museu Luís de Camões – 224 (x2), 225, 226 (x2), 227, 228
Noticias de Macau – 229
Livraria Francisco Franco – 231
Pittsburgh Post Gazette – 253
Courtesy of Meghan Walsh Gerard – 273
Reno Gazette Journal – 276
Ultimata Hora – 280
Jonathan Cape Publishing – 285
Sydney Morning Herald – 286

Also by Paul French

DESTINATION SHANGHAI
ISBN 978-988-77927-5-8

DESTINATION PEKING

ISBN 978-988-79639-6-7

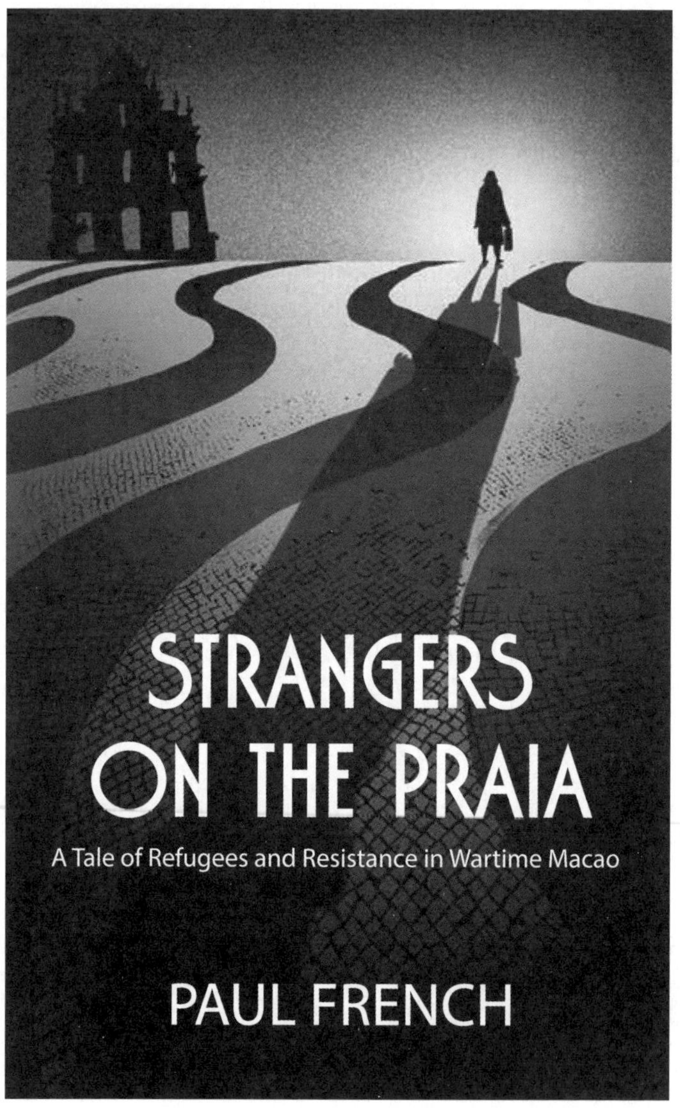

STRANGERS ON THE PRAIA
ISBN 978-988-79638-9-9

Forthcoming: DESTINATION SINGAPORE

by PAUL FRENCH

Including:

A Night on Cad's Alley – When Raffles was slightly less respectable
Georgette Chen and the birth of the Nanyang Style (1951-1980)
Up in Court – Nellie Farren and the Alsagoff Case (1928)
Clavell in Changi – James Clavell (1941-1945)
On Tour with The Quaints – John Mills & Noël Coward (1930)
The King of Kitsch and the Green Chinese Lady – Vladimir Tretchikoff (1936)
A Brief Affair – Gertrude Bell and Frank Swettenham (1903-1904)
A War Artist in Bukit Timah – Tsuguharu Foujita (1941)
Madame Blanche Charms All Singapore – Blanche Arral on Tour (1904)
Aiming for China; Finding Singapore – Helmut Newton (1939)
Judging Bertha Hertogh – How a Young Dutch Girl's Fate was Decided in a Singapore Courtroom and Sparked a Riot (1950)
Orchids for the Emperor – EJH Corner and the Botanic Gardens at War (1942-1945)
The War Artists' Advisory Committee's Man in Singapore – Leslie Cole (1945)